MLIWK

An Introd
and Pragmatics

Edinburgh Textbooks on the English Language

General Editor
Heinz Giegerich, Professor of English Linguistics (University of Edinburgh)

Editorial Board
Laurie Bauer (University of Wellington)
Derek Britton (University of Edinburgh)
Olga Fischer (University of Amsterdam)
Norman Macleod (University of Edinburgh)
Donka Minkova (UCLA)
Katie Wales (University of Leeds)
Anthony Warner (University of York)

TITLES IN THE SERIES INCLUDE

An Introduction to English Syntax
Jim Miller

An Introduction to English Phonology
April McMahon

An Introduction to English Morphology
Andrew Carstairs-McCarthy

An Introduction to International Varieties of English
Laurie Bauer

An Introduction to Middle English
Simon Horobin and Jeremy Smith

An Introduction to Old English
Richard Hogg

An Introduction to Early Modern English
Terttu Nevalainen

An Introduction to English Semantics and Pragmatics

Patrick Griffiths

Edinburgh University Press

© Patrick Griffiths, 2006

Edinburgh University Press Ltd
22 George Square, Edinburgh

Typeset in Janson and Neue Helvetica
by Norman Tilley Graphics and
printed and bound in Great Britain
by Antony Rowe Ltd, Chippenham, Wilts

A CIP record for this book is available from the British Library

ISBN-10 0 7486 1631 4 (hardback)
ISBN-13 978 0 7486 1631 2
ISBN-10 0 7486 1632 2 (paperback)
ISBN-13 978 0 7486 1632 9

The right of Patrick Griffiths
to be identified as author of this work
has been asserted in accordance with
the Copyright, Designs and Patents Act 1988.

Contents

List of figures and tables

Figures

Tables

Preface

I chose Edinburgh University for postgraduate studies because I wanted to learn semantics from John Lyons, one of whose books I had read. It turned out that he was not teaching semantics the year that I took the taught graduate course, but there were eventually seminars of his that I could attend, and I read more of his work. His influence can be traced in this book. It was Martin Atkinson, a fellow research assistant on an Edinburgh University Linguistics Department project, who first explained to me how the study of meaning can be split between semantics and pragmatics. Semantics is concerned with the resources (vocabulary and a system for calculating phrase-, clause- and sentence-meanings) provided by a language, and pragmatics is concerned with how those resources are put to use in communication. My grasp got firmer when I began to teach semantics and pragmatics myself at York University (UK), and later at the University of the South Pacific, York St John and Beppu University (Japan). Finding examples that communicate a point but which cannot easily be dismissed or misunderstood by students is a valuable discipline, especially when one tries to figure out, in relation to particular theoretical notions, what it takes to be a good example.

I am grateful that Heinz Giegerich, general editor of this series, came up with the idea of introductory textbooks offering compact descriptions of English unobtrusively grounded in defensible theory – it is an approach congenial to my ways of teaching and learning. My contribution to the series aims to present a reasonably detailed first look at the main features of the meaning system of English and the pragmatics of using that system. I owe thanks to Anthony Warner for encouraging me to write the book. In lunchtime conversations that I used to have with him at York University, he several times straightened out muddled ideas of mine regarding meaning. Beppu University provided me with an environment conducive to writing. Professor Kenji Ueda, Head of the English Language and Literature Department, encouraged me and also kindly authorised the purchase of some of the books that I needed to consult.

Pragmatics deals with inferences that listeners and readers make, or that – when speaking or writing – they invite others to make. These inferences are often conscious, so pragmatics tends to be easier to understand than semantics, because the latter is about abstract potential meanings that are often best described by means of notations drawn from logic and set theory. Linguistic meaning cannot usefully be studied by someone who knows only about pragmatics, however. A view widely shared among linguists is that semantics and pragmatics are essential components that work together in a full description of meaning.

In this book, I attempt to integrate semantics with pragmatics, but I hold back a detailed exposition of pragmatics until near the end (Chapter 8), with a detailed illustration of it in the closing chapter (Chapter 9). But Chapter 1 has a brief introduction to pragmatics and it is mentioned in all chapters – sometimes there is rather more than a mention: for instance, Chapter 5 introduces presupposition and puts the notion to work. The pragmatics is Gricean, supplemented by Austin-Searle speech acts, and making use in a couple of places of ideas from Relevance Theory.

The point of the early concentration on semantics is to encourage readers to grapple with semantics before they have seen pragmatics as a possible "soft option". Chapter 1 introduces entailment as the foundation of semantics, together with compositionality and scope, the latter seeing some service in Chapters 2 and 7. Chapters 2 and 3 show how lexical sense relations are based on entailment. Throughout, but particularly in Chapter 4 (on verbs and situation types), the text presents not just analyses of meanings, but the evidence and reasoning that motivates them. Exercises at the end of each chapter, with suggested solutions at the end of the book, are intended for consolidation and to encourage further exploration. Chapter 5 is a short account of figurative elaborations of meaning, mainly through a non-technical retelling of Josef Stern's theory of metaphor. Chapter 6 treats the basics of English tense and aspect. Chapter 7, on the inter-related topics of modality, scope and quantification, is the semantic summit of the book, including a short introduction to Generalised Quantifier Theory.

Theoretical concepts and technical terms are introduced to the extent needed for making essential points in the description of meaning in English. Though the book is a self-standing introduction to English semantics and pragmatics, I hope that readers will be interested enough to want to learn more. For any who have the opportunity to do additional reading, the terminology introduced here should suffice for them to make headway with a range of intermediate-level books about semantics and pragmatics. At the end of each chapter there is a section of recommendations for further reading. Bold printed items in the index point to places in the text where technical terms are explained – not just when they first come up, but also to any subsequent elaborations.

Sarah Edwards, Commissioning Editor at Edinburgh University Press, provided clear guidance and responded efficiently to queries. She earned even greater gratitude from me for her forbearance in the face of my repeated failures to deliver chapters on time. Norman Macleod, as a member of the Editorial Board, scrutinised first drafts of all the chapters and read a revised version of the whole book too. Norman made very concise suggestions for improvements and alerted me to a number of subtleties in English meaning and usage. It was he who reminded me that a reversing dog is not followed by its tail (see Chapter 2). Heinz Giegerich kindly read a near-final version of the whole text. I thank James Dale, the Managing Desk Editor, and Sarah Burnett, the Copy Editor, for quality control on the text. Near the end, Andrew Merrison, doing it simply as a favour for a fellow linguist, read the book and passed on a list of inconsistencies, mistypings and questionable punctuations, many of which have now been eliminated. Sole responsibility for the published wording and content lies with me, however.

"Slow food", with time lavished on it in the growing, preparation and savouring, tastes better. It took me a long time to write this book. Unfortunately, not all of it was composed in a measured and reflective way. Some was done in haste because other jobs and projects demanded attention. I hope that there are enough considered bits to make it an interesting read and that the "fast food" intrusions will not be too off-putting.

Janet Griffiths, my spouse, supported me throughout and was the person most available for verification (or a headshake) of my intuitions about meaning. She checked drafts of several of the chapters and diagnosed confusing wording in quite a few places. I thank her with all my heart. Jane Griffiths visited around the time that I finished a second version of Chapter 5. She read it and offered comments that I appreciated. Thanks, Jane.

1 Studying meaning

Overview

This is a book about how English enables people who know the language to convey meanings. Semantics and pragmatics are the two main branches of the linguistic study of meaning. Both are named in the title of the book and they are going to be introduced here. **Semantics** is the study of the "toolkit" for meaning: knowledge encoded in the vocabulary of the language and in its patterns for building more elaborate meanings, up to the level of sentence meanings. **Pragmatics** is concerned with the use of these tools in meaningful communication. Pragmatics is about the interaction of semantic knowledge with our knowledge of the world, taking into account contexts of use.

Bold print for explanations of terms
In the index at the back of the book, bold printed page numbers indicate places where technical terms, such as **semantics** and **pragmatics** in the paragraph above, are explained. The point is to signal such explanations and to make it fairly easy to find them later, should you want to.

Example (1.1) is going to be used in an initial illustration of the difference between semantics and pragmatics, and to introduce some more terms needed for describing and discussing meanings.

(1.1) Hold out your arm. That's it.

Language is for communicating about the world outside of language. English language expressions like *arm* and *your arm* and *hold out* are linked to things, activities and so on. A general-purpose technical term that will appear fairly often in the book is **denote**. It labels the connections between meaningful items of language and aspects of the world – real or imagined – that language users talk and write about. *Hold out your arm*

1

denotes a situation that the speaker wants; *hold out* denotes an action; *arm* denotes a part of a person; *your arm* denotes 'the arm of the person being spoken to'; and so on. An **expression** is any meaningful language unit or sequence of meaningful units, from a sentence down: a clause, a phrase, a word, or meaningful part of a word (such as the parts *hope*, *-ful* and *-ly* that go together to make the word *hopefully*; but not the *ly* at the end of *holy*, because it is not a separately meaningful part of that word.)

That's it at the end of Example (1.1) is an expression which can mean 'OK (that is correct)', or 'There is no more to say', but for the moment I want to discuss the expressions *That* and *it* separately: what do they denote? *That* denotes something which is obvious to whomever is being addressed – perhaps the act of holding out an arm – yes, acts and events can be spoken of as if they were "things". (There is a question over which arm, since most people have two.) Other possibilities for what *that* could denote are the arm itself, or some other thing seen or heard in the surroundings. The word *it* usually denotes something that has recently been spoken about: the arm or the act of holding it out are the two candidates in (1.1). Without knowing the context in which (1.1) occurred, its meaning cannot confidently be explained much more than this.

In fact, (1.1) is a quotation from the first of J. K. Rowling's Harry Potter books.[1] It is spoken to Harry by Mr Ollivander, a supplier of fine wands. In the book it comes just after Mr Ollivander, taking out a tape measure, has asked Harry 'Which is your wand arm?' The contextual information makes it pretty certain that *your arm* denotes Harry's wand arm (his right arm, Harry guesses, as he is right-handed). Immediately after Mr Ollivander has said what was quoted in (1.1), he begins to measure Harry for a wand. This makes it easy in reading the story to understand that Harry complied with the request to hold out his arm, and "That's it" was said to acknowledge that Harry had done what Mr O. had wanted. This acknowledgement can be unpacked as follows: *That* denotes Harry's act done in response to the request – an obvious, visible movement of his arm, enabling Mr O. to use the measuring tape on Harry's arm; *it* denotes the previous specification of what Harry was asked to do, the act of holding out his arm; and the *'s* (a form of *is*) indicates a match: what he had just done was what he had been asked to do. Table 1.1 summarises this, showing how pragmatics is concerned with choices among semantic possibilities, and how language users, taking account of context and using their general knowledge, build interpretations on the semantic foundation.

The reasoning in the right-hand column of Table 1.1 fits a way of thinking about communication that was introduced by the philosopher H. P. Grice (1989 and in earlier work) and is now very widely accepted

Table 1.1 Semantic information and pragmatic considerations in the interpretation of Example (1.1)

Semantics	Pragmatics
arm – 'upper limb' or 'horizontal side bar on some types of chair'	Mr O.'s earlier question was about wand wielding, so *arm* is most likely 'upper limb'.
your arm – 'left upper limb' or 'right upper limb' *hold out* – 'extend', or 'refuse to capitulate'	Preferred hand is probably the one for wands and Harry is right-handed. Mr O. has a tape measure out and measuring Harry's arm will require access to his arm, so Mr O. wants him to extend his right upper limb.
That denotes something obvious in the situation.	If Harry has just complied and moved his arm outwards, that would be a noticeable event, so the word probably denotes that act.
is – 'equates to' (there are other meanings of *is*, but they are not relevant here). *it* usually denotes something previously mentioned.	It would fit the context if Mr O. now means that Harry's act with his right arm is what was wanted, so the word *it* probably recalls the previous specification; and Mr O. is acknowledging Harry's compliance.

in the study of pragmatics. According to this view, human communication with language is not like pressing buttons on a remote control and thereby affecting circuits in a TV set. Instead it requires active collaboration on the part of any person the message is directed to, the **addressee** (such as a reader of (1.1) in its context in J. K. Rowling's book, or a listener, like Harry Potter hearing what Mr Ollivander said in (1.1)). The addressee has the task of trying to guess what the **sender** (the writer or speaker) intends to convey, and as soon as the sender's intention has been recognised, that's it – the message has been communicated. The sender's task is to judge what needs to be written or said to enable the addressee to recognise what the sender wants to communicate.

There are three consequences of this:

- There are different ways of communicating the same message (and the same string of words can convey different messages) because it depends on what, in the context at the time, will enable the addressee to recognise the sender's intention. It is not as undemanding as remote control of a TV set.
- The active participation of the addressee sometimes allows a lot to be communicated with just a little having been said or written.
- Mistakes are possible. In face-to-face interactions the speaker can monitor the listener's (or listeners') reactions – whether these are grins

or scowls, or spoken responses, or actions like Harry obediently holding out his arm – to judge whether or not the sending intention has been correctly guessed, and can then say more to cancel misunderstandings and further guide the addressee towards what is intended. Such possibilities are reduced but still present in telephone conversations and, to a lesser extent, in internet chat exchanges; even writers may eventually discover something about how what they wrote has been understood, and then write or say more.

The rest of this chapter introduces other concepts that are important in the study of linguistic meaning and indicates which later chapters take them further. Technical terms are going to be brought in, but only ones needed for getting a reasonable initial grasp on semantics and pragmatics and to set you up for reading basic books in this area.

Competent users of a language generally employ it without giving thought to the details of what is going on. Linguists – and semantics and pragmatics are branches of linguistics – operate on the assumption that there are interesting things to discover in those details. This approach can seem like an obsession with minutiae, and maybe you felt that way when the first example was discussed. It is a project of trying to bring to accessible consciousness knowledge and skills that are most of the time deployed automatically. This close inspection of bits of language and instances of usage – even quite ordinary ones – is done with a view to understanding how they work, which can be fascinating.

1.1 Pragmatics distinguished from semantics

1.1.1 Utterances and sentences

In our immediate experience as language users, the things that have meaning are utterances, and (1.2) presents three examples.

(1.2) a. "Not so loud."   (Something I said to a student who was speaking rather loudly, in Room 420, in the afternoon on 6 May 2005.)

   b. "In H101."   (I recall hearing a student say this, about seven years ago.)

   c. "People who buy these tickets often don't have loads of money." (According to a BBC website report,[2] the policy manager of the Rail Passengers Council said this towards the end of 2004.)

Utterances are the raw data of linguistics. Each utterance is unique, having been produced by a particular sender in a specific situation.

(Though it may seem a bit strange, I will use the term utterance to cover not only spoken utterances but also individual stretches of written language up to sentence-size, done by a particular person at a particular time.) Because they are tied to a sender and a time, utterances can never be repeated. When early in the morning on 6 May 2005 I said, in our apartment, "Not so loud", because I was worried that the noise of our TV might bother the neighbours, that was a different utterance from (1.2a). Even when someone is held to have said (or written) "the same thing twice", as in the case of people who "repeat themselves" (or someone who repeats what someone else has uttered), there is going to be more than one utterance constituting the repetition – differing in time, or having been made by a different speaker. No-one keeps a record of every utterance, but in principle they are all distinguishable.

Notation
When it matters, I use:

" " double quotes for utterances,
italics for sentences and words considered in the abstract,
' ' single quotes for meanings.

I also use single quotes when quoting what various authors have written about semantics or pragmatics. Such quotations can usually be identified by the nearby citation of the author's surname.

And an additional use for double quotes is to mark something as not strictly accurate but usefully suggestive, as when, earlier, I described semantics as a "toolkit".

The abstract linguistic object on which an utterance is based is a **sentence**. My recollection is that the utterance "In H101" mentioned in (1.2b) was based on the sentence *The class will be in Room H101*, because it was said in response to me asking "Where's the class going to be?" We talk of repetition when two or more utterances are based on the same sentence.

Utterances are interpreted in context. The context of (1.2c) indicated clearly that *often* was to be understood as modifying what followed it, to mean '… are often not rich', rather being a modifier of what came before: 'People who buy these tickets often …'. I read about (1.2c) in a report on the internet. If I had heard the utterance, it is likely that the speaker's delivery would have signalled which of the two meanings was intended. For the 'frequent purchaser' meaning, there would probably have been an intonational break straight after *often*, one that the report writer could have marked with a comma. Without such a break, either interpretation would be possible, but the absence of a break could be taken as a pointer towards the 'often not well off' interpretation. Nonetheless, intonation does not obviate the need to consider context: we tend to use context to check that we have heard the intonation correctly, and to treat intonation as a clue regarding which contextual information to use.

1.1.2 Three stages of interpretation

The essential difference between sentences and utterances is that sentences are abstract, not tied to contexts, whereas utterances are identified by their contexts. This is also the main way of distinguishing between semantics and pragmatics. If you are dealing with meaning and there is no context to consider, then you are doing semantics, but if there is a context to be brought into consideration, then you are engaged in pragmatics. **Pragmatics** is the study of utterance meaning. **Semantics** is the study of sentence meaning and word meaning.

To illustrate this, the interpretation of (1.3) will be discussed in terms of three distinguishable stages. The first stage is a semantic one: literal meaning. The others are two kinds of pragmatic interpretation: explicature and implicature.

(1.3)   *That was the last bus.*

The **literal meaning** of a sentence is based on just the semantic information that you have from your knowledge of English. Among the things that people who know English should be able to explain about the meaning of (1.3) are the following: something salient (*That*) is equated, at an earlier time (*was* is a past tense form), to either the final (*last*) or the most recent (*last*) bus. That meaning is available without wondering who might say or write the words, when or where. No consideration of context is involved.

An **explicature** is a basic interpretation of an utterance, using contextual information and world knowledge to work out what is being referred to and which way to understand ambiguous expressions, such as the word *last*. Two possible contexts for using an utterance based on the sentence in (1.3) will be considered. They lead to different explicatures.

Firstly, Ann sends a text message to Bess: "missed 10 pm bus" and Bess responds "That was the last bus". In this situation, Bess's reply can probably be interpreted as meaning 'that was the final bus on tonight's schedule going to where I know you were intending to travel'.

Secondly, Charley says to the driver of a bus about to pull out of a busy terminus: "Some of these buses go via Portobello; is this one of them?"

The driver's hurried reply is "That was the last bus", probably interpretable as 'The previous bus that departed from here was one of those
that goes via Portobello'.
These explicatures of utterances go beyond the literal meaning of
the sentence *That was the last bus*. They are interpretations based on the
linguistic context (Ann's and Charley's utterances respectively) and the
non-linguistic context (it is late at night in Ann's case; Charley and the
bus driver can both see bus after bus departing). Background knowledge
comes in too (buses generally stop running at some late hour; Bess knows
where Ann was going and takes it that Ann knows that she knows). Since
context has to be considered, this is pragmatics. Context facilitates
disambiguation (between the 'final' and 'previous' meanings of *last*) and
helps establish what things are referred to when the second individual
in each scenario uses the expressions "That" and "the last bus". As with
other pragmatic interpretations, there are uncertainties over explicature,
which is why I used the word *probably* in both of the previous paragraphs.
  In working out an **implicature**, we go further and ask what is hinted
at by an utterance in its particular context, what the sender's "agenda" is.
We would have to know more about the kind of relationship that Ann and
Bess have, and about Charley and the look on the driver's face, but if we
had been participants in these exchanges we would have been able to
judge fairly confidently whether Bess's reply conveyed sympathy or a
reprimand or an invitation to spend the night at her place, and whether
the driver meant to convey annoyance or apology by his response to
Charley. Fairly obviously, the bus driver's answer can be taken as an
implicit 'No' in answer to Charley's question. These are inferences
derived by trying to understand, in the light of contextual and background information, the point of a sender producing utterances that, in
context, are likely to have particular explicatures. We cannot forget about
the literal meaning of the sentence in (1.3) because literal meaning is the
foundation for explicature, on which implicatures are based, but it is
important to note that it cannot be claimed that the sentence *That was the
last bus* generally means 'Spend the night at my place' or 'No'.
  Each stage is built on the previous one and we need to develop
theories of all three: literal meaning – the semantics of sentences in the
abstract; explicature – the pragmatics of reference and disambiguation;
and implicature – the pragmatics of hints.

1.1.3 A first outline of pragmatics

A crucial basis for making pragmatic inferences is the contrast between
what might have been uttered and what actually was uttered. Example

(1.4) was a short, headed section from an information flyer about a restaurant. (Double quotes have been omitted because they would spoil the appearance, but this counts as a sequence of utterances. Remember that I am allowing utterances to be in speech, writing or print.)

(1.4)   Alcohol & Smoking
You are welcome to bring your own alcohol
provided you are buying a meal. There is no
charge for doing so.

The leaflet then switches to another topic, inviting us to infer that no provision is made for smoking. We cannot be certain. They might simply have forgotten to add something permissive that they intended to say about smoking, but it could be a pointedly negative hint to smokers. Nothing in the leaflet actually says that smoking is unwelcome or disallowed; so this implicature from (1.4) and its context is an elaboration well beyond the literal meaning of what appears in the leaflet.

Explicature, the second of the stages of interpretation described in Section 1.1.2, would have included working out that the heading in (1.4) is about alcoholic beverages, not, for instance, hospital-grade alcohol to sterilise the table tops.

Example (1.5) shows a kind of pragmatic inference generally available when words can be ordered on a semantic scale, for instance the value judgements *excellent* > *good* > *OK*.

(1.5)   A: "What was the accommodation like on the work camp?"
B: "It was OK."
A: "Not all that good, hey?"

Speaker A draws an implicature from B's response because, if the accommodation was better than merely OK, B could have used the word *good*; if it was very good B could have used the word *excellent*. Because B did not say *good* or *excellent*, A infers that the accommodation was no better than satisfactory. At the time of utterance, A might well have heard and seen indications to confirm this implicature – perhaps B speaking with an unenthusiastic tone of voice or unconsciously hunching in recollection of an uncomfortable bed. Such things are also contextual evidence for working out implicatures.

The stage of explicature – before implicature (see Section 1.1.2) – would have involved understanding that, in the context of A's question, B's utterance in (1.5) has as its explicature 'The work camp accommodation was OK', the work camp being one that B had knowledge of and which must previously have been identified between A and B, probably earlier in the conversation.

The pragmatic inferences called **implicatures** and **explicatures** occur all the time in communication, but they are merely informed guesses. It is one of their defining features that they can be cancelled. In (1.5), B could have come back with "No, you've got me wrong; the accommodation was good". This would cancel the implicature, but without contradiction, because accommodation that is 'good' is 'OK', so it is not a lie to say of good accommodation that it was OK. (Pragmatics is the focus of Chapters 8 and 9, but it also figures in sections of most of the other chapters. Explicature plays a significant role in Chapter 5's account of figurative language.)

1.2 Types of meaning

Sender's meaning[3] is the meaning that the speaker or writer intends to convey by means of an utterance. Sender's meaning is something that addressees are continually having to make informed guesses about. Addressees can give indications, in their own next utterances, of their interpretation (or by performing other actions, like Harry Potter extending his right arm between the two utterances in Example (1.1)). The sender or fellow addressees or even bystanders will sometimes offer confirmation, corrections or elaborations, along the lines of "Yes, that's part of what I meant, but I'm also trying to tell you …" or "You've misunderstood me" or "The real point of what she said was …" or "Yes, and from that we can tell that he wanted you to know that …" or "The way I understand the last sentence in this paragraph is different". Sender's meanings, then, are the communicative goals of senders and the interpretational targets for addressees. They are rather private, however. Senders will sometimes not admit that they intended to convey selfish or hurtful implicatures and, at times, may be unable to put across the intention behind an utterance of theirs any better than they have already done by producing the utterance.

Sender's thoughts are private, but utterances are publicly observable. Typed or written utterances can be studied on paper or on the screens of digital devices. Spoken utterances can be recorded and played back. Other people who were present when an utterance was produced can be asked what they heard, or saw being written. We cannot be sure that sender meaning always coincides with addressee interpretation, so there is a dilemma over what to regard as the meaning of an utterance. Is it sender's meaning or the interpretation that is made from the utterance, in context, by the addressee(s)? We cannot know exactly what either of these is. However, as language users, we gain experience as both senders and addressees and develop intuitions about the meaning an utterance is likely to carry in a given context. So **utterance meaning** is a necessary fiction that linguists doing semantics and pragmatics have to work with. It is the meaning – explicature and implicatures – that an utterance would likely be understood as conveying when interpreted by people who know the language, are aware of the context, and have whatever background knowledge the sender could reasonably presume to be available to the addressee(s).

Utterances are the data for linguistics, so linguists interested in meaning want to explain utterance meaning. But, because utterances are instances of sentences in use, an important first step is an account of the meanings of sentences. I will take **sentence meaning** to be the same as **literal meaning** (already introduced in Section 1.1.2: the meanings that people familiar with the language can agree on for sentences considered in isolation). As an illustration of how utterance meaning relates to sentence meaning, consider the sentence *That's it*, the basis for part of (1.1). I hope you agreed that, when context is ignored, the sentence has the meaning shown in (1.6a), but that, after learning that it was used for an utterance by Mr Ollivander while measuring up Harry Potter for a wand, you agreed that its explicature (the basic utterance meaning) could reasonably be represented as in (1.6b).

(1.6)   a.   'something obvious = something previously mentioned'
        b.   'you, Harry Potter, have extended your right arm as I asked'
        c.   'the addressee's recognition of the sender's communicative intention = the communication of that intention'

When I was discussing Table 1.1 – in the paragraph that also introduced the terms addressee and sender – I used the same sentence as the basis for an utterance "that's it" in the text of this book. That utterance – also based on the sentence meaning represented in (1.6a) – had as its explicature (1.6c), considerably different from (1.6b). (What could the implicatures have been? Mr O. was probably conveying 'stop moving now', Harry by then having moved his arm out to the desired angle, and he was giving Harry a nod of approval, somewhat like calling him "a good boy". With my utterance, I wanted you to see that the addressee's recognition of the sender's intention brings sudden closure to what otherwise looks like a complicated process.)

Ordinary language users have readily accessible intuitions about sentences. Among other items of information that people proficient in English can easily come to realise on the basis of their knowledge of the language is that the sentence in example (1.7a) has two meanings (it is **ambiguous**), shown in (1.7b) and (1.7c).

(1.7) a. *He is a conductor.*
    b. 'He is a public transport ticket checker'
    c. 'He regulates the performance of a musical group'

Ordinary language users' access to the meanings of words is less direct. The meaning of a word is the contribution it makes to the meanings of sentences in which it appears. Of course people know the meanings of words in their language in the sense that they know how to use the words, but this knowledge is not immediately available in the form of reliable intuitions. Ask non-linguists whether *strong* means the same as *powerful* or whether *finish* means the same as *stop* and they might well say Yes. They would be at least partly wrong. To have a proper feeling for what these words mean, it is best to consider sentences containing them, as in (1.8a–d). (All four are sentences, so there is no need to distinguish them from utterances or meanings, which is why I have not put them in italics.)

(1.8) a. Mavis stopped writing the assignment yesterday, but she hasn't finished writing it yet.
    b. *Mavis finished writing the assignment yesterday, but she hasn't stopped writing it yet.
    c. This cardboard box is strong.
    d. ?This cardboard box is powerful.

Notation
The asterisk at the beginning of (1.8b) is important. In semantics it marks examples that are seriously problematic as far as meaning goes; (1.8b) is a contradiction. A question mark at the beginning, as in (1.8d), signals oddness of meaning, but not as serious a problem as an asterisk does.

Examples (1.8a, b) are evidence that *finishing* is a special kind of *stopping*: 'stopping after the goal has been reached'. Examples (1.8c, d) are part of the evidence showing that *strong* is an ambiguous word, meaning either 'durable' or 'powerful'. Only one of the two meanings is applicable to cardboard boxes.

1.2.1 Denotation, sense, reference and deixis

Near the beginning of this chapter, expressions – sentences, words and so forth – in a language were said to denote aspects of the world. The **denotation** of an expression is whatever it denotes. For many words, the denotation is a big class of things: the noun *arm* denotes all the upper limbs there are on the world's people, monkeys and apes. (Yes, there is a noun *arms* that has a lot of weapons as its denotation, but it always appears in the plural form.) If expressions did not have denotations, languages would hardly be of much use. It is the fact that they allow us to communicate about the world that makes them almost indispensable.

Because languages have useful links to the world, there is a temptation to think that the meaning of a word (or other kind of expression) simply is its denotation. And you would stand a chance of elucidating the meaning to someone who did not know the body part meaning of *arm* by saying the word each time as you point to that person's arms, one at a time, and wave one of your own arms then the other. In early childhood our first words are probably learnt by such processes of live demonstration and pointing, known as **ostension**. It is not plausible as a general approach to meaning, however, because:

- It ignores the fact that after early childhood we usually use language, not ostension, to explain the meanings of words (*"Flee* means 'escape by running away'").
- When people really do resort to ostension for explaining meanings, their accompanying utterances may be carrying a lot of the burden. (*"Beige* is this colour" while pointing at a piece of toffee; or think of the legend near a diagram in a book indicating what it is that one should see in the diagram. It would be easier to avoid the misunderstanding that the word *arm* means 'move an upper limb' if you produced sentence-sized utterances: "This is your arm", "This is my right arm" and so on, while doing the pointing and showing.)
- There are all kinds of abstract, dubiously existent, and relational denotations that cannot conveniently be shown. (Think of the denotations of *memory, absence, yeti* and *instead of.* These are only a tiny sample of a large collection of problems.)

There are two general solutions, which are compatible, but differ in their preoccupations. The most rigorous varieties of semantics (called **formal semantics** because they use systems of formal logic to set out descriptions of meaning and theories of how the meanings of different sorts of expressions are constructed from the meanings of smaller expressions; see Lappin 2001) accord importance to differences between kinds of denotation. Thus count nouns, like *tree*, may be said to denote sets of things (and it is the denotation being a set that is of interest, rather than what things are in the set); property words, like *purple*, also denote sets (sets of things that have the property in question); singular names denote individuals; mass nouns, like *honey*, denote substances; spatial relation words, like *in*, denote pairs of things that have that spatial relation between them; the most straightforward types of sentence, like *Amsterdam is in Holland*, can be analysed as denoting either facts or falsehoods; and so on. (Chapters 2, 3 and 4 offer a little more about this, but without the formal logical apparatus.) Another approach, which I believe is a valuable start in the linguistic study of meaning, will be presented in this book in a version that forms a reasonable foundation for anyone who, later, chooses to learn formal semantics. In this approach the central concept is **sense**: those aspects of the meaning of an expression that give it the denotation it has. Differences in sense therefore make for differences in denotation. That is why the term sense is used of clearly distinct meanings that an expression has. Example (1.7), for instance, illustrated two senses of *conductor*, and a third sense of this word denotes things or substances that transmit electricity, heat, light or sound.

There are different ways in which one might try to state "recipes" for the denotations of words. One way of doing it is in terms of **sense relations**,[4] which are semantic relationships between the senses of expressions. This is the scheme that is going to be used in the book. It harmonises well with the fact that we quite commonly use language to explain meanings. In (1.9) some examples of items of semantic knowledge we have from knowing sense relations in English are listed. Notice that they amount to explanations of meanings.

(1.9) an *arm* is a *limb*
       an *arm* is an *upper limb*
       a *leg* is a *limb*
       a *leg* is a *lower limb*
       a *person* has an *arm*
       an *arm* has a *hand* and a *wrist* and an *elbow* and *biceps*
       extend is a synonym of *hold out*
       pursue is the converse of *flee*

Sense relations between words (and some phrases, such as *upper limb* in (1.9)) will be further explained and illustrated in Chapters 2, 3 and 4, dealing successively with adjectives, nouns and verbs. The reason for thinking that such ties between senses have a bearing on denotation is the following: with words interconnected by well-defined sense relations, a person who knows the denotations of some words, as a start in the network of relationships, can develop an understanding of the meanings (senses) in the rest of the system.

Reference is what speakers or writers do when they use expressions to pick out for their audience particular people ("my sister") or things ("the Parthenon Marbles") or times ("2007") or places ("that corner") or events ("her birthday party") or ideas ("the plan we were told about"); examples of **referring expressions** have been given in brackets. The relevant entities outside of language are called the **referents** of the referring expressions: the person who is my sister, the actual marble frieze, the year itself, and so on. Reference is a pragmatic act performed by senders and interpreted at the explicature stage (see Section 1.1.2). Reference has to be done and interpreted with regard to context. Consider (1.10) as something that might have been written in a letter.

(1.10) "We drove to Edinburg today."

The letter writer would have to be sure that the recipient knows they live in Indiana – where there is an Edinburg – if the utterance is not to be misunderstood as about a trip to the Edinburg in Illinois, or the one in Texas, or even Edinburgh in Scotland. When using the pronoun *we*, the writer of (1.10) refers to herself, or himself, and associates. The recipient of the letter can work out the reference by knowing who wrote it and can pragmatically infer the time reference of "today" from knowledge of when the letter was written. Imagine, however, that the letter is eventually torn up and a stranger finds a scrap, blowing in the wind, with only (1.10) on it. Uncertain about the situation of utterance, the stranger will not know who the travellers were, which Edinburg they drove to, or when they did so.

Deictic expressions are words, phrases and features of grammar that have to be interpreted in relation to the situation in which they are uttered, such as *me* 'the sender of this utterance' or *here* 'the place where the sender is'.

A course bulletin board once carried a notice in Week 1 of the academic year worded as in (1.11).

(1.11) "The first tutorial will be held next week."

The notice was not dated and the tutor forgot to take it down. Some students who read it in Week 2 failed to attend the Week 2 tutorial meeting because "next week" had by then become Week 3. *Next week* is a deictic expression meaning 'the week after the one that the speaker or writer is in at the time of utterance'.

Deixis[5] is pervasive in languages, probably because, in indicating 'when', 'where', 'who', 'what' and so on, it is very useful to start with the coordinates of the situation of utterance. There are different kinds of deixis, relating to:

time: *now, soon, recently, ago, tomorrow, next week*
place: *here, there*, two kilometres *away, that side, this way, come, bring, upstairs*

participants, persons and other entities: *she, her, hers, he, him, his, they, it, this, that*

discourse itself: *this* sentence, the *next* paragraph, *that* was what they told me, I want you to remember *this* ...

Our semantic knowledge of the meanings of deictic expressions guides us on how, pragmatically, to interpret them in context. Thus we have *yesterday* 'the day before the day of utterance', *this* 'the obvious-in-context thing near the speaker or coming soon', *she* 'the female individual' and so on. As always in pragmatics, the interpretations will be guesses rather than certainties: when you infer that the speaker is using the word *this* to refer to the water jug he seems to be pointing at, you could be wrong; perhaps he is showing you the ring on his index finger.

Deixis features in the account of metaphor presented in Chapter 5. Tense (for instance, past tense *told*, in contrast to *tell*) is deictic too and forms one of the two topics in Chapter 6. More will be said about reference in most chapters, but especially in Chapter 9.

1.3 Semantics

Semantics, the study of word meaning and sentence meaning, abstracted away from contexts of use, is a descriptive subject. It is an attempt to describe and understand the nature of the knowledge about meaning in their language that people have from knowing the language. It is not a prescriptive enterprise with an interest in advising or pressuring speakers or writers into abandoning some meanings and adopting others (though pedants can certainly benefit from studying the semantics of a language they want to lay down rules about, to become clear on what aspects of conventional meaning they dislike and which they favour). A related point is that one can know a language perfectly well without knowing its history. While it is fascinating to find out about the historical currents and changes that explain why there are similarities in the pronunciations or spellings of words that share similarities in meaning – for example: *arms*$_{body\ parts}$, *arms*$_{weapons}$, *army, armada* and *armadillo* – this kind of knowledge is not essential for using present-day English, so it is not covered in this book. Historical linguists investigating language change over time sometimes concern themselves with semantic (and pragmatic) matters. They are then doing historical (linguistic) semantics (and/or pragmatics).

Semantic description of language knowledge is different from the encyclopedia maker's task of cataloguing general knowledge. The words *tangerine* and *clementine* illustrate distinctions that are not part of our knowledge of English, but rather a fruiterer's kind of expertise, which some other people also know, but which most users of English do not have to know. As long as they are aware that these are citrus fruits, they do not need English lessons on this point.

1.3.1 Propositions

Different sentences can carry the same meaning, as in (1.12a–c).

(1.12) a. Sharks hunt seals.
       b. Seals are hunted by sharks.
       c. Seals are prey to sharks.
       d. These chase and kill these others.

Proposition is the term for a kind of core sentence meaning, the abstract idea that remains the same in cases such as (1.12a–c). Propositions in this technical sense are very abstract, not tied to particular words or sentences: the proposition carried by (1.12a, b) can be expressed without using the verb *hunt*, as shown in (1.12c). A young child who is unsure about which are seals and which are sharks could, while watching a (somewhat gory) nature programme, point at sharks and seals, respectively, for the two occurrences of *these* in (1.12d) and, without using any of the words in (1.12a–c), bring the same proposition into play.

The only feature that all **propositions** have – and this is a litmus test for propositions – is that it is reasonable to wonder whether they are true or false. I am not saying that anybody need be well enough informed to know for certain whether or not a given proposition is true, just that propositions are, in principle, either true or false. I have been told that the proposition in (1.12a–c) is true. I think it is, but notice that we have to know what is being spoken or written about before we can judge whether a proposition is true or false. The proposition expressed by a sentence is not known until an explicature has been worked out for it: reference and ambiguities both cleared up using contextual information. The explicatures for generic sentences such (1.12a–c) are relatively easy to get at: something like 'for all typical sharks and all typical seals, when they are engaging in typical behaviour, the former hunt the latter'. That is why I presented generic sentences to start with. But with (1.12d) you would need to know what is referred to by "These" and "these others" before it becomes sensible to ask whether it is true, and that is going to require information about the particular context in which an utterance based on the sentence is used.

The sentences in (1.12) (and very many others in this book) are declaratives, the sentence pattern on which **statements** (utterances that explicitly convey factual information) are based. Once they have been explicated, it is easy to see that they express propositions, because reactions such as the following can reasonably be made to them: "Yes, that's true" or "That's a lie" or "Is that really true?" Utterances based on some other sentence patterns cannot comfortably be reacted to like this. Try imaginary conversations in which such responses are made to examples like those in (1.13) (for example: A "What's your name?" B "That's a lie.").

(1.13) a. What's your name?
        b. Please help me.

Even though most conceivable explicatures of the sentences in (1.13) would not express propositions, they nonetheless involve propositions. The question in (1.13a) carries a proposition with a gap 'addressee's name is ___' and cooperative addressees supply their name to fill the gap. The request (1.13b) presents a proposition 'addressee help sender' and the sender hopes that the addressee will act to make that proposition come true. (See the section on speech acts in Chapter 8, for more about nondeclaratives, such as the examples in (1.13).)

Ambiguities are another reason for needing the concept of propositions. Example (1.14) can express, at least, two different propositions because *right* is ambiguous: 'correct' or 'right-hand'.

(1.14) She took the right turn

1.3.2 Compositionality

We need to account for sentence meaning in order to develop explanations of utterance meaning, because utterances are sentences put to use. The number of sentences in a human language is potentially infinite; so our account cannot be a list of all the sentences with an interpretation written next to each one. We have to generalise, to try to discover the principles that enable people to choose sentences that can, as utterances in particular contexts, have the intended meanings and that make it possible for their addressees to understand what they hear or read.

Semanticists, therefore, aim to explain the meaning of each sentence as arising from, on the one hand, the meanings of its parts and, on the other, the manner in which the parts are put together. That is what a **compositional** theory of meaning amounts to. The meaningful parts of a sentence are clauses, phrases and words; and the meaningful parts of words are **morphemes**.

Consider an analogy from arithmetic: the numbers that go into a sum affect the answer, as in (1.15a); so do the operations such as addition and multiplication by which we can combine numbers (1.15b). With more than one operation, the order they are performed in can make a difference (1.15c), where round brackets enclose the operation performed first.

(1.15) a. 3 + 2 = 5   but 3 + 4 = 7
        b. 3 + 2 = 5   but 3 × 2 = 6
        c. 3(2 + 4) = 18   but (3 × 2) + 4 = 10

The examples in (1.16) show something similar in the construction of words from morphemes – similar but not identical, because this is not addition and multiplication, but an operation of negation or reversal performed by the prefix *un-*, and the formation of "capability" adjectives by means of the suffix *-able*.

(1.16) a. *un(lock able)* 'not able to be locked'
        b. *(un lock)able* 'able to be unlocked'

The analysis indicated by the brackets in (1.16a) could describe a locker with a broken hasp. The one in (1.16b) could describe a locked locker for which the key has just been found. The brackets indicate the **scope** of the operations: which parts of the representation *un-* and *-able* operate on. In (1.16a) *un-* operates on *lockable*, but *-able* operates only on *lock*. In (1.16b) *un-* operates on just *lock*, and *-able* operates on *unlock*. The meaning differences based on scope differences in (1.16) are not a quirk of the word – or pair of words – *unlockable*. The same bracketing will yield corresponding meanings for *unbendable*, *unstickable* and a number of others.

In syntax too there can be differences in meaning depending on the order that operations apply. Example (1.17a) is an unambiguous sentence. It covers the case of someone who was awake for two days. But (1.17b), containing the same words, is ambiguous, either meaning the same as (1.17a) or applying to someone who was asleep, but not for two days (possibly for only two hours or maybe for three days).

(1.17) a. For two days, I didn't sleep.   'for two days (it was not so
                                            (that I slept))'
        b. I didn't sleep for two days.   'for two days (it was not so
                                            (that I slept))'
                                        or 'it is not so (that for two days
                                            (I slept))'

The 'meanings' indicated to the right of the examples are not in a standard notation. They are there to informally suggest how the overall meanings are built up. In (1.17a) the listener or reader first has to consider a negation of sleeping and then to think about that negative state – wakefulness – continuing for two days. To understand the second meaning given for (1.17b), first think what it means to sleep for two days, then cancel that idea. Syntactically, *for two days* is an adjunct in (1.17a) and also for the first of the meanings shown for (1.17b). When it is a complement to *slept*, we get the second meaning of (1.17b). Try saying (1.17b) with stress on *two* if you initially find the second meaning difficult to get.

The interpretations in (1.17) are not one-off facts regarding a particular sentence about sleeping – or not sleeping – for two days. Other sentences involving the operation of negation and a prepositional phrase that is either an adjunct or a complement have corresponding meanings. For instance, when we lived in a village some distance from town, I once overheard a member of my family say (1.18) over the phone.

(1.18)   I won't be in town until 4 o'clock.   'until 4 p.m. (it is not so (that (I be in town))' or 'it is not so (that until 4 p.m. (I be in town))'

I couldn't tell which of the meanings – parallel to the two given for (1.17b) – was intended: being out of town until 4 pm and arriving in town only then or later, or arriving in town at some earlier time and then not staying in town as late as 4 pm. If the speaker had instead said "Until 4 o'clock, I won't be in town", it would have been unambiguous, as with (1.17a). (There is more about compositionality and scope in Chapters 2 and 7.)

Idioms are exceptions. An expression is an **idiom** if its meaning is not compositional, that is to say it cannot be worked out from knowledge of the meanings of its parts and the way they have been put together. *Come a cropper* means 'fall heavily' but we cannot derive this meaning from the meanings of *come*, *a*, *crop* and *-er*. *Browned off* (meaning 'disgruntled'), and *see eye to eye* (meaning 'agree') are other examples. Idioms simply have to be learned as wholes (see Grant and Bauer 2004 for more discussion). Ordinary one-morpheme words are also, in a sense, idioms. The best we can hope to do for the word *pouch* is to pair it with its meaning, 'small bag'. The meaning of *pouch* cannot be worked out compositionally from the meaning of *ouch* and a supposed meaning of *p*.

1.3.3 Entailment

Entailment is a centrally important type of inference in semantics. While the pragmatic inferences called explicatures and implicatures are cancellable (as pointed out near the end of Section 1.1.3), an **entailment** is a guarantee.

Notation
⇒ represents entailment

Using the notation ⇒ for entailment, (1.19a) indicates that when *The accommodation was excellent* is true, we can be sure that it (the same accommodation at the same point in time) was very good. The statement in (1.19b) signifies that if it was excellent, it was (at least) good; and (1.19c) signifies that it was (at least) OK.

(1.19) a. The accommodation was excellent ⇒ The accommodation was very good
        b. The accommodation was excellent ⇒ The accommodation was good
        c. The accommodation was excellent ⇒ The accommodation was OK

Strictly speaking, **entailment** holds between propositions (see Section 1.3.1). However, explicated utterances based on declarative sentences express propositions and no great harm will come from the shortcut of thinking about a sentence as entailing other sentences (provided each sentence is considered in just one of its meanings, which amounts to it being an explicated utterance (see Section 1.1.2)).

Contrast the cancellability of the 'not all that good' guess that A made in (1.5) with the certainty of the inferences in (1.19).

The examples in (1.20) illustrate further points about entailment:

(1.20) a. Moira has arrived in Edinburgh.
        b. Moira is in Edinburgh.
        c. Moira has arrived in Edinburgh ⇒ Moira is in Edinburgh
        d. *Moira has arrived in Edinburgh and she is not in Edinburgh.

When (1.20a) is true we can be sure that (1.20b) is also true (provided it is the same Moira and the same city). This is shown in (1.20c) as a statement about entailment. Attempting to cancel an entailment leads to contradiction, as in (1.20d). If the first clause in (1.20d) is true, it entails the proposition expressed by a non-negative version of the *and* ... clause. Tacking on the negative clause yields a contradiction.

Examples (1.21a, b) show other entailments of (1.20a).

(1.21) a. Moira has arrived in Edinburgh ⇒ Moira is not in Birmingham
        b. Moira has arrived in Edinburgh ⇒ Moira went to Edinburgh

The word *arrived* is an important contributor to (1.20a) having the entailments shown. For instance, if *lived* or *been* were substituted for *arrived*, the entailments would be different. If someone not fully proficient in English asks what *arrive*, means, a sentence like (1.20a) could be given as an example, explaining that it means that Moira journeyed from somewhere else (Birmingham perhaps) and is now in Edinburgh. (The construction with *has* in (1.20a), called present perfect in grammar books, is crucial to the entailment in (1.20c); see Chapter 6.)

If (1.20a) is understood and accepted as true, then none of the entailments in (1.20c) and (1.21a, b) needs to be put into words. They follow if (1.20a) is true; they can be inferred from it; they derive from the meaning of *arrive*. It would be fair to say that the main point of choosing which words to use when talking or writing is to select among entailments. The **sense** of a word can now be defined in terms of the particular entailment possibilities that sentences get from containing that word: whatever aspects of the word's meaning are responsible for the sentences having those entailments are its sense. (Chapters 2, 3 and 4 explore the senses of different kinds of word. The notion of entailment will appear again in all chapters.)

Summary

Listeners and readers have the task of guessing what the sender of an utterance intends to communicate. As soon as a satisfactory guess has been made, the sender has succeeded in conveying the meaning. Pragmatics is about how we interpret utterances and produce interpretable utterances, either way taking account of context and background knowledge. Such interpretations are informed guesses. They can be mistaken. Explicature is the basic stage of pragmatic interpretation, involving disambiguation and working out what is being referred to. Referring and understanding other people's acts of reference usually require us to use and pragmatically interpret deictic words, ones that have meanings tied to the situation of utterance. A further stage of pragmatic elaboration yields implicatures, guesses as to what the point of an utterance is.

Semantics is the study of context-independent knowledge that users of a language have of word and sentence meaning. The meanings of constructions are compositionally assembled out of the meanings of smaller units, and what comes into the scope of which operations can influence the meaning of a construction.

Semantics is descriptive, and not centrally concerned with how words came historically to have the meanings they do. Nor do semanticists aim to write encyclopedic summaries of all human knowledge. An explicated utterance (based on a declarative sentence) expresses a proposition, which can be true or false. The central kind of inference in semantics is entailment. Entailments are propositions guaranteed to be true when a given proposition is true, though we can, loosely, think of entailing as a connection between sentences.

The sense of a word determines what it denotes (how it relates to the world outside of language) and the entailment possibilities that the word gives to sentences. In this book, sense will be approached through meaning relations that hold within a language, between the senses of expressions, in ways that should become clearer in later chapters.

Exercises

1. Here are two sets of words: {*arrive, be in/at, leave*} and {*learn, know, forget*}. There is an overall similarity in meaning – a parallel – between them. Can you see it? Here is a start: someone who is not at a place gets to be there by arriving; what if the person then leaves? Once you have found the similarities between the two sets, answer this subsidiary question: was this a semantic or a pragmatic task?

2. Student: "How did I do in the exam?" Tutor: "You didn't fail." What the tutor opted to say allows the student to guess at the sort of grade achieved. Do you think the grade was high or low? Briefly justify your answer. In doing this, were you doing semantics or pragmatics?

3. *Pick the right lock* is an ambiguous sentence. State at least two meanings it can have. How many different propositions could be involved?

4. The word *dishonest* means 'not honest'. The following five words also all have 'not' as part of their meaning: *distrust, disregard, disprove, dislike, dissuade*. Write a two-word gloss for the meaning of each, similar to the one given for *dishonest*. Thinking of sentences for the words will probably help. There are two different patterns. Use the term scope (which was introduced in 1.3.2) to describe the difference.

5. Here is an unsatisfactory attempt to explain the meaning of *not good enough*:

> *not good* means 'bad or average'; *enough* means 'sufficient(ly)'; so *not good enough* means 'sufficiently bad-or-average'.

With the aid of brackets, explain why the phrase actually means 'in-adequate'.

6. For class discussion. Someone once said to me: "You and I are well suited. We don't like the same things." The context indicated – and I checked by asking – that the speaker meant to convey 'You and I are well suited, because the things we don't like are the same'. *We don't like the same things* is ambiguous, but notice that *We dislike the same things* would not have been ambiguous in the relevant respect. Explain the ambiguity, and comment on unambiguous alternatives.

7. Which of the following sentences entail which?
    1. The students liked the course.
    2. The students loved the course.
    3. The rain stopped.
    4. The rain ceased.

Recommendations for reading

Worthwhile textbooks offering more detail are Kearns (2000) and Saeed (2003). Both include introductions to formal semantics, Kearns's being particularly good in this respect. Cruse (2000) offers many interesting insights into word meanings. Blakemore (1992), chapter 4, sets out the three stages of interpretation: literal meaning, explicature, implicature. Grundy (2000) is an accessible book on pragmatics. Wales (1986) is an interesting paper on deixis in child language.

Notes

1. J. K. Rowling (1997), *Harry Potter and the Philosopher's Stone*, London: Blooms-bury, p. 94.

2. Clare Babbidge, BBC News online (World Edition), 1 December 2004, < http://news.bbc.co.uk >.

3 This is commonly called *speaker-meaning* (see Lycan 2000: 103), but as the notion applies to both speaking and writing, I prefer to talk of sender's meaning.

4. This approach was given impetus in the 1960s, 1970s and 1980s by the writings of the semanticist Sir John Lyons. See Lyons 1977, for instance.

5. *Deixis* is an abstract noun corresponding to the adjective *deictic.*

2 Adjective meanings

Overview

Cruse (2000: 289) notes that adjective meanings are often one-dimensional. Think of pairs like *thin–thick, fast–slow, cool–warm, young–old, true–false*. Thickness concerns only a minor dimension, not length or width; for speed, one can ignore temperature, height, age; and so forth. This makes adjectives a good starting point for trying to understand word meaning. This chapter concentrates on various kinds of meaning relationship between adjectives, mainly relationships of similarity and oppositeness. Three other topics are broached: meaning postulates, gradability, and how to account for the meanings that arise when adjectives modify nouns.

2.1 Using language to give the meanings of words

(2.1) little – small, not big; not much
      small – little in size
      big – large in size
      much – large in quantity
      large – ample in extent
      ample – large in extent
      tiny – very small
      short – 1. not long; 2. small in stature, not tall

The fragments of entries shown in (2.1) could plausibly appear in a dictionary. In the entry for *short*, the numbers 1 and 2 distinguish two different senses of the word. It is unlikely you would look up words as familiar as these, but the items in (2.1) illustrate the circularity of a monolingual dictionary. It is reminiscent of a puppy chasing its own tail. Nonetheless, such a dictionary can give useful indications of word meanings. The cryptic hints in (2.1) catalogue relationships between word meanings, such as that all these words have something to do with size/quantity/extent; that *little* and *small* have closely similar meanings, as do *large* and *big*, that *big* is opposite in meaning to *little*, and so on. If the network can be anchored in a few places – if the meanings of some basic words are known – then it is a useful system.

In early childhood we come to know the denotations of our first words in the course of close encounters with the world, painstakingly mediated by our caregivers (sometimes with point-and-say demonstrations of the kind called ostension in Chapter 1). But once we have a start in a language, we learn the meanings of most other words through language itself: by having them explained to us (as when a child is told that *tiny* means 'very small') or by inference from the constructions words are put into (for example, when an older child realises from the title of Gerald Durrell's book *My Family and Other Animals* that there is a view according to which people are classified as animals).

The focus of the present book is the systematic description of meaning relationships within a language, between the senses of expressions (mainly words, but some phrases too). The aim is to state economically and insightfully which expressions are equivalent in meaning to which others – or contrast with them in various ways – according to the linguistic knowledge of individuals competent in the language.

Most of Chapter 2 is about sense relations between adjectives, but Section 2.3.2, discussing the modification of nouns by adjectives, touches on compositional issues (Section 1.3.2 of Chapter 1 introduced compositionality).

What about denotation? Semanticists tend to regard the building up of links between words and the world, and the perceptual processes that allow us to recognise the "things" that are denoted by words, as a matter for psychologists. However, the semantic study of sense relations contributes to this because the sense of a word places limits on what it can denote. And formal semantics is relevant too because the compositional senses of larger expressions delimit what they can denote.

2.2 Sense relations relevant to adjectives

The notion of entailment was introduced in Chapter 1, and it was pointed out that word senses affect the entailments that a sentence carries. Entailments are propositions that follow when a given proposition is true, just as the dog's tail follows whenever the dog comes in (unless the dog enters backwards). If it is true that a particular person has arrived in Edinburgh, then it must be true that the person is in Edinburgh at that time and made a journey from somewhere else. Entailments are willy-nilly understood and do not have to be expressed (a great saving of time when we are communicating). The account of sense relations in this chapter and the next one will be framed in terms of entailment possibilities.

2.2.1 Synonyms

Synonymy is equivalence of sense. The nouns *mother*, *mom* and *mum* are synonyms (of each other). When a single word in a sentence is replaced by a **synonym** – a word equivalent in sense – then the literal meaning of the sentence is not changed: *My mother's/mum's/mom's family name was Christie.* Sociolinguistic differences (such as the fact that *mom* and *mum* are informal, and that *mom* would typically be used by speakers of North American English while *mum* has currency in British English) are not relevant, because they do not affect literal meaning. (As explained in Chapter 1, literal meaning is abstracted away from contexts of use.)

Sentences with the same meaning are called **paraphrases**. Sentences (2.2a, b) are paraphrases. They differ only by intersubstitution of the synonyms *impudent* and *cheeky*.

(2.2)   a.   Andy is impudent.
      b.   Andy is cheeky.
      c.   (2.2a $\Rightarrow$ 2.2b) & (2.2b $\Rightarrow$ 2.2a)
      d.   *Andy is impudent but he isn't cheeky.
      e.   *Andy is cheeky but he isn't impudent.

(Remember that $\Rightarrow$ represents entailment, and an asterisk at the beginning of a sentence signals that it has serious meaning problems.)

Sentence (2.2a), if it is true, entails – guarantees the truth of – sentence (2.2b), provided it is the same Andy at the same point in time. When (2.2a) is true, (2.2b) must also be true. To establish paraphrase we have to do more, however, than show that one sentence entails another: the entailment has to go both ways, (2.2a) entails (2.2b) and it is also the case that (2.2b) entails (2.2a), as summarised in (2.2c). In normal discourse,[1] both (2.2d) and (2.2e) are contradictions, because entailments cannot be cancelled. When an entailed sentence is false, sentences that entail it cannot be true.

What has been said about the synonyms *impudent* and *cheeky* can be employed in two different directions. One way round, if you are doing a semantic description of English and you are able to find paraphrases such as (2.2a, b) differing only in that one has *cheeky* where the other has *impudent*, then you have evidence that these two adjectives are synonyms of each other. Alternatively, if someone else's description of the semantics of English lists *impudent* and *cheeky* as synonyms, that would tell you that they are predicting that sentences such as (2.2a, b) are paraphrases of one another, which is to say that the two-way entailments listed in (2.2c) hold. The claim that *impudent* is a synonym of *cheeky* predicts that sentences such as (2.2d, e) are contradictions; or the contradictions can be cited as evidence that the two words are synonymous.

Paraphrase between two sentences depends on entailment, since it is defined as a two-way entailment between the sentences. The main points of the previous paragraph are that entailments indicate sense relations between words, and sense relations indicate the entailment potentials of words.

How can one find paraphrases? Well, you have to observe language in use, think hard and invent test sentences for yourself, to try to judge whether or not particular entailments are present. The examples in (2.3) show how the conjunction *so* can be used in test sentences for entailment.

(2.3) a. You said Andy is cheeky, so that means he is impudent.
      b. You said Andy is impudent, so that means he is cheeky.

So generally signals that an inference is being made. When we are dealing with sentences out of context, as in cases when it does not matter who the Andy in (2.3a, b) is, then the inferences are entailments rather than some kind of guess based on knowledge of a situation, or of the character of a particular Andy.

Sentence (2.3a) is an entirely reasonable argument. People who accept it as reasonable accept (tacitly at least) that *Andy is cheeky* entails that 'Andy is impudent'. Sentence (2.3b) is also an entirely reasonable argument. People who accept it as reasonable are accepting that *Andy is impudent* entails 'Andy is cheeky'. If both of the arguments (2.3a, b) are accepted as reasonable, then we have two-way entailment – paraphrase – between *Andy is cheeky* and *Andy is impudent* and we can conclude that the two adjectives are synonymous with each other. (People who do not accept (2.3a, b) as reasonable arguments perhaps do not know either or both of the adjectives in question, or use meanings for one or both of these words that are different to those used by the author of this book, or they are focusing on a difference that is the concern of other branches of linguistics: sociolinguistics and stylistics.)

Some other pairs of synonymous adjectives are listed in (2.4).

(2.4) silent   noiseless
      brave   courageous
      polite   courteous
      rich   wealthy

It is important to realise that the two-way, forward-and-back entailment pattern illustrated in (2.2c) is defining for synonymy. *Huge* and *big* are related in meaning, but they are not synonyms, as confirmed by the fact that, while *The bridge is huge* entails *The bridge is big*, we do not get entailment going the other way; when *The bridge is big* is true, it does not have to be true that *The bridge is huge* (it might be huge, but it could be big without being huge).

Synonymy is possible in other word classes, besides adjectives, as illustrated in (2.5).

(2.5) truck   lorry   (nouns)
       depart   leave   (verbs)
       quickly   fast   (adverbs)
       outside   without   (prepositions)

In principle, synonymy is not restricted to pairs of words. The triplet *sofa*, *settee* and *couch* are synonymous.

2.2.2 Complementaries

Figure 2.1 is meant to depict the fact that, at any given point in time, the whole domain of whatever is capable of moving or being stationary is divided without remainder between two non-overlapping sets (which might or might not be equally big): the moving things and those that are stationary. In the world as it is ordinarily experienced and talked about in English, *moving* versus *stationary* is a stark opposition. (I am ignoring possibilities in physics and science fiction of multiple reference points and relativity.)

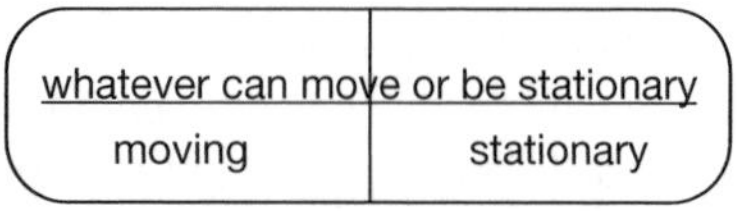

whatever can move or be stationary

moving | stationary

Figure 2.1 Complementaries divide their domain without remainder

Some other adjective contrasts that also divide their relevant domains sharply and without residue are listed in (2.6).

(2.6) same   different
       right   wrong
       true   false
       intact   damaged
       connected disconnected

These are pairs of complementary terms. (Note the spelling. The second vowel is an *e*. This has nothing to do with free tickets!) **Complementaries** are defined in terms of a pattern of entailment illustrated in (2.7c).

(2.7) a. Maude's is the same as yours.
  b. Maude's is different from yours.
  c. (2.7a ⟹ NOT2.7b) & (NOT2.7a ⟹ 2.7b) & (2.7b ⟹ NOT2.7a) & (NOT2.7b ⟹ 2.7a)

It may be a bit tedious, but let me spell out how all four of the entailments in (2.7c) follow logically, assuming that the people and possessions are unchanged between explicatures of the two sentences (2.7a, b). When (2.7a) is true, which is to say when Maude's is the same as yours, then it must be true that Maude's is not different from yours (represented in (2.7c) as 'NOT2.7b'). When Maude's is not the same as yours (NOT2.7a), then (2.7b) must be true: Maude's is different from yours. When Maude's is different from yours (2.7b), then Maude's is not the same as yours (NOT2.7a); and when Maude's is not different from yours (NOT2.7b), then Maude's is the same as yours (2.7a).

In comparison with what happens in synonymy, notice that (2.7c) provides evidence for two **paraphrase** pairs (sentences with the same meaning, or – another way of stating it – sentences that express the same proposition). If the two-way pair of entailments (2.7a ⟹ NOT2.7b) and (NOT2.7b ⟹ 2.7a) holds, then (2.7a) is a paraphrase of (NOT2.7b), which is to say that *Maude's is the same as yours* paraphrases *Maude's is not different from yours*. And if there is the mutual entailment summarised in (NOT2.7a ⟹ 2.7b) & (2.7b ⟹ NOT2.7a), then *Maude's is not the same as yours* is a paraphrase of *Maude's is different from yours*. Thus, complementaries can be viewed as negative synonyms.

In the discussion of synonyms, in Section 2.2.1, the sentence frame that the adjectives were put into was kept constant: *Andy is _____*, but for complementaries the example frame changed slightly between (2.7a) *Maude's is the _____ as yours* and (2.7b) *Maude's is _____ from yours*. These are differences brought about by details of English grammar. They do not have semantic significance in the present discussion. You would probably understand a non-proficient learner of English who made errors such as "Maude's is same from yours". My explanation of complementaries could, alternatively, have been made in terms of expressions bigger than a single word, *the same as* and *different from*, which could then have been seen as fitting into an unchanged frame in (2.7a,b).

With complementaries we get entailments from affirmative sentences (the ones lacking NOT in (2.7c)) to negative sentences (the ones with NOT in 2.7c) and back again from negative to affirmative. It will be seen in the next section that the kind of opposite that I am calling *antonyms* exhibit a pattern with parallels to only two of the four entailments shown in (2.7c).

2.2.3 Antonyms

The term antonymy is sometimes employed to mean any kind of oppositeness. I follow the practice of most semanticists in applying it to one particular sort of opposition, exemplified by *noisy* and *silent* in (2.8).

(2.8) a. The street was noisy.
       b. The street was silent.
       c. (2.8a $\Rightarrow$ NOT2.8b) & (2.8b $\Rightarrow$ NOT2.8a)
       d. ~~(NOT2.8a $\Rightarrow$ 2.8b) & (NOT2.8b $\Rightarrow$ 2.8a)~~

(The scoring through of 2.8d is deliberate and will be explained below.)

Antonymy is defined by a pattern of entailments such as the one in (2.8c): if we know that (2.8a) is true, then we can be sure that, with regard to the same (part of) the same street at the same time, (2.8b) is false, or equivalently that the negation of (2.8b) is true (2.8a $\Rightarrow$ NOT2.8b). And if we know that (2.8b) is true, it follows – again provided that we keep the place and time constant – that the street was not noisy (NOT2.8a).

Both of the entailments shown in (2.8c) go from an affirmative sentence to a negative one. With antonym pairs, we do not get the entailments in (2.8d). They are have been scored through to indicate that they do not hold. The reason that they do not hold is because there is middle ground between what *noisy* denotes and what *silent* denotes, as I try to suggest in Figure 2.2.

whatever can be noisy or silent		
noisy	neither noisy nor silent	silent

Figure 2.2 There is middle ground between antonyms

Imagine a complaint to the mayor that a particular street is noisy. The mayor denies this and the complainant then says "Well, it's not silent". The mayor can reasonably respond by saying "Agreed, but it is not noisy either". There is a middling range of sound levels that are not loud enough to count as *noisy*, but that also cannot be said to be *silent/noiseless*.

Some other antonym pairs are listed in (2.9).

(2.9) thick   thin
       rich   poor (or, since *wealthy* is a synonym of *rich*:
                      wealthy–poor)
       polite   rude (because of synonymy between *courteous* and *polite*, this is the same opposition as: *courteous–rude/discourteous/impolite*)

humble	vain/proud/boastful
rare	frequent/common
patient	impatient
brave/courageous	cowardly
early	late
harsh/severe	lenient
stubborn/obstinate	compliant
happy	sad
full	empty

The list in (2.9) is longer than the ones given in (2.4) and (2.6). All three lists could easily be extended, but a list of antonym pairs can easily be made longer than lists of either synonyms or complementaries. The explanation for there not being all that many synonyms is that they are something of a luxury. *Courteous* offers the same entailments, no more and no fewer, that we get from using the word *polite*. Thus we could do without one of them if the transmission of information was our only concern. Synonyms are perhaps tolerated because they allow us to speak and write expressively: varying the way we convey the same information and manipulating assonances, rhymes, alliterations and rhythms. Similar considerations make it something of a luxury to have both members of a complementary pair. Whatever information we can convey with, for instance, the word *false* can be can be put across by saying *not true*, or vice versa. However, there are considerations of perspective that make either a negative or an affirmative more appropriate in some circumstances, so we might not all that willingly give up one member of each complementary pair.

2.2.4 Converses

A general feature of the members of antonym pairs is that they have what grammarians term comparative forms, with the comparative suffix *-er* (*thicker, poorer, humbler*, for instance) or in the construction *more* + adjective (for example, *more humble, more patient, more obstinate*, with some words, like *humble*, forming the comparative by either method). The comparative forms of an antonym pair have an interesting sense relation between them, called converseness. The pair {*richer, poorer*} is used as an illustration in (2.10).

(2.10)   a. California is richer than some countries.
        b. Some countries are poorer than California.
        c. (2.10a $\Rightarrow$ 2.10b) & (2.10b $\Rightarrow$ 2.10a)

The entailment pattern illustrated in (2.10) defines **converseness**. Firstly, note that (2.10c) represents a two-way entailment, from (2.10a) to (2.10b) and also back from (2.10b) to (2.10a). This makes (2.10a) and (2.10b) paraphrases of each other. In this respect, it is a similar relationship to synonymy, but there is an important additional difference between (2.10a) and (2.10b). Not only has *richer* been replaced by *poorer* in going from (2.10a) to (2.10b), but the noun phrases *California* and *some countries* have been exchanged. Converses are thus a species of synonym that requires reordering of noun phrases. (The change from *is* to *are* is a detail of English grammar that is not semantically relevant here.)

Converseness is found not only between comparative adjectives but also in other word classes. Some examples are noted in (2.11).

(2.11) parent of   child of   (nouns)
        precede   follow   (verbs)
        above   below   (prepositions)

2.2.5 Four sense relations compared

No more sense relations are going to be introduced in this chapter, so this is an appropriate point to take stock. Table 2.1 compares the sense relations dealt with so far in terms of a number of features that have been mentioned in this chapter. (In Chapter 3, three more sense relations are going to be brought in.)

Table 2.1 The patterns of entailment that define four different sense relations

| | Patterns of entailment | | | |
Sense relation	two-way entailment	affirmative to negative	negative to affirmative	how paraphrases are created
synonyms	yes			by substitution
complementaries	yes	yes	yes	by substitution and negation
antonyms		yes		do not yield paraphrases
converses	yes			by substitution and reordering of noun phrases

In (2.12) the defining patterns of entailment for these four sense relations are recapitulated to make it easier to relate them to the entries in the table, with relevant example numbers given for the illustrative sentences used earlier.

(2.12) Synonyms: $(2.2a \Rightarrow 2.2b)$ & $(2.2b \Rightarrow 2.2a)$ (was 2.2c)
Complementaries: $(2.7a \Rightarrow NOT2.7b)$ & $(NOT2.7a \Rightarrow 2.7b)$ & $(2.7b \Rightarrow NOT2.7a)$ & $(NOT2.7b \Rightarrow 2.7a)$
(was 2.7c)
Antonyms: $(2.8a \Rightarrow NOT2.8b)$ & $(2.8b \Rightarrow NOT2.8a)$
(was 2.8c)
Converses: $(2.10a \Rightarrow 2.10b)$ & $(2.10b \Rightarrow 2.10a)$
(was 2.10c)

2.2.6 Meaning postulates

Meaning postulates were developed by the philosopher Rudolf Carnap (1891–1970) as a way of integrating into logical systems the entailment information that comes from word meanings. A short account of this should help you appreciate some of the wider significance of semantic description. First, we need to distinguish between inferences that depend solely on structure and inferences that depend also upon the meanings of particular words.

(2.13)   Rupert is a friend of mine
          and if he is a friend of mine then I am willing to lend him my bicycle.
          Therefore I am willing to lend Rupert my bicycle.

The inference at the end of (2.13) – after the word *Therefore* – depends entirely on the structure of that three-line discourse. The reasoning is valid simply because it fits a particular pattern that always yields true conclusions if the premises (initial statements) are true. The pattern is set out in (2.14).

(2.14)   p
          & (if p then q)
          Therefore q

When both of the premises – in the first two lines – are true, then the conclusion must be true. To emphasise that it is the structure of the discourse that ensures validity here, rather than the individual words or the particular ideas being spoken about, (2.15) is another instance of the same pattern.

(2.15)   We are sailing towards the Arctic
and if we are sailing towards the Arctic then we are sailing
northwards.
Therefore we are sailing northwards.

By contrast with (2.14) and (2.15), (2.16) is an inference that depends
crucially upon the meanings of particular words.

(2.16)   The A380 is bigger than a B747.
(+ unstated fact about the sense relation between 'bigger' and
'smaller')
Therefore a B747 is smaller than the A380.

Leaving out the material in brackets gives an argument which is
accepted as valid by people who know English: *The A380 is bigger than a
B747, therefore a B747 is smaller than the A380* (even if they do not realise that
the reference here is to two kinds of aircraft). However, it is an argument
that does not follow from the structure of the discourse. The discourse
has the structure 'p therefore q' and that is certainly not a generally valid
line of reasoning. If the formula 'p therefore q' was generally valid, then
it should yield satisfactory arguments no matter what we substitute for
p and q, but in fact this pattern can yield nonsense, as suggested by (2.17).

(2.17)   Rupert is a friend of mine.
Therefore we are sailing northwards.

A meaning postulate is needed between p and 'therefore q' before the
reasoning in (2.16) can be seen to be valid. The particular meaning postulate required for (2.16) has to represent a linguistic fact about English:
that 'when any thing, x, is bigger than some other thing, y, then y is
necessarily smaller than x; and vice versa'. This is, in effect, the information summarised in the sense relation of converseness. In formal
systems of logic there are ways of representing this and the other sense
relations that have been discussed above. See Cann (1993: 218–24) for an
account that explicitly accommodates sense relations (but without some
study of symbolic logic, you are likely to find the details hard to grasp).

2.3 Constructions with adjectives

2.3.1 Gradability

The comparative forms discussed in Section 2.2.4 are an aspect of something more general: many adjectives (and also adverbs, though they are
ignored here) are **gradable**, which is to say that the language has ways of
expressing different levels or degrees of the qualities that they denote.

Examples are given in (2.18), with the relevant indicators of gradability in italics.

(2.18) Card is thick*er than* paper.
Showers will be *more* frequent tomorrow.
He is the rud*est* person I've ever met.
They are *too* rare to stand any chance of survival.
Just *how* patient do you have to be?
The conditions were *very* harsh.

The adjectives in the examples given in (2.18) are all members of antonym pairs. They denote regions towards either end of scales. For instance, there is a scale of thickness, with *thick* denoting values towards one end, *thin* denoting values towards the other end, and a region in between that is neither thick nor thin. Interestingly, there is frequently one member of each pair that signals bias regarding the answer if it is used in asking questions about positions on the scale, whereas the other member of the pair is used in asking unbiased questions. See the short conversations in (2.19).

(2.19) a. A: "How thin is that piece of wood?" B: "It's very thin."
b. C: "How thin is that piece of wood?" D: "It's not thin; it's as thick as my forearm."
c. E: "How thick is that piece of wood?" F: "It's very thick."
d. G: "How thick is that piece of wood?" H: "It's pretty thin, about 4 millimetres."

The questions with *thin* (2.19a, b) show a bias: the senders, A and C, expect answers that place the piece of wood somewhere in the 'thin' region. That is why it is natural for speaker D, who is faced with a thick piece of wood, to first negate C's expectation by saying "It's not thin". But the unbiased question with *thick* (2.19c, d) simply enquires where the piece of wood is on the thin–thick scale, without bias towards an answer in the thick region. Thus, there is no pressure for speaker H to begin the reply by saying "It's not thick".

The members of complementary pairs (*same–different, right–wrong* and so on) are resistant to grading. See the examples in (2.20).

(2.20) *Twins are sam*er*/*more* same than siblings.
*That is the right*est* answer I have heard today.
*The jury heard evidence that was *too* false to accept.
?*How* disconnected is this kettle from the power supply?
?They left the door *very* open.

Superlatives (such as *best* and *fastest*) and covert superlatives (such as *freezing*) denote extreme ends of scales. Some examples are given in (2.21) of their tendency towards non-gradability.

(2.21)   *The other team was best*er* than ours.
          *In the inner city walking is *more* fastest.
          *The presentation was *very* excellent.
          ?The hospital kitchen was *too* spotless.
          **How* scorching was the weather in Luxor?

There are some adverbs that will go with both complementaries and covert superlatives, but not with most ordinary antonyms. The "maximisers" *absolutely* and *completely* are among these adverbs. Some examples are presented in (2.22).

(2.22) with antonyms: *The shrink wrapping was absolutely thin.
                                     *Her friends were completely proud of her.

        with complementaries: You'll look completely different with your hair restyled.
                                     What you say is absolutely true.

        with covert superlatives: ?Digital sound reproduction is completely perfect.
                                     The weather has been absolutely freezing.

2.3.2 Adjectives modifying nouns

How are noun and adjective meanings put together when an adjective modifies a noun as in *green bicycles*? Just enough will be said here to show that interesting issues arise in this area. A simple interpretation in terms of the intersection of sets, as depicted in Figure 2.3, will work in some cases.

In Figure 2.3, the left-hand oval represents the set denoted by *green*, all the green entities that there could be. The right-hand oval represents the

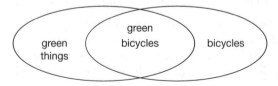

Figure 2.3 Simple cases of an adjective modifying a noun are like the intersection of sets

set of entities denoted by *bicycle*, all bicycles. The intersection of the two ovals encompasses things that are included in both sets, things that are green and also bicycles. This is a satisfactory enough account of how these two meanings are put together. Adjectives that fit this scheme of interpretation are called **intersective** adjectives.

Some adjectives are straightforwardly non-intersective: *former, imaginary, fake. Former champions* are no longer denoted in an uncomplicated way by the word *champion*; a *fake Stradivarius* is not a Stradivarius. Lappin (2001) gives a short overview of some proposals in formal semantics for handling such cases.

Two further types of non-intersective modification will be mentioned here. One class arises from what can be called relative adjectives (Cruse 2000: 290). Two examples are given in (2.23).

(2.23)   A big molecule is a small thing.
    A narrow shipping lane can be a wide stretch of water (if you are thinking of swimming it).

The problem for an intersective account of modification with *small* or *big, wide* or *narrow*, or any of numerous other relative adjectives is that the adjective is interpreted relative to the norms of the entities denoted by the noun: 'big as molecules go', 'narrow when compared to an average shipping lane'.

Another set of cases where an intersective explanation of modification is not feasible is illustrated by the ambiguity of (2.24).

(2.24)   He's the best politician in the country.

One can use (2.24) either to describe someone who is skilled at politicking, whether or not one approves of him as a person, or of someone who is good and happens to be a politician, whether or not he is competent in the practice of politics. The first meaning appears to rely on there being characteristic roles, duties, activities or functions for certain classes of people: a politician engages in politics, an embroiderer embroiders, a farmer farms, a plumber installs and repairs water systems. Now some adjectives can be taken as qualifying the extent to which the characteristic role is carried out (on this reading the *best politician* is the one who practises politics best). There is an ambiguity if the same adjective could also be used to describe the nature of people as people (the *best politician* could be understood as the most virtuous one). When the noun denotes something inanimate, then the only interpretation is likely to be the one in which its function is qualified by the adjective, for example a *good shovel* is one that is better than averagely suited for shovelling.

2.3.3 Larger sets than pairs

Most of the adjectives discussed in this chapter have been ones that come in pairs, though I pointed out that synonymy is not restricted to pairs. In Chapter 3 another sense relation that holds between the meanings of sets of words that can be larger than pairs will be introduced. It is called incompatibility. In advance of that discussion it should be noted that some adjectives with apparently interesting interrelationships in meaning occur in sets of more than two; for examples, see (2.25).

(2.25)   {black, purple, blue, brown, green, yellow, orange, red, pink, white, grey}
          {circular/round, triangular, rectangular}
          {previous, current, next}

If one is truthfully told that a particular rock is yellow, then it follows that it is not any of the other colours listed in the first set of (2.25). Is this blindingly obvious? Is it not always true that if something is said to have one property, then it does not have others? No, that only holds within such sets: a yellow rock could perfectly well be triangular, and, it could be the previous, current or next specimen in a batch being examined by a geologist.

Summary

The framework presented in this chapter for systematising adjective meanings is one that explains meanings in terms of a limited number of relationships between the senses of words. The following four sense relations were defined and illustrated: synonymy, complementarity, antonymy and converseness. In the process of doing semantic description, entailments between sentences are the evidence for sense relations between words. And, going the other way, the sense relations in a semantic description indicate the entailment potentials of words. In formal semantics, meaning postulates carry this information. Gradability – a feature of antonyms, but not of complementaries – was explained. It was observed that the modification of nouns by adjectives cannot be fully accounted for in terms of the intersection of sets denoted by the words.

Exercises

1. Provide example sentences and write out a pattern of entailments (comparable to (2.2c)) that establishes *soundless*, *silent* and *noiseless* as synonymous.

2. Are *awake* and *asleep* complementaries? Give reasons for your answer. Whether you have answered yes or no, how would you include *half-awake*, *half-asleep* and *dozy* in an account of the meanings of *awake* and *asleep*?

3. The adverb *quite* has two different meanings when it modifies adjectives. In one sense it is a "downtoner": *quite friendly* can be glossed as 'moderately friendly'. In another sense, it is a "maximiser": *quite exceptional* is synonymous with 'exceptional to the fullest extent'.

Assume that the judgements shown in the following table are correct about the meaning which arises when *quite* modifies the given adjectives (and, in one instance, a past participle). Comment on the relevant meaning difference between the forms in the two columns?

Quite can only be a "downtoner" with the forms below	*Quite* can only be a "maximiser" with the forms below
clever	right
late	finished
small	impossible
unusual	alone

4. Class exercise. Unless everyone is very well-informed, half the class should find out how Roget's *Thesaurus* is organised, in particular how synonymy and oppositeness are used in it. The other half of the class should find one or more "synonym dictionaries" (sometimes called "synonym finders"). Both groups should prepare themselves to give short descriptions of these in class, with examples.

5. Which of the following adjectives would normally yield biased *How adjective is/was x?* questions, and which not? Justify your responses. It could be that both adjectives in a pair are biased.

old	young
miserable	pleasant
unpalatable	tasty
weak	strong

6. Giving reasons, say which of the following phrases can handled by an intersective account of modification?

royal visitor
royal correspondent
heavy eater
wise fool

Recommendations for reading

Chapter 9 in Cruse (2000) is a thorough discussion of oppositeness in meaning. Griffiths (1986) discusses infants' learning of the meanings of words in their initial vocabularies. Lappin (2001) provides a good overview of formal semantics, and chapter 10 in Saeed (2003) complements this by dealing in greater detail with a limited number of topics. Quite a lot can be learnt about meaning as it is tied to particular word classes (adjectives, nouns, verbs), by looking through the relevant sections of major grammars of English, such as Quirk et al. (1985) and Huddleston and Pullum (2002).

Notes

1. The qualification 'in normal discourse' is there because languages are to some extent open to negotiation between language users, especially when language itself is temporarily the topic. At the level of pragmatics, if a sender is speaking or writing in apparent seriousness but appears to be treating synonyms as if they differ in meaning, addressees will generally try hard to find a rational interpretation. Thus, there could be non-contradictory uses of (2.2d) or (2.2e) if stylistic or register differences between *cheeky* and *impudent* are somehow relevant in a particular discussion.

3 Noun vocabulary

Overview

Nouns form a majority of the words in the vocabulary of English. In contrast to the unidimensional meanings of adjectives explored in Chapter 2, nouns typically 'denote rich, highly interconnected complexes of properties' (Cruse 2000: 289). This chapter outlines ways of describing the complexity, starting with a sense relation that I will call the *has*-relation.[1] The "things" denoted by some nouns have parts, which may figure in the nouns' meaning. For example, a *square* has four equal sides and it has 90° angles, and in saying what a *square* is, one cannot avoid talking about its four sides and right angles. Also dealt with in the chapter is the way nouns are grouped into semantic categories, for example *squares, circles* and *triangles* belong together as *shapes*. In semantic terms to be introduced below, *square, circle* and *triangle* are **hyponyms** of the **superordinate** word *shape*. Contrasts between the different kinds under a given superordinate are mainly captured through a sense relation called *incompatibility*, also to be explained. The chapter ends with a discussion of meaning differences between count and mass nouns. **Mass nouns** are ones that English treats as denoting substances – as not having distinguishable parts.

3.1 The *has*-relation

The everyday words *square, circle* and *triangle* are also technical terms in geometry, where they have tight definitions. For example, a closed, straight-sided figure is a triangle if, and only if, it has exactly three sides. This underpins entailments such as: *That figure is a triangle* ⇒ *That figure has three sides.* For many words, however, we can only be sure that all the parts are there if the *has*-relation is stated in terms of prototypes. **Prototypes** are clear, central members of the denotation of a word.

Think of what you might advise a child drawing a face to put in: probably eyes, a nose and a mouth. How about a child drawing a house?

Probably you would expect there to be a roof, a door (or doors) and windows. Prototypes among the things denoted by the English word *face* have eyes, a nose and a mouth. The face of a Cyclops, with its single eye, is a *face*, but it is not a prototype face. I have seen a windowless house (the Black House of Arnol, on the Isle of Lewis). It is incontestably a house, but it is not a prototype for the denotation of *house* in contemporary English. The information that needs to be built into meaning postulates (see Chapter 2) to reflect these semantic facts is listed in (3.1).

(3.1)   A prototype face has two eyes.
        A prototype face has a nose.
        A prototype face has a mouth.
        A prototype house has a roof.
        A prototype house has a door.
        A prototype house has windows.

I grant that prototype faces and houses may have other parts besides those listed in (3.1), for example cheeks and a chin (for faces), perhaps a bedroom and kitchen (for houses). I have merely tried to list the main ones. Importantly, there are also many things that the prototypes do not have, like blemishes and a carport, even though these may be parts of many real faces and houses, respectively.

Restricted to prototypes, the **has-relation** makes available entailments. Some examples are given in (3.2).

(3.2)   *There's a house at the corner* ⇒ 'If it is like a prototype for *house* then it has a roof'
        The child drew a face ⇒ 'If the face was prototypical, then the child drew a mouth'

In Chapter 1, entailments were introduced as guarantees. Here the guarantees are weakened by making them conditional on prototypicality. The entailed propositions in (3.2) start with 'if' because it seems that average English words are not as tightly defined as technical words like *triangle*. Given that the *has*-relation has to be restricted to prototypes for some words, it simplifies matters to do the same for all words that enter this relation.

3.1.1 Pragmatic inferences from the has-relation

The *has*-relation, restricted to prototypes, is the basis for some of our pragmatic expectations in language use. This can be seen in a switch from indefinite to definite articles. A noun phrase that first brings something into a conversation is usually indefinite (for example, marked by means of an indefinite article, *a* or *an*), but on second and subsequent mention of the same thing in the conversation it will be referred to by means of a definite noun phrase (marked by, for example, the definite article *the*), as in (3.3a, b).

(3.3) a. A: "I've bought a house." B: "Where's the house?" (not: "Where's a house?")
       b. C: (a child showing off a drawing): "I drawed a face." D: (responding to the child and commenting on the drawing): "I like the face you drew." (not: "I like a face you drew.")

However, if a whole that has a part has been mentioned, then the part can, on first mention, be referred to by means of a definite noun phrase, as illustrated by the use of *the* in the responses of B and D in (3.4a, b).

(3.4) a. A: "I've bought a house." B: "I hope the roof doesn't leak."
       b. C: "I drawed a face." D: "Where's the nose?"

3.1.2 Parts can have parts

Words denoting wholes bear the *has*-relation to the labels for their parts, but the parts can, in turn, have parts, and a whole can be a part of a larger whole, as illustrated in Figure 3.1.

I have not posited an inverse relation to the *has*-relation, one that would guarantee the existence of the relevant larger whole whenever a part of it is present. This is because parts can exist in the absence of the larger whole: for instance, newly-cast or hewn kerb stones can be lying around and not be part of any street; a builders' merchant keeps stocks of

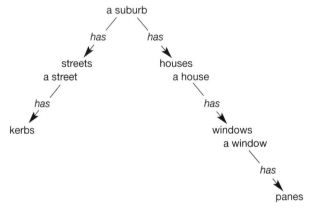

Figure 3.1 Suburbs and houses: parts can have parts

windows for houses that have not yet been built. Furthermore, the same kind of part can belong to different kinds of whole, a given kerb need not be part of a street; it could be part of an off-street parking lot.

3.1.3 Spatial parts

A prototype *thing*, such as a rock, can be said to have a *top*, a *bottom* (or *base*), *sides* and a *front* and *back*. Two points need to be noted about these words. One is that they are general: very many different kinds of thing – *windows, heads, faces, feet, buses, trees, canyons*, to randomly name just a few – have *tops, bottoms, sides, fronts* and *backs*. In Section 3.2 this will be explained in terms of a *thing* having spatial parts, making the possession of such parts characteristic of prototypes in the *thing*-category. The other notable feature of spatial part words is that they are often deictic.

Pragmatics enters the interpretation of deictic words. As explained in Chapter 1, the meaning of a deictic word is tied to the situation of utterance. The *front* of a rock faces the speaker and the *back* of a rock faces away from the speaker, and the *sides* are to the left and right from the point of view of the speaker. What counts as the *top* of the rock and what counts as the *bottom* or *base* of the rock depends on which way up the rock happens to be lying at the time of utterance. However, many things – *bus* is a good example – inherently have a non-deictic *top, bottom, front* and *back*, and *sides*. The *top* of a bus is its roof, even in the dire case of one lying overturned at the side of the road; the *front* of a bus is the driver's end of it, regardless of where the speaker is viewing it from; and so on. It is with things that do not inherently have these parts that the deictic *top, bottom, front, back* and *sides* come into play. Notice that a rescue worker who is standing "on top" (as one might say deictically) of an overturned bus is not on *the top (part)* of the bus. The list in Table 3.1 gives further examples.

There are additional subtleties that would have to be dealt with in a

Table 3.1 Examples of two kinds of spatial parts

having inherent spatial parts	*having spatial parts only deictically*
people	balls
houses	planets (in the talk of amateurs looking through a telescope)
trees (top, base, sides)	trees (front, back)
hills (top, base, sides)	hills (front, back)
animals	
pianos	

fuller account. For instance, it is possible to cede deictic centrality to someone being addressed, as when – speaking from behind a tree – a person says: "Just open your eyes and you'll see the notice: (from where you are) it's pinned on the front of the tree."

3.1.4 Ends and beginnings

Long thin things have *ends*, and sometimes two different kinds of *end* are distinguished: *beginnings* and *ends*. A list of some of the things that proto-typically have *ends* is given in (3.5).

(3.5) ropes
(pieces of) string
ships (though mariners have special words for them, *stern* and *bows*)
roads
trains
planks

Nouns denoting periods of time have *beginnings* and *ends*. They also have *middles*. Some examples are listed in (3.6a).

(3.6) a. day, week, month, era, term, semester, century
b. conversation, demonstration, ceremony, meal, reception, process

The words in (3.6b) do not denote concrete entities that you could touch or stub your toe on, but the events and processes that they can be used to refer to are nonetheless located in time and space, which is to say that it is reasonable to wonder when and where conversations, demonstrations and so forth took place. They can also have *beginnings*, *middles* and *ends*, which in Chapters 4 and 6 will be seen to be involved in verb meanings.

3.1.5 Some other parts

The body is a source of metaphors (see Chapter 5), for instance *lose one's head*, meaning 'panic'. The *has*-relation applies between various words denoting body parts. *Person* is an ambiguous word denoting either a physical person – who can, for instance, be *big* or *ugly* – or the psychological individual – who can be *kind* or *silly* and so on. The physical person proto-typically has a *head*, has a *torso*, has *arms*, has *legs*, has *genitals* and has a *skin*. These parts and some of the parts that they, in turn, prototypically have are set out in (3.7).

(3.7)   a person *has* a head, a torso, arms, legs, genitals, skin
a head *has* a face, hair, forehead, jaw
a face *has* a mouth, nose, chin, eyes, cheeks
a mouth *has* lips
a torso *has* a chest, back, belly, shoulders
an arm *has* an upper arm, forearm, biceps, elbow, wrist, hand
a hand *has* a palm, fingers, knuckles
a person's skin *has* pores

In Chapter 1 it was pointed out that semantic description is different from the compilation of an encyclopedia. Semantics is not an attempt to catalogue all human knowledge. Instead, semanticists aim to describe the knowledge about meaning that language users have simply because they are users of the language. Anatomists, osteopaths, massage practitioners and similar experts have a far more detailed vocabulary for talking about body parts than just the terms in (3.7). It is safe to assume that any competent user of English knows the meanings of the words in (3.7), and the *has*-relations listed there are the basis for inferences. If you are told that the mountain at Machu Picchu looks like a face, you can expect it to have parts corresponding to a mouth, nose, chin, eyes and cheeks, but, in an ordinary conversation, it would be unreasonable to expect that there should be parts corresponding to everything shown in an anatomy book's treatment of the face.

For the sake of clarity, I avoided using the word *body* in (3.7) because *body* is ambiguous and two of its several different senses could have been used in that example. One sense (and, to keep track of the difference, I'll call it *body*$_1$) is synonymous with *(physical) person* and another sense (*body*$_2$ for convenience of reference) is synonymous with *torso*. The first line of (3.7) could have been written as 'a body$_1$ *has* a head, a body$_2$, arms, legs, genitals, skin'. Readers who use the word *body*$_2$ in preference to *torso* might have liked that better.

A prototype *chair* has a *back*, *seat* and *legs*. Interestingly the words *back* and *legs* are also body part labels. The body part labels *head*, *neck*, *foot* and *mouth* are used to label parts of a wide range of things: for example, a *mountain* has a *head* and *foot*; *lampposts* and *bottles* both have *necks*; *caves* and *rivers* have *mouths*. Presumably this indicates a human tendency to interpret and label the world by analogy with what we understand most intimately, such as our own bodies.

3.2 Hyponymy

This relation is important for describing nouns, but it also figures in the description of verbs (see Chapter 4) and, to a lesser extent, adjectives. It is concerned with the labelling of sub-categories of a word's denotation: what kinds of Xs are there and what different kinds of entities count as Ys. For example, a *house* is one kind of *building*, and a *factory* and a *church* are other kinds of *building*, *buildings* are one kind of *structure*, *dams* are another kind of *structure*.

The pattern of entailment that defines hyponymy is illustrated in (3.8).

(3.8)   a.   There's a house next to the gate.
        b.   There's a building next to the gate.
        c. $(3.8a \Rightarrow 3.8b)$ & $\overline{(3.8b \Rightarrow 3.8a)}$

If it is true that there is a house next to the gate, then (with respect to the same gate at the same point in history) it must be true that there is a building next to the gate; it cannot be otherwise. On the other hand, if we are given (3.8b) as true information, then we cannot be sure that (3.8a) is true. It might be true, but there are other possibilities: the building next to the gate could be a barn or any other kind of building. That is why the second half of (3.8c) has been scored out; to show that – though it could follow – (3.8a) does not have to follow from (3.8b). Terminology: *building* is a superordinate[2] for *house* and nouns labelling other kinds of building. *House*, *barn*, *church*, *factory*, *hangar* and so forth are hyponyms of *building*.

It is possible to generalise about the pattern shown in (3.8): a sentence, such as (3.8a), containing a **hyponym** of a given superordinate entails a sentence that differs from the original one only in that the **superordinate** has been substituted for its hyponym, as in (3.8b). The sentence with the hyponym entails the corresponding sentence with the superordinate replacing it, but the entailment goes one way only – not from the sentence containing the superordinate. This generalisation is not watertight. There are some other conditions that would have to be stated, for instance the sentences must not be negative. With reference back to (3.8), if we knew that it was true that *there isn't a building next to the gate*, then we could be sure that (talking about the same gate at the same time) *there isn't a house next to the gate*. Because of the negative, *n't*, the entailment goes the other way round: from the sentence with the superordinate to the corresponding one with the hyponym. Incidentally, this highlights the fact that there being a building by the gate is a necessary condition for there to be a house by the gate. If there is no building at the gate, then there cannot be a house there. Intuitively it is reasonable to say that 'building' is a component of the meaning of *house*: a *house* is a 'building for living in'.

Prototypicality has to be brought into consideration for the *has*-relation, but is not needed for hyponymy.

3.2.1 Hierarchies of hyponyms

House is a hyponym of the superordinate *building*, but *building* is, in turn, a hyponym of the superordinate *structure*; and, in its turn, *structure* is a hyponym of the superordinate *thing*. A superordinate at a given level can itself be a hyponym at a higher level, as shown in Figure 3.2.

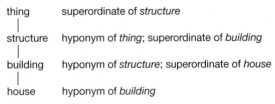

Figure 3.2 Superordinates can be hyponyms and vice versa

The hyponymy relation passes through intermediate levels in the hierarchy, which means that *house* is not only a hyponym of *building*, but is also a hyponym of *building*'s immediate superordinate, *structure*; and, via *structure*, *house* is also a hyponym of *thing*. *Thing* is a superordinate for all the words on lines that can be traced down from it in the hierarchy, and so on, as shown in Figure 3.3.

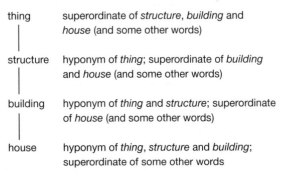

Figure 3.3 Hyponymy passes through intermediate levels

The significance of hyponymy passing through intermediate levels is that a hierarchy of this kind guarantees numerous inferences. Thus if someone who is speaking the truth tells us about a house, we know, with certainty and without having to ask, that the entity in question is a building, that it is a structure and that it is a thing.

The phrase *and some other words* is used in Figure 3.3 because the diagram shows only a fragment of the hierarchy. There are other kinds of *thing* besides *structures* (for example, *plants* are *things*); there are other kinds of *structures* besides *buildings* (for example, *dams* are *structures*); there are also words that are hyponyms of *house* (for example, *cottage* and *bunga-low*). In Section 3.2.2, it will be seen that this interacts in an interesting way with the *has*-relation, making further inferences possible.

High in the hierarchy, the senses of words (the specifications that determine their denotation; see Chapter 1) are rather general and un-detailed, which has the consequence that these words denote many different kinds of entity. At successively lower levels, the meanings are more detailed and, therefore, the words denote narrower ranges of things (see Figure 3.4).

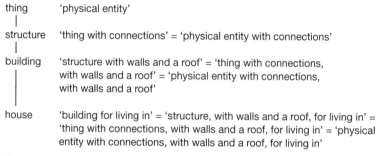

thing   'physical entity'
│
structure   'thing with connections' = 'physical entity with connections'
│
building   'structure with walls and a roof' = 'thing with connections, with walls and a roof' = 'physical entity with connections, with walls and a roof'
│
house   'building for living in' = 'structure, with walls and a roof, for living in' = 'thing with connections, with walls and a roof, for living in' = 'physical entity with connections, with walls and a roof, for living in'

Figure 3.4 Hyponym senses get successively more detailed

Please take 'with connections' as short for 'with connections between its parts'. Notice that the meaning of a **hyponym** is the meaning of its immediate superordinate elaborated by a modifier; so the meaning of *house* is the meaning of *building* modified, in this case by the modifier 'for living in'. Because *building* is itself a hyponym one level below *structure*, its meaning is that of *structure* plus a modifier, 'with walls and a roof'; and so on.

Figure 3.5 shows more of the hyponym hierarchy for nouns in English, though still only a small fraction of it. (Compound words like *garden tool* and *postgraduate* enter into semantic relations in the same way as simple words do.)

The ways in which Figure 3.5 is incomplete are obvious. There are different kinds of *places* (*islands*, *summits*, *fields* and *villages*, for instance). There are different kinds of *times* (for example, *dawn*, *noon*, *evening*). There are other *products* besides *tools* and *vehicles* (items of *furniture*, for instance). *Buildings* and *dams* are not the only kind of *structures* that exist (*bridges* are another). *Students* are not the only kind of *person*₁; and so on. *Person* appears twice, in recognition of the ambiguity mentioned in Section 3.1.5: 'physical person', shown in Figure 3.5 as *person*₂, a

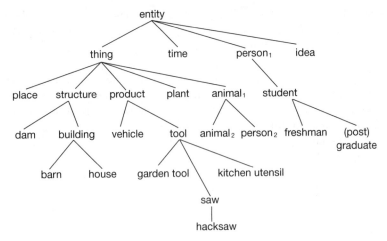

Figure 3.5 Part of the hyponym hierarchy of English nouns

hyponym of *animal₁*, and 'psychological individual', shown as *person₁*, the immediate superordinate of *student*. *Animal* appears twice in the tree because it has two senses in ordinary English usage: *animal₁* 'living thing other than plants', which, of course, includes humans; and *animal₂* 'animal₁ other than humans'. It is *person₂* that bears the *has*-relation to the body parts discussed in Section 3.1.5.

Miller and Fellbaum (1991) report on the development of WordNet, a substantial and systematic computer database of English word meanings. By 1991 WordNet contained entries for more than 54,000 different words. In creating the database, they found that a hyponym hierarchy with twenty-six high-level superordinates, such as *time, plant, animal* and so forth, 'provides a place for every English noun' (1991: 204). The highest three levels in Figure 3.5 are largely based on their description of the hyponym hierarchy for nouns in English. To keep the diagram manageable, however, I have omitted nineteen of their twenty-six high-level superordinates; so Figure 3.5 represents merely a tiny sample of the full picture.

3.2.2 Hyponymy and the has-relation

These two semantic relations should not be confused: hyponymy is about categories being grouped under superordinate terms (for example, *tandems, ATBs, tourers* and *racers* are kinds of *bicycle*; and *bicycles, unicycles* and *tricycles* are kinds of *cycle*), but the *has*-relation concerns parts that prototypical members of categories have (for instance, a prototype *cycle* has *wheel(s)*, a *frame*, *handlebars* and *pedals*; a prototype *bicycle* has these parts too and also has a *chain*). Of course, a *bicycle* does not have *tandems*, and a *chain* is not a kind of *bicycle*, as someone who confused the *has*-relation and hyponymy might think!

There is nonetheless a link between the two relations: hyponyms "inherit" the parts that their superordinates have (Miller and Fellbaum 1991: 206). If a prototype superordinate has certain parts then prototype members of that superordinate's hyponyms also have those parts. The information in Figure 3.6 can be used to illustrate this.

At the bottom of the hierarchy in Figure 3.6, a prototypical *house* has a *kitchen* and at least one *bedroom*. A prototypical *house* also has the parts that its prototypical superordinates have: *walls* and a *roof* (because prototypical *buildings* have those), *connections* between the parts ("inherited" from *structure*, one of its higher-level superordinates) and a *top*, *base*, *front*, *back* and *sides* (inherited from *thing*). What has just been said is not offered as a full account of the parts linked to *house* by the *has*-relation; for instance, prototypes in the *building* category also have *doors* and *floors*, and prototype houses have those too, by inheritance.

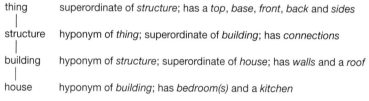

Figure 3.6 Parts that some superordinates have

In (3.7) a *person* (in the sense of a person's body, something that I later labelled *person₂*) was said to have a *head*, a *torso*, *arms*, *legs*, *genitals* and a *skin*. Except for *arms and legs*, all of these are parts tied to *animal₁* by the *has*-relation. A prototypical *person₂* *has* these parts because of being one kind of *animal₁*. (You might find it useful to look back to Figure 3.5 to remind yourself of which senses of *animal* and *person* were given which subscripts.)

With reference to Figure 3.5, a prototypical *tool* has a handle, and prototypical members of hyponyms of *tool* have handles too, by inheritance. In this way prototypical *saws* have handles; prototypical *garden tools*, such as *rakes*, have *handles*; prototypical *kitchen utensils*, such as *spatulas* and *egg whisks*, have *handles*. A non-prototypical *kitchen utensil*, such as a *mixing bowl*, however, need not have a *handle*.

For an example from nature, consider the tree name *oak*. Part of the meaning of this word comes via the *has*-relation: a prototypical *oak* has *acorns*. A prototypical *oak* also has a *trunk*, but this is by inheritance from *tree*; and, inherited from *plant*, a prototypical *oak* has *leaves*.

Note that the inheritance discussed here passes down through hyponymy. It does not pass down to parts of parts. A prototype in the *hand* category has a *palm* and *fingers*, but that does not lead us to expect prototype *palms* to have their own *palm* and *fingers*!

As a final point about interactions between the *has*-relation and hyponymy, it must be pointed out that part words can enter directly into superordinate and hyponym relations. *Wrists, knuckles, knees* and *ankles* are hyponyms of the superordinate *joint*. *Limb* is a superordinate for *arm* and *leg*. *Lid* is a hyponym of *top* – it is the 'top of a container'.

3.3 Incompatibility

A small hyponym hierarchy is shown in Figure 3.7. There are alternative labels and perhaps even different kinds of meals that could have been included (for example, *supper*, *high tea* and *brunch*), but the ones given will do for present purposes.

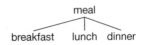

Figure 3.7 Some hyponyms of *meal*

Breakfast, lunch and *dinner* are hyponyms of *meal*, their immediate superordinate word. Hyponymy guarantees that if we hear that some people had a *breakfast* in Calais, then we know that they had a meal in Calais, because a *breakfast* is one kind of *meal*. However, there is no similarly straight entailment from a sentence with the superordinate – from a sentence containing *meal* to the corresponding sentence with one of its hyponyms. If we are told that some people had a meal in Calais, we cannot conclude, just from that, that they had breakfast there; it might have been a lunch or a dinner.

What about relations between hyponyms, like *breakfast, lunch* and *dinner*? A semantic relation called incompatibility holds between the hyponyms of a given superordinate. Hyponymy is about classification: *breakfast, lunch* and *dinner* are kinds of *meal*. **Incompatibility** is about contrast: *breakfast, lunch* and *dinner* are different from each other within the category of meals; they are eaten at different times of day. The pattern of entailment that provides the test for incompatibility is exemplified in (3.9).

(3.9) a. This is Nameera's breakfast.
  b. This is Nameera's lunch.
  c. This is Nameera's dinner.
  d. (3.9a $\Rightarrow$ NOT3.9b) & (3.9a $\Rightarrow$ NOT3.9c) & (3.9b $\Rightarrow$ NOT3.9a) & (3.9b $\Rightarrow$ NOT3.9c) & (3.9c $\Rightarrow$ NOT3.9a) & (3.9c $\Rightarrow$ NOT3.9b)
  e. ~~(NOT3.9a $\Rightarrow$ 3.9b) & (NOT3.9a $\Rightarrow$ 3.9c) & (NOT3.9b $\Rightarrow$ 3.9a) & (NOT3.9b $\Rightarrow$ 3.9c) & (NOT3.9c $\Rightarrow$ 3.9a) & (NOT3.9c $\Rightarrow$ 3.9b)~~

The six entailments in (3.9d) capture the fact that (provided the reference of *This* stays constant), if one of the sentences (3.9a–c) is true , then the other two sentences – made by substitution of incompatible words – must be false. The scoring through in (3.9e) indicates that a comparable set of entailments is not available from negative versions of sentences (3.9a–c). Knowing that a particular container in the freezer is not Nameera's breakfast does not allow one to infer that it must be her lunch; it might be her dinner, or my lunch (or even a frozen birthday cake).

3.3.1 Further points about incompatibility

The relation of antonymy, introduced in Chapter 2, exhibits the same pattern of entailment: there are entailments from affirmative sentences to negative sentences containing the antonym, but not from negative sentences to the corresponding affirmatives. For example, *long* and *short* are antonyms. Notice the way that the following entailments that these two words give us fit the larger pattern shown in (3.9d, e): a *long* ladder is not *short* and a *short* ladder is not *long*. However, a ladder that is *not long* is not necessarily *short*; it could just be middling in length. And a ladder that is *not short* is not necessarily *long*; it could be somewhere between *long* and *short*. Antonymy holds between many pairs of adjectives (and adverbs, for example *quickly* and *slowly*). It would be correct to say that *long* and *short* are incompatible, but, as most semanticists use the special term antonymy for incompatibility between pairs of adjectives (or adverbs), it is easier to keep with tradition. When adjectives occur in larger sets than pairs – as with {*black, purple, blue, brown, green, yellow, orange, red, pink, white, grey*} – then the appropriate term for the relation holding within the set is incompatibility.

Synonyms, introduced in Chapter 2, yield an exception to the generalisation that hyponyms of a given superordinate are incompatible with each other. The following are all hyponyms of *seat*: *chair, bench, stool, sofa, settee*. The relation of incompatibility holds between most of them: for example, if we know that Hazel is sitting on a chair, then we know that she is not (at that moment) sitting on a bench, stool, sofa or settee. If she is on a bench, then she is not (at that moment) on a chair, stool, sofa or settee; and so on. However *sofa* and *settee*, because they are synonyms, are not incompatible with each other. If Hazel is sitting on a sofa, then she is sitting on a settee, and vice versa.

(Non-synonymous) hyponyms of a word immediately superordinate to them are not only incompatible with each other but are also incompatible with hyponyms of their higher-level superordinates. The lists in (3.10) can be used to illustrate this.

(3.10) | Superordinate | Hyponyms |
|---|---|
| drinking vessel | glass, cup, mug |
| glass | wineglass, martini glass, tumbler |
| cup | coffee cup, tea cup |
| mug | coffee mug, beer mug |

A *tea cup* is not only not a *coffee cup* or any other kind of *cup*. It is also not a *glass* or a *mug*, nor any of the hyponyms of *glass* or *mug*. It might seem that this is boringly obvious: no given thing can be something else. That is not true, however. A *cup* can be a *present*, a *possession*, a *piece of crockery* and various other things.

Incompatibility is not pure unconstrained difference. Incompatibility is difference against a background of similarity. Remember that hyponyms of any superordinate have as their meaning the meaning of the superordinate plus some modification, for instance a *tumbler* is a 'glass without a stem' and a *glass* is a 'drinking vessel made of glass'. In the meaning given here for *tumbler*, the modifier 'without a stem' records the difference between a *tumbler* and other *glasses*, and 'glass' represents the similarity that the meaning of *tumbler* has with the meanings of *wineglass*, *martini glass* and all the other kinds of *glasses*.

3.4 Count nouns and mass nouns

In the grammar of English, there is a clear distinction between count nouns, exemplified by *loaf* and *coin* in Table 3.2, and mass nouns, exemplified by *bread* and *money*. The whole noun vocabulary divides into words that are almost always count nouns (*garment* for instance), ones that are almost always mass nouns (like *clothing*) and ambiguous ones which can be used as either mass or count nouns (like *cake*).

The question marks in Table 3.2 are there because of a special use allowable with some mass nouns, as when *bread* is taken to denote 'distinct variety of bread'. For example, one might say of a bakery that it produces

Table 3.2 Distinguishing between count and mass nouns

Count nouns	Mass nouns
This is a loaf.	?This is a bread.
This is a coin.	*This is a money.
How many loaves are there?	?How many breads are there?
How many coins are there?	*How many monies are there?
a large number of loaves	?a large number of breads
a large number of coins	*a large number of monies
six loaves	?six breads
six coins	*six monies
*How much loaves are there?	How much bread is there?
*How much coins are there?	How much money is there?

Notation
In Table 3.2

* marks severe ungrammaticality.
? is for a lesser level of ungrammaticality.

Ungrammatical signifies that we do not assemble our sentences that way in English, even if you could understand what was meant. This is different from the notation elsewhere in the book, where * and ? mark meaning problems.

"six breads" to mean that it produces 'six types of bread': wholewheat, focaccio, French sticks, and so on. *Six breads* is ungrammatical for attempting to express the meaning 'six loaves'.

Mass nouns resist being quantified with numbers and plural suffixes or the word *many* or the singular indefinite article *a* (right-hand column in Table 3.2), while **count nouns** (in the left-hand column) can be quantified in this way. Count nouns denote distinguishable whole entities, like beans or people or shirts. They can be counted. Mass nouns are quantified with the word *much*. They denote undifferentiated substance, like dough or water or lava.

Table 3.2 shows that the difference between count nouns and mass nouns is partly a matter of how the speaker or writer chooses to portray reality. What is out there in the world is pretty much the same whether you are referring to a *loaf* or to *bread*; likewise, the denotation of the words *coins* (and *banknotes* or *bills*) is pretty much the same as that of the word *money*. However, count nouns portray what we are talking about as consisting of individually distinct wholes (loaves, coins, banknotes, bills and so on), while talking about almost the same reality with mass nouns represents it as homogeneous substance, undifferentiated "stuff". Another pair that could have been selected to illustrate this is *drinks* (count) and *booze* (mass).

It is certainly not the case that when people use mass nouns to talk or write about *clothing* or *bread* or *money* or *scenery*, that they become incapable of distinguishing shirts from socks, or one sock from another, or seeing boundaries between the lakes, mountains and seascapes that go to make up scenery. They are merely treating scenery or money or whatever as if "how much" were the only difference there could be between one "dollop" of the stuff and any other dollop of it.

Hyponymy and incompatibility have been illustrated in this chapter almost entirely with count nouns. However, these two relations exist among mass nouns too. *Velvet* 'cloth with a silky nap', *corduroy* 'cloth with a corrugated nap', *gingham* and so on are mass nouns that are incompatible hyponyms of the mass noun *cloth*. (The mass noun *cloth* is the one seen in *How much cloth is produced annually?* There is a count noun *cloth* too, for instance in *You'll never use all these old cloths for wiping oil off your bicycle; throw some of them away.*)

Only individuated wholes are represented in English as having parts. Homogenous substance is not separable into distinct parts. Therefore, only count nouns bear *has*-relations to labels for their parts; mass nouns do not enter the *has*-relation (except in physical chemistry, but that is another story).

Summary

Chapter 3 has introduced three semantic relations that are important sources of entailment possibilities contributed to sentences by nouns: the *has*-relation, concerned with the parts that prototype members of categories have; hyponymy, which links words into hierarchies where superordinate words group together the kinds that comprise them; and incompatibility, which is the relation holding between the different (non-synonymous) hyponyms of any superordinate. Antonymy (introduced in Chapter 2) is a special case of incompatibility. It was shown that words denoting parts can themselves bear *has*-relations to their own parts, that they can be superordinates to their own hyponyms, and that hyponyms "inherit" parts from their superordinates. The distinction between count nouns and mass nouns was explained as a way of portraying the world. Labelling with a mass noun treats what is referred to as homogeneous substance, and therefore as not having distinct parts. Though they do not enter the *has*-relation, mass nouns can figure in hyponymy and incompatibility just as count nouns do. In Chapter 4 it will be seen that there is a similar distinction in verbs to the count-versus-mass distinction in nouns.

Exercises

1. What parts does a prototype *shoe* have? Do those parts have parts?

2. The following strikes me as a reasonable non-technical statement, even if a rather long-winded one, of the meanings of some spatial-part words:

> The *top* of a thing is one of its *sides*: the side that is uppermost. The *bottom* of a thing is one of its *sides*: the side that is down. The *front* is one of the *sides*: the side that faces forwards. The *back* is one of its *sides*, the side that faces away from the front.

If so, what sense relations hold between the words *side, top, bottom, front* and *back*? Give reasons to support your answer.

3. *Parent* is a superordinate for *mother* and *father*. At the level immediately below *parent* there are only those two hyponyms. What is the semantic relation between *mother* and *father*? Is it incompatibility or antonymy? Justify your answer.

4. For class discussion. The following words are hyponyms of *footwear*: *shoes, sneakers, trainers, sandals, slippers, boots, galoshes*.
a. Is *footwear* the superordinate that you use for all of the hyponyms or do you use the word *shoe* in a general sense that we might distinguish as *shoe₁*, as the superordinate? (After all, the kind of shop that could sell all of them is a *shoe shop*.)
b. Find as many other hyponyms of *footwear* (or *shoe₁*) as you can.
c. Draw up a hyponym hierarchy, similar to Figure 3.5, for the given words and any additional ones you have found.
d. Try to provide a brief characterisation of the meaning of each word in the hierarchy, in the form of its immediate superordinate plus a modifying phrase. Avoid getting into encyclopedic description.

5. *Paper, glass* and *cheese* are ambiguous between a count sense and a mass sense.
a. Devise a pair of example sentences for each of them that clearly brings out the count-mass difference.
b. Find some hyponyms for each of the words in each of its senses and,

on the basis of these, comment informally on the meanings of the super-ordinates.

Recommendations for reading

You might find Grandy (1987) a fairly difficult article, but it is valuable for proposing solutions to various problems that arise for simple accounts of hyponymy like the one in this chapter. Cruse (2000) provides detailed and thoughtful discussion of meronymy (the part-to-whole relation), hyponymy and incompatibility. Kearns (2000) is an excellent source for more about differences in meaning between count and mass nouns. Imai (2000) reports on an interesting series of experiments on count and mass noun meanings, comparing speakers of English and Japanese, children as well as adults.

Notes

1. Some semanticists (Cruse 2000, for instance) distinguish between *holonyms* (words for wholes) and *meronyms* (words for parts). My *has*-relation could be called *holonymy*. I use a different label because I have not paired it with its usual inverse, *meronymy* – the relation of parts "belonging" to wholes. See the end of section 3.1.2 for justification.

2. *Hypernym* and *hyperonym* are alternatives occasionally found in semantics books, instead of the term *superordinate*. *Hyperonym* makes it clear that it belongs in a pair with *hyponym*, but *superordinate* is an easy term to learn and students are not then faced with remembering a distinction between two somewhat confusible terms, *hyperonym* and *hyponym*.

4 Verbs and situations

Overview

This chapter is about verb meanings. A simplified account of the semantic ingredients that make a clause (such as *Robby brought me the news*) is that a verb (*brought*, in this case) "says something about" – that is, interrelates – the entities referred to by noun phrases (here *Robby*, *me* and *the news*). Among the reasons why this is only partly correct is that not all noun phrases are referring expressions (for instance, in *Blinko was a famous clown*, the noun phrase *a famous clown* puts Blinko into a category, rather than being used to refer to some clown), and it is not only verbs that categorise or interrelate entities (for example, most of the meaning of the preposition *on* in *Those cups are on the shelf* could alternatively be carried by a verb, *The shelf supports those cups*; and the sentence *They made a fool of him*, containing the noun *fool*, has a paraphrase with a verb *They fooled him*). There is nonetheless enough truth in the idea to justify talking of a clause as expressing a proposition by having a verb as its semantic centre and some accompanying referential expressions.

Verbs differ in whether they demand one, two or three noun phrases (italicised in Examples (4.1) and (4.2). Later discussion will show that this can have systematic effects on meaning.

(4.1) *Billy* lies. (meaning that he tells untruths; one noun phrase)
       Benjamin Franklin told *the truth*. (two noun phrases)
       I offered *her a scone*. (three noun phrases)

In place of noun phrases, some verbs will accept preposition phrases (for example *to her* in 4.2a). And sometimes positions are filled by embedded clauses (like the *that*-clauses in 4.2c–e). A **clause** usually has a verb of its own and can carry a proposition, for example *Spring has come early* carries a proposition about the start of a season. In (4.2c, e) the same clause is not free-standing, but has been **embedded** (which is to say "packed into") another clause as object of the verb *confirm*. In (4.2d, e) we see a clause embedded as the subject. The word *that* is one of the markers made available by English grammar to mark a clause as embedded.

(4.2) a. *I* offered *a scone to her.*
   b. *This evidence* confirms *my hunch.*
   c. *It* confirms *that spring has come early.*
   d. *That the daffodils are blooming* confirms *my hunch.*
   e. *That the daffodils are blooming* confirms *that spring has come early.*
   f. Offer *him a scone.*

The term **argument** is used to cover all kinds of obligatory, potentially-referential constituents that verbs require, whether they are noun phrases (like *This evidence*) or embedded clauses (like *that the daffodils are blooming* or *that spring has come early*) or preposition phrases. (In this context *argument* does not mean 'dispute'.) Example (4.2a) has three arguments. The main clauses in (4.2b–e) each have two arguments. Example (4.2f) has three arguments, because the "understood" subject 'you' counts as an argument.

Especially with verbs, meaning is a property not just of individual words, but is affected by the constructions they appear in. The following is an instance showing how the array of arguments in a clause can influence the way the meaning of a verb is understood. Until I read a newspaper headline *Robbers spray victims to sleep* (*Fiji Post,* 1 June 1995), the verb *spray* was not, for me, one that took an embedded clause. However, on seeing it with the clause *victims to sleep* as its second argument, I immediately understood that *spray* was causative here: the robbers caused the victims to fall asleep by spraying something at them.

Section 4.1, below, discusses causative verbs, with and without an embedded clause indicating the situation caused. With causatives, the proposition carried by the embedded clause is entailed by the whole sentence: thus, if it is true that 'the robbers sprayed the victims to sleep', it must also be true that 'the victims slept'. Section 4.2 is about research based on Zeno Vendler's influential account (1967) of ways that verbs and their arguments indicate how a situation is structured in time. **Aspect** is the general term for the encoding in language of the time profiles of events, for example whether things build up to a climax or just continue unchanged. It is aspect as a property of English words[1] that is considered in this chapter. Chapter 6 takes the discussion further, focusing mainly on aspect as marked in the grammar of English.

4.1 Causatives

The sentences in the left-hand column of Table 4.1 are causatives and each one entails the sentence to its right.

Table 4.1 Examples of causative sentences with an entailment from each

Causatives	Entailments
The thought made her gleeful.	She was gleeful.
The children got the kite to fly.	The kite flew.
Bad weather forces us to cancel the picnic.	We are cancelling the picnic.
His inexperience is causing the decisions to go unactioned.	The decisions are going unactioned.
I had the students read this article.	The students read this article.
The lock prevented him from opening the door. (a negative causative)	He did not open the door (that time).

The sentences on the right in Table 4.1 have either one or two arguments (in the special sense of argument introduced above) and they describe states or events. The causatives on the left differ from the corresponding sentences on the right in several ways:

- They include a causative verb (*make, get, force, cause, have, prevent* in these examples).
- The subject (*the thought, the children, bad weather* and so on) is an extra argument – in addition to the arguments of the corresponding sentence on the right.
- The subject of the causative sentence is used to refer to whatever – human, abstract or concrete – brings about the situation described by the sentence on the right.
- The causative has an embedded clause carrying the same proposition as the sentence to its right in the table. This is most clearly seen in *I had (the students read this article)*, where the embedded clause is in parentheses. (Even here there has been a change. Think of how *read* is pronounced: in the causative as /riːd/, the untensed base form of the verb, but as a past tense verb /rɛd/ in the entailed free-standing clause.)

So the meaning expressed by a **causative** sentence is: a situation is brought about – caused – by whatever the subject noun phrase refers to, and the caused situation is described by the embedded clause.[2] For example, the person referred to as *I* caused the situation 'the students read this article' to come about.

The verb in the main clause of a causative sentence is a **causative verb**. *Cause* is arguably a superordinate for the other causative verbs in Table 4.1, for example the causative verb *force* can be taken to mean 'cause an unwanted consequence', where the hyponym's meaning given in single quotes is (as noted in Chapter 3) the meaning of the superordinate with a modifier. It would take more space than is available here to present the case properly. But, accepting *cause* as the superordinate, we have the entailment pattern shown in (4.3), where X is the referent of the subject of the causative sentence and the single quotes enclose propositions – clause meanings.

(4.3)   'X cause ('clause')' $\Rightarrow$ 'clause'

Of course, the relevant details of the entailed clause need to stay the same on either side of the arrow: 'clause' is the same proposition both times, even if the wording changes from, for example, *the kite to fly* (left-hand column in Table 4.1) to *The kite flew* (right-hand column). (You might wonder how the two propositions can be the same, given that *The kite flew* is past tense, unlike *the kite to fly*. Past tense, matching *flew*, is on the verb *got* in *The children got the kite to fly* – and the embedded clause *the kite to fly*, falling within the scope of *got*, receives past tense from the main clause verb.)

The embedded clause – the one in brackets in (4.3) – is an argument of the causative verb. Semantically, causative verbs have a minimum[3] of two arguments: one denoting the causer and one denoting the caused state or event. I'll call the latter argument the **embedded situation**. The embedded situation itself contains arguments; for two of the examples discussed in the previous paragraphs they are *the students, this article* and *the kite*.

4.1.1 Adverbial diagnostics

Consider (4.4a). (Perhaps Lucinda is an anaesthetist who needed access to a particular store-room for the week in question.) Example (4.4a) entails (4.4b), a causative construction, and I am going to suggest that (4.4a) is itself a causative construction, even though it lacks an embedded clause. Tenny (2000) proposes that a justification for this sort of claim can be found by looking at what is modified by certain adverbials, such as the preposition phrase *for the week* in (4.4a).

(4.4)   a.   The staff nurse gave Lucinda a key for the week.
        b.   The staff nurse caused Lucinda to have a key for the week.
        c.   Lucinda had a key for the week.

Because (4.4b) is a causative fitting the pattern to the left of the entailment arrow in (4.3), we should expect (4.4b) to entail (4.4c), and intuitively it does.

Giving is not the only way of causing someone to have something;

a malicious individual who "plants" an incriminating key on Lucinda would also 'cause her to have' it. So, while (4.4a) entails (4.4b), the entailment does not go in the reverse direction: starting from knowledge that (4.4b) is true would not guarantee that (4.4a) is true. Recall from Chapter 3 that a one-way pattern of entailment, with the rest of the sentence kept constant, defines the semantic relationship of hyponym to superordinate. *Give* is a hyponym of *cause ... to have.*

There are several possible interpretations available for (4.4a), but on the most obvious one the staff nurse gave Lucinda a key once and Lucinda retained possession of it for the week. On this interpretation, what does *for the week* have its modifying effect on? A reasonable answer is seen in the entailed sentence (4.4b), where *for the week* modifies the clause with *have* to indicate how long Lucinda had the key. The modifier does its work on the meaning carried by the entailed clause, the one describing the caused situation.

If we think of the verb *cause* in (4.4b) as describing a single event[4] in which the staff nurse hands over a key to Lucinda (or "plants" it in Lucinda's coat pocket), then that is likely to take only seconds and it would be implausible to think that *for the week* says how long that event lasts. It is the same with (4.4a): if *for the week* modifies *give* as a handing-over event, then the situation is far-fetched: the staff nurse very, very slowly takes up the key and – over a period of days – passes it across to Lucinda. For the ordinary way of understanding (4.4a), it is reasonable to say that the durational preposition phrase *for the week* does not modify the handing over, but instead modifies an "understood" embedded situation 'Lucinda to have a key', and the effect of this modification can be expressed by (4.4c).

In a sentence like (4.4b), as well as adverbial modification operating on the embedded situation clause – the clause with *have* – there could be separate adverbial modification on the main clause – the one with the causative verb *cause* – as exemplified in (4.5).

(4.5)   The staff nurse a year earlier caused Lucinda to have a key in 2005.

The sentence in (4.5) is a possible way of talking about a staff nurse doing something in 2004 – perhaps through inattention misplacing a key – and Lucinda, who might never have had any interaction with that staff nurse, getting the key a year later, for example taking it from where it is hanging on the wrong hook in the hospital ward's key cupboard. Whatever the scenario, the point is that two-clause causatives like (4.4b) and (4.5) can be used to describe **indirect causation**: someone does something and – perhaps unintentionally; maybe after a long interval – causes a situation which can be traced back to that person's act. By contrast, a one-clause causative, such as *The staff nurse gave Lucinda a key*, describes **direct causation**, so (4.4a) is not suitable for expressing Lucinda getting a key in an event that was caused by an act distant in time and not intended to result in her having the key.

In Table 4.1 the causative sentences each had an overt embedded clause. But in Table 4.2 the causative sentences are like (4.4a) in having only one clause syntactically, though for each of them there is an entailed proposition about a caused situation – an entailment that could be expressed by means of the corresponding sentence in the right-hand column of Table 4.2. In view of these entailments, it is reasonable to call the sentences in the left-hand column causative. And bearing in mind the relationships illustrated in (4.4a–c), the entailed propositions can be taken as "understood" embedded situations in the causatives.

Table 4.2 Three kinds of one-clause causative with an entailment from each

Causatives	*Entailments*
different verbs (e.g. *feed–eat*)	
She fed the baby some mashed banana.	The baby ate some mashed banana.
The bank has lowered its interest rate.	The bank's interest rate dropped.
Drought killed the lawn.	The lawn died.
morphologically related verbs and adjectives (e.g. *enrich–rich*)	
Nitrogen spills have enriched the soil here.	The soil is rich here.
The graphic artist enlarged the logo.	The logo became larger.
His job deafened Dougie.	Dougie became deaf (to an extent).
same verb form used causatively and non-causatively (e.g. *walk–walk*)	
The guide walks tourists through the eco park.	Tourists walk through the eco park.
The gardener grew several vines.	Several vines grew.
He chipped one of his teeth.	One of his teeth chipped.

Imagine that a brand new bank starts business offering a low interest rate on its credit card accounts. A year later difficult financial circumstances obliges it to raise its interest rate. After a few months it proves to be possible to drop the rate back to its original level. Notice, in the scenario just sketched, that this bank's rate is decreasing for the first time ever. Nonetheless, this first fall can be reported as *The bank has lowered its interest rates again*. There are other ways of wording the report, but – perhaps surprisingly – it is possible to use the adverb *again*. This use of *again* is called **restitutive**: there is restitution of a previously existing state (Tenny 2000). For the case in question, the rate was low, then it rose, then it was low. Because it had been low before, it is appropriate to use *again* even to describe the first ever decrease in the rate. This is a reason for thinking that part of the meaning of the *bank* sentence is an embedded proposition which is not syntactically visible as an embedded clause. When there is reversion back to an earlier state, the restitutive adverb *again* can operate on the embedded situation, and this is evidence that the embedded situation is part of the meaning of the clause.

To be considered next are differences between the entailed sentences in the right-hand column of Table 4.2 in terms of the number and types of arguments demanded by their verbs. The first sentence *The baby ate some mashed banana* is the only one that is **transitive**, which is to say that it is a clause with a subject argument (*The baby*) and a direct object argument (*some mashed banana*). *Tourists walk through the eco park* also has two arguments (*You* and *through the eco park*) but, because of the preposition *through*, the constituent *through the eco park* is not a direct object; so the sentence is **intransitive**, rather than transitive. Other intransitive sentences here are *The bank's interest rate dropped*, *The lawn died*, *Several vines grew* and *One of his teeth chipped*. They will be discussed soon. The other sentences on the right in Table 4.2 have copula verbs, *be* or *become* (see Miller 2002: 30–2). Semantically, these copula sentences indicate that the referent of the subject belongs in a category that is often labelled by an adjective, for instance *The soil is rich here* designates the soil here as being in the category 'rich'; likewise, for the logo coming into the sub-category of 'larger (things)' and Dougie becoming 'deaf (to an extent)'.

Intransitive clauses have been divided into two rather opaquely-named kinds (Trask 1993: 290–2) on the basis of the kind of the subject argument that their verbs require:

- An **unergative** verb requires a subject that is consciously responsible for what happens. *Walk* is such a verb and *Tourists walk through the eco park* is an unergative clause. A good test is acceptability with the adverb *carefully*, because taking care is only a possibility when an action is carried out deliberately. *Tourists carefully walk through the eco park* is unproblematic.
- **Unaccusative** verbs are seen in *The bank's interest rate dropped*, *The lawn died*, *Several vines grew* and *One of his teeth chipped*. These intransitives will not easily take the adverb *carefully*. *The bank's interest rate carefully dropped*, *The lawn carefully died*, *Several vines carefully grew*, *One of his teeth carefully chipped*. Even if the subject argument is a human being, the sentence will be peculiar when *carefully* is put into construction with

an unaccusative verb, for example *Mort carefully died. With an un-accusative verb, the subject is affected by the action but does not count as responsible for it.

The last two lines of Table 4.2 show causatives entailing unaccusatives with the same verb form: *Gardeners grow vines* ⇒ *Vines grow*; *He chipped a tooth* ⇒ *A tooth chipped*. Fellbaum, who has done extensive studies of English vocabulary, says there are thousands of such pairs (2000: 54). Some more are listed in (4.6).

(4.6)   bend, break, dry, hang, hurt, lean, pop, spill, split, turn

With the verbs in (4.6) a systematic semantic connection – causative-to-unaccusative entailment – is paralleled by a morphological link, in this case no change (also called **conversion** or **zero derivation**), as in *He spilt the coffee* ⇒ *The coffee spilt*. Regular patterns like this prompt the search for similar semantic ties even when the word forms are unrelated, as with *kill* and *die* in Table 4.2.

4.2 Situation types

The historical starting point for this section is an article by Zeno Vendler (1967) called 'Verbs and times'. Much of his discussion concerned verb phrases, rather than verbs in isolation. He classified verb phrases into four kinds, differing according to how the denoted states or actions are distributed in time: almost instantaneous switches between states (as with *notice a mistake*), simple existence of a state (for example, *hate hypocrisy*), ongoing actions (like *ring handbells*) and goal-directed actions that culminate (*cook dinner*, for example). It is worth extending the domain from verb phrases to clauses, because the subject of the clause can be important too: for instance, while *Jo cooked dinner* describes a culminating activity, if *First one home cooked dinner* was the rule for a household, then the latter sentence denotes a state rather than an activity.

Vendler's (1967) paper is a classic, the basis for a substantial field of research on the interface between syntax and semantics. Vendler's labels and much of his framework continue to be used, but no attempt is made here to distinguish the original version from subsequent changes. Instead, a sketch will be given of the semantic side of this work as it was around the turn of the century. (My account owes quite a lot to Levin and Rappaport 1998, Tenny and Pustejovsky 2000, and Huddleston and Pullum 2002).

The four sentences in (4.7) illustrate Vendler's four kinds of situation. His labels are given in parentheses. They are technical terms that are going to be explained here. Though *achievement* and *accomplishment* have positive connotations in ordinary usage, they are evaluatively neutral when we are talking about **situation types**.

(4.7) a. She got her ankle sprained. (achievement)
b. She had a sprained ankle. (state)
c. She had physiotherapy. (activity)
d. She got better. (accomplishment)

Get and *have* are among the most frequently used English verbs (Leech et al. 2001: 282) and both have several meanings, but for present purposes it is essential to keep with a single meaning for each of the sentences in (4.7). Think of (4.7a) as a description of a one-off sports accident and of (4.7d) as expressing the person's recovery from the accident. The main verb in both is *get*, but different senses of *get* are in play. The accident (4.7a) is a sudden transition from ankle being okay to ankle being sprained. In a transition of this kind – an **achievement** – there is not usually enough time to avoid the outcome by stopping partway through. This shows in the unacceptability of * *She stopped getting her ankle sprained.* It is different with the **accomplishment** meaning of *get* (seen in 4.7d): there is nothing linguistically strange about *She stopped getting better.* The culmination is a state of good health, but *getting better* also encodes a healing process that leads up to it, and English allows us to talk of stopping during that process, before the end result has been reached.

A subsidiary point needs to be made about the phrase *get better* in (4.7d), which, in the way I asked you to understand it, has the idiomatic meaning 'recover one's health' (see Chapter 1 for the term *idiom*). *Ill* and "health-recovery *better*" form a pair of complementaries (see Chapter 2 for the term). We can reasonably wonder whether a person who was ill is *completely better*, and in ordinary conversation I have heard the argument made that "If you are not completely better, then you are still ill". No matter how gradual or constant the rate at which someone recovers, the sentence *She got better* encodes it as if a sharp boundary into good health is eventually crossed. With a gradable adjective such as *bigger*, the adverb *completely* yields semantically dubious sentences: * *Tokyo is completely bigger than London.* (If *She got better* is taken as a description of improvement in someone's volleyball playing, then *better* is the comparative form of a gradable adjective and, just like *bigger*, rejects modification with *completely*.)

Another indication that English treats achievements, like (4.7a), as if they were instantaneous, but accomplishments, like (4.7d), as having a pre-culmination phase spread out in time is the contrast between * *She was getting her ankle sprained* – no good on the one-off accident reading – and the normality of *She was getting better*. This is because **progressive**

aspect marking (BE + Verb-*ing*) highlights the durative phase of an event and ignores its termination (see Chapter 6 for more on this). Achievements are encoded as not having duration, so progressive aspect is inapplicable to (4.7a), while the lead-in phase of an accomplishment has duration, allowing progressive marking on (4.7d).

Progressive aspect marks not only duration – extendedness in time (and hence its unacceptability with the abrupt changes called achievements) – it also signals dynamism. Progressive marking does not go well with clauses describing situations where nothing happens, where there is no dynamism. **State** sentences such as (4.7b) do not readily accept progressive marking: *She was having a sprained ankle.* On the other hand, the progressive is freely applicable to the **activity** use of *have* in (4.7c): *She was having physiotherapy.* (Going back to (4.7b) and the progressive: consider the possibility of a speaker saying in all seriousness: *She was having a sprained ankle.* In real conversations one does not usually say "That's an asteriskable sentence. Please try something different." Instead, an interpretation could be made along the following lines: progressive aspect indicates a dynamic performance; so what is being described cannot be the state that we expect *have a sprained ankle* to denote, it must have been an activity; so perhaps the person with the sprained ankle was making a big show of her suffering.)

Stop was one of the tests mentioned for distinguishing achievements (4.7a) from accomplishments (4.7d). Both states (4.7b) and activities (4.7c) can be stopped: *She stopped having a sprained ankle; She stopped having physiotherapy.* The first of these might not be the best way to say that the person in question no longer had a sprained ankle, but I think it is good enough for a plus sign to go under *stop* in the states row of Table 4.3. Add a query mark if you wish; states will still be distinguished from the other situation types.

Examination of the first two columns of asterisks and pluses in Table 4.3 shows that these two tests alone are not sufficient to distinguish activities from accomplishments: both are double-plus. The possibility of first-time use of restitutive *again*, introduced in Section 4.1.1, makes the distinction. An activity, such as (4.7c), modified by *again* can only be understood as the activity happening for a second or subsequent time: *She had physiotherapy again. (It worked for her before; so let's hope it does this time.)* But if an accomplishment, such as (4.7d), results in restitution of a state that the subject was in before, first-time use of *again* is possible: *She got better again. (I'm so glad, because she had never had health problems before.)* This suggests that, similarly to causatives, accomplishments have an "understood" embedded situation: 'she be in good health' for (4.7d). There is no named causer in (4.7d), but as with the causatives, this embedded

Table 4.3 Tests to distinguish four verb-based situation types (with indications in parentheses of why the tests work)

situation types	stop (interruptability)	progressive aspect (duration and dynamism)	first-time use of restitutive again (embedded situation)
achievements	*	*	+
states	+	*	*
activities	+	+	*
accomplishments	+	+	+

+ semantically unproblematic
* semantically wrong

situation is entailed: *She got better* ⇒ *She was better*. The time for the tense of the embedded proposition comes from *got*, the overt verb of (4.7d); so *She was better* to the right of the entailment arrow is taken as becoming true at the time that *She got better* became true.

Table 4.3 shows states and activities asterisked in the restitutive-*again* column. This does not mean that the wording is ruled out. It is simply that *She had a sprained ankle again* and *She had physiotherapy again* are false (a serious semantic problem) if we are talking about the first time she had a sprained ankle or had physiotherapy. To understand why achievements have a plus under restitutive *again*, imagine a foetus developing, from the beginning, with a sprained ankle and therefore being born with one. Imagine that physiotherapy sorts out the problem and the infant stops having a sprained ankle,[5] but learning to walk about a year later there is an accident and she sprains her ankle. Even if this is the child's first accident of any kind, it can be reported using restitutive *again* on the achievement sentence (4.7a): *She got her ankle sprained again.*

4.2.1 Accomplishments contain activities and achievements, which in turn contain states

When an unwell person gets better (an accomplishment), there is a phase of healing or taking medicine or whatever (an activity) which culminates in a transition from ill to well (an achievement), and immediately after that the person is in good health (a state). A compact representation of this is offered in (4.8): states and activities are taken as simple situations; an achievement is more complex because it contains a state as an embedded proposition; and an accomplishment is even more complex because it contains both an activity and an achievement.

(4.8)   accomplishment = activity (achievement (state))

The pattern is not restricted to getting well after injury. The scheme of four situation types is much more general, and another set of examples (4.9) will now be discussed to begin to illustrate this.

(4.9)   a.   He joined the band. (achievement)
        b.   He was a member of the band. (state)
        c.   I talked to him about it. (activity)
        d.   I got him to join the band. (accomplishment)

An achievement, such as (4.9a), incorporates an implicit end-state, (4.9b) in this instance: joining the band results in him being a member of the band. There is an entailment here: as soon as (4.9a) becomes true, (4.9b) does too, provided *he* refers to the same person in both sentences and the referent of *the band* remains constant. The part of an accomplishment, such as (4.9d), that works towards the goal is an activity, like (4.9c): one way – not the only way – of getting people to join a band is to talk to them about it. The goal of an accomplishment is an entailed achievement, here (4.9a).

If you applied the tests of Table 4.3 to the sentences in (4.9), then perhaps you judged *He was joining the band* – the progressive version of (4.9a) – as okay, which, of course, would not fit with the second asterisk in the achievements row of Table 4.3. It is worth explaining why this judgement does not undermine the proposed test. Three possibilities would allow progressive marking to be added to (4.9a) unproblematically:

• Joining this particular band may be a drawn-out process. You do not just get accepted the first time you turn up for a practice. Instead there are auditions, forms to fill in and committee approval to be obtained. If so, it becomes an accomplishment situation instead. As noted in Table 4.3, accomplishments accept progressive marking, which then operates on the rigmarole that precedes the achievement.

• *He was joining the band at the beginning of every semester and dropping out after a couple of weeks.* Extended in this way (4.9a) has an interpretation called **habitual**, which could alternatively be expressed with *used to*: *He used to join the band at the beginning of every semester* … This converts the sequence of his joinings into an activity. As an activity, it should be acceptable with *stop*. It is: *He has stopped joining the band at the beginning of every semester.* So a more rigorous version of the Table 4.3 criteria would exclude habitual interpretations. (Chapter 6 has more on habituality.)

- In certain circumstances we can use progressive aspect to talk about the future, notably when something is scheduled, for example *The timetable says there's another bus arriving in an hour.* So (4.9a) with progressive marking could have been a scheduled event at some time in the past: *He was joining the band, so he bought a new trombone.* This usage would have to be ruled out too in applying the Table 4.3 tests.

The point of this discussion is that doing semantics calls for careful thought. Asking why a test seems to fail can lead to deeper understanding and a better specification of the conditions under which the test does work. Or it can show that a test should be discarded, though I do not think this is the case here.

As well as being an accomplishment, the sentence in (4.9d) is a causative on the pattern of those in Table 4.1. I regard causative sentences as a subspecies of accomplishments. It is not possible to pursue the issue here, but it appears that all the causatives in Tables 4.1 and 4.2 fit the criteria for accomplishments given in Table 4.3.

4.2.2 Agents and goals

Table 4.4 presents a selection of further examples of the four situation types and classifies them according to goal-directedness and whether or not there is an instigator (termed an *agent*).

Table 4.4 The four situation types classified on presence of goals and agents

	states (−goal)	*achievements (+goal)*
−agent	Axel owned a pair of jeans. You sound hoarse. Even small contributions count.	Axel received a pair of jeans. I heard a bang. She realised that 512 was 8 cubed.
	activities (−goal)	*accomplishments (+goal)*
±agent	This machine embroiders. Someone was listening. He slept.	The river flooded the meadow. The court heard all the evidence. They planted the field with rye. The hikers walked to Crianlarich. The campers are packing up.

The referent of an argument is an **agent** if the language encodes it as consciously responsible for what happens. Without naming it, the concept was introduced earlier in connection with unergative clauses, which have agent subjects, and unaccusatives, which do not. *Carefully* was offered as a test for agency. It produces strange results with all six of the sentences in the top half of Table 4.4, for example *Even small contributions carefully count*, *I carefully heard a bang*, indicating that the subjects of states and achievements are not agents, which is why they have been given a minus for the feature agent. If such sentences are intransitive, like *Even small contributions count*, then they are unaccusative. Activities and accomplishments are annotated ± for agency because some of them have agents but some do not: courts can carry out their functions carefully and someone can listen carefully, but some of the other sentences in the lower half of the table are semantically weird with *carefully*, for example *He carefully slept*, *The river carefully flooded the meadow*. Although ±agent is not a very interesting characterisation of activities and accomplishments, the absence of agency from states and achievements does identify one feature of their meaning clearly.

By the way, even though sleeping is a rather inert process, it is nonetheless encoded in English as an activity. It passes the tests in Table 4.3 and it can be used to answer *What ... do?* questions: "What did he do?" "He slept". But this is inappropriate with states: "He owned a pair of jeans" is not a reasonable answer to "What did Axel do?"

Achievements and accomplishments are directed towards **goals**[6] – end-points after which the event is over: for instance the event encoded in *Axel received a pair of jeans* has been achieved the moment Axel has those jeans; the action of the meadow flooding has been accomplished when the meadow reaches a flooded state. Among the tests that Vendler (1967) put forward for distinguishing among situation types were time preposition phrases with *in* and *for*.

Acceptability with an *in*-time phrase, such as *in twenty seconds* or *in four hours*, diagnoses the presence of a goal. *She realised in twenty seconds that 512 was eight cubed* indicates that the flash of realisation came twenty seconds after some point that is not actually specified in the achievement sentence – perhaps timing started when she was set an arithmetical puzzle. And it is the same with achievement sentences generally: an *in*-phrase specifies, from some prior point external to the encoded situation, how long it takes before the achievement happens. For another example, here is (4.7a) with an *in*-phrase: *She got her ankle sprained in ten minutes* – perhaps from the start of the game.

With accomplishments an *in*-time phrase represents the time taken up with the activity that leads to the achievement (see (4.8) if you need a reminder about the components encoded in an accomplishment). Thus *The court heard all the evidence in four hours* says there was a four-hour listening phase (including note-taking and whatever other legal activities normally form part of it) at the end of which there was an achievement –

all the evidence had been heard and the evidence then had the status (a word related to *state*) of 'heard evidence'. It is the same with other accomplishments, for example (4.7d), modified with an *in*-time phrase: *She got better in ten days*; the healing activity that culminated in her regaining good health lasted for ten days.

It is different when an *in*-phrase is put with situation types that lack a goal (states and activities). This leads either to semantic oddity or it pushes them over into the achievement class. *You sound hoarse in five minutes* could be taken as a warning that some kind of vocal malpractice leads rapidly to hoarseness, but that kind of transition is an achievement, not a state. Instead of being understood as an activity clause, *He slept in five minutes* is likely to be interpreted as an achievement clause meaning 'He fell asleep in five minutes'.

States and activities go comfortably with *for*-phrases, however. These specify the duration of the state or activity: for example *Axel owned a pair of jeans for a week*, *He slept for an hour*. Because a goal is not part of the meaning, no sudden change at the end is encoded: Axel might or might not have got rid of his jeans at the end of the week; the person who slept could wake up after the hour or sleep on for another hour; the end is not made explicit.

For-duration phrases with achievements and accomplishments lead to mixed results, depending on whether they are interpreted as indicating the length of the end-state or – with accomplishments – the length of the activity phase. The achievement *Axel received a pair of jeans for a week* can be understood as meaning that the goal state of his having the jeans lasted for a week; after that he was expected to give them up. With an accomplishment, like *They planted the field with rye for a week*, two interpretations are generally possible: 'the goal-state of the field being planted with rye lasted for a week' and after that they replaced it with oats; or the field was enormous and the work was slow, so 'the activity of planting rye in the field lasted for a week' – the goal was to plant the whole field with rye, but the sentence with the *for*-phrase having the activity as its scope does not say whether the goal was reached. (Given that the speaker could just as easily have explicitly signalled completion by saying *They planted the field with rye in a week*, there is a pragmatic inference – an implicature – encouraged by the use of the *for*-phrase, namely that planting on the occasion in question stopped before the goal was achieved.)

Locative goal phrases, like *to the corner*, *on to the plateau* or *home*, when used with motion verbs like *walk*, *crawl*, *swim* or *fly*, have a role in accomplishment clauses. They specify the goal that ends the activity phase of the accomplishment. In the accomplishment encoded by *The hikers walked to Crianlarich*, this instance of walking activity ends with an understood embedded achievement 'they got to Crianlarich', which itself includes an understood end-state 'they were [then] in Crianlarich'. The **completive particle** *up* in *The campers are packing up* does a similar job of specifying the goal.

With many accomplishments a direct object noun phrase – particularly if it is definite – delimits the activity. *The field*, direct object in *They planted the field with rye*, gives the measure of the rye-planting activity: it is over when the field is planted. A superficially similar sentence is *They planted rye in the field*. Here the **locative argument** *the field* is no longer direct object; what we could call the **"material" argument** *rye* is the direct object. There is an interesting meaning difference here and, to highlight it, indefinite *rye* has been made definite *the rye* in (4.10).

(4.10)   a.   They planted the field with the rye. (meaning 'the whole field was done')
         b.   They planted the rye in the field. (meaning 'all the rye was used up')

When *the field*, direct object in (4.10a), has been completely planted, the goal has been accomplished, even if there is some rye left over. On the other hand, with *the rye* in direct object position (4.10b), the activity phase is over when the rye has been completely used up, even if a part of the field is left without rye. *Spray*, *smear* and *load* are among other verbs that pattern in the same way – either the locative argument or the "material" argument appears as direct object, and the other one of these two comes as a preposition phrase (*with the rye* or *in the field*).

Chapter 3 introduced the distinction between mass and count nouns, partly a matter of different words (for instance, *bread* is a mass noun, but *loaf* is a count noun) and partly a matter of grammatical marking (*I don't eat much cake* illustrates a mass use of the noun *cake*, but *cake* is a count noun in *I don't eat many cakes*). At a rather abstract level, there is a parallel with some of what was noted above regarding goals. The language treats both states and activities as homogenous, like mass uses of nouns: asking how long the state or activity went on for is similar to asking how much cake or bread is involved. On the other hand, similar to count uses of nouns, we saw that accomplishments and achievements are delimited (sometimes overtly by means of *in*-time phrases, definite direct objects and so on) and individuated (remember the discussion of restitutive *again*). As with mass–count in nouns, goal-directedness is partly a matter of using different verbs (*smile* – activity, but *explode* – achievement) and partly a matter of how the clause is constructed (*The children counted aloud* – activity, but *The cashier counted the day's takings* – accomplishment).

Summary

This chapter has been about verbs in the encoding of situations, concentrating on how what is talked about is packaged in time, part of the study of aspect (to be taken further in Chapter 6). States and activities are the simplest kind. The language treats them as existing without change for periods of time, somewhat like the homogeneous "stuff" that mass nouns (see Chapter 3) denote. Contrasting with them are two kinds of situation that end when goals are reached (thus exhibiting a general similarity to the bounded entities denoted by count nouns): achievements encoding abrupt entry into a state, and accomplishments, which comprise an activity phase that culminates in an achievement. Discussion began with a subtype of accomplishments called causatives. Causatives entail a caused situation brought about by the referent of the subject. Sometimes the embedded state proposition in an achievement is carried by a visible embedded clause, for example *I realised* (*it was after midnight*) and the same is true for the achievement embedded in an accomplishment. It was shown how the semantic existence of such components – even when there is not an overt embedded clause – can be argued for by considering what various adverbial modifiers must be operating on.

Exercises

1. In February 2002 a UK government minister announced the resignation of a senior civil servant in his department. According to one report, it was only from listening to the radio on his way back to work from a hospital appointment that the civil servant heard about his own alleged resignation. This led to a question in the media: ? *Who is going to be resigned next?* (The question mark at the beginning marks the sentence as semantically odd.) The civil servant eventually resigned in May 2002. Resigning is supposed to be a conscious act performed by the person who quits the post, but if, in talking about the situation described, someone had used the expression ? *The minister resigned the civil servant,* would the sentence have been causative? Would it have the same meaning as *The minister made the civil servant resign?*

2. Assume that Humpty Dumpty was an egg that got broken. The nursery rhyme says 'All the king's horses/ And all the king's men/ Couldn't put Humpty together again'. Why *again?* Eggs grow biologically. The soldiers had not put the egg together on some previous occasion. What kind of verb is *put* in this sentence?

3. What is each of the following sentences: unaccusative or unergative? (a) *The kite flew.* (b) *My heart sank.* (c) *The students were reading.* Give reasons for your answers.

4. Classify the following as achievements, states, activities or accomplishments: (a) The kid was having a tantrum. (b) The band had a makeover. (c) I caught a cold. (d) Part of the Louvre resembles a pyramid. (e) The music stopped. (f) He got the joke the second time. (g) Khalid played the violin.

5. Here are two imaginary mini-conversations with an actor: (a) "Have you finished learning your lines?" "No, but I've stopped for today." (b) "Have you finished playing teenage roles?" "Yes, I've stopped." The *No* in (a) indicates that stopping learning your lines is different from finishing learning your lines. The *Yes* in (b) indicates that stopping playing teenage roles is the same as finishing playing them. Comment on the difference in terms of situation types.

6. Two instructions in a cookery book[7] are worded as follows: (a) 'Combine 3 Tbs. flour and spices, and <u>sprinkle this into the peaches</u>. Mix gently but thoroughly.' (b) 'Butter the bottom of a 9-inch springform pan, and <u>dust it lightly with flour</u>.' In terms of accomplishment goals, discuss the meanings of the two underlined verb phrases and how they differ with regard to the quantity and distribution of flour.

Recommendations for reading

Kearns (2000) and Huddleston and Pullum (2002) both offer illuminating accounts of matters dealt with in this chapter. Miller (2002: ch. 13) gives a clear summary of situation types. Vendler (1967) is accessible and still an inspiring read. Tenny and Pustejovsky's (2000) chapter is a survey of approaches and issues in the study of causatives and situation types. Dowty (2000) is an interesting short article (by a pioneer investigator of situation types) on so-called argument alternations, the pattern that was illustrated in (4.10): *plant the field with the rye* ~ *plant the rye in the field.*

Notes

1. The German term **Aktionsarten** is widely used in semantics to distinguish word-based aspect from aspect marked by grammatical inflection. It is often translated into English as *event types.* I use the term *situation types* because states are included and it grates a bit to talk of a state as a kind of event.

2. The sequence *her gleeful*, in *The thought made her gleeful*, is of a kind that some linguists call a "small clause", one that has a subject (*her* in this case) but lacks any marking of tense – this one does not even have a verb to carry tense marking. In Table 4.1 the clauses with *to*, like *the kite to fly* in *The children got the kite to fly*, are infinitival clauses. Some linguists say that you cannot have a clause without a tensed verb, so the idea of infinitival clauses is a bit controversial, and small clauses are more so.

3. The qualification 'a minimum' is there because some analyses see an indirect object in some of these sentences, for example *us* in *Bad weather forces us to cancel the picnic*, but this has no bearing on matters discussed in the text.

4. Another reading of (4.4a) is **habitual**: 'The staff nurse gave her a key repeatedly' or 'kept giving her a key'. On the habitual interpretation it is reasonable to understand *for the week* as saying how long the repeated giving of the key – perhaps every morning – went on for. (See Chapter 6 for more on habitual aspect.)

5. In earlier discussion of the *stop*-test applied to a state (4.7b), I admitted that *She stopped having a sprained ankle* might strike some people as infelicitous, but the same wording fits naturally into the text here, doesn't it?

6. Many authors use the term **telic** – derived from the Greek word *telos* 'end' – to characterise the goal-directedness of achievements and accomplishments.

7. Katzen, Mollie (2000), *The New Moosewood Cookbook*, Berkeley: Ten Speed Press, pp. 205, 208.

5 Figurative language

Overview

Jenny Diski's grandfather would pour tea from his cup into the saucer before drinking it. Diski[1] used the metaphor in (5.1) to describe her mother's reaction to this.

(5.1) "My mother's face curdled."

The metaphor is abundantly evocative in comparison to a literal alternative such as *My mother grimaced*. Metaphors tend to provoke thought and feeling to a greater extent than more literal descriptions do.

Curdling liquid thickens into lumps. Small muscles tightening in a person's face could look like that. In Britain tea is usually served with milk, and curdled milk is, by common consent, unpleasant in tea; for one thing, it is sour. The reaction to tasting tea with curdled milk could be a grimace. Blood is among the substances sometimes said to curdle, as a symptom of fear. Blood is an ingredient, below the surface, of one's face. Visibly-tensed muscles around a scowling mouth could betray apprehension of further embarrassment and might be thought of as caused by blood getting lumpy around there, that is to say curdling. Diski's metaphor conveys a vivid image and, very economically, also indicates that her mother's face signalled distaste and trepidation. (Exercise 1, at the end of the chapter, invites you to take the interpretation of this metaphor a bit further.)

The account of metaphor to be offered in this chapter is loosely derived from elements of a detailed theory proposed by Stern (2000), according to which metaphorical interpretation is somewhat similar to deixis (a term introduced in Chapter 1).[2] Examples of deixis are "I" used to indicate the speaker or writer of the utterance in which it occurs and the demonstrative "that" to refer to something obvious to the interlocutors (because it is pointed out, has just arrived on the scene, or has just been mentioned). In (5.1) Diski could be understood as using the word *curdled* to "point" to assumptions about the process of curdling, with the intention that readers should, on the basis of those assumptions, work out her meaning. From the areas of their own experience that she has pointed to, they should be able to imagine – or even picture or mimic – the facial expression involved. Stern writes 'Like a picture, a metaphor *displays* rather than *describes* its content' (2000: 290).

A distinction was made in Chapter 1 between semantics, the study of word and sentence meaning in the abstract, and pragmatics, the use of utterances in context. Understanding how figurative uses of language work requires us to supplement semantics with pragmatics. Four kinds of figurative usage will be looked at in this chapter, the first two quite briefly: irony, metonymy, metaphor and simile. According to a traditional – and, as will be seen (in Section 5.2.1), not entirely satisfactory – definition, an **ironic** utterance is one intended to be taken as conveying the "opposite" of its literal meaning. Oppositeness links this topic back to the meaning relations called complementarity and antonymy (in Chapter 2). For metonymy, I will concentrate (in Section 5.2.3) on metonymies that depend on the *has*-relation (introduced in Chapter 3). Metaphor – the topic to which the rest of the chapter leads – depends largely on encyclopedic knowledge. Metaphor and simile are discussed in Section 5.3.

As a preliminary, the contrast between literal and figurative meaning needs to be examined, and this is done in Section 5.1, below.

5.1 Literal and figurative usage

We learn word meanings in context and our memory records of words certainly bear encyclopedic connotations picked up from the contexts in which we have encountered them and from communications that those words contributed to. The distinction made in Chapter 1 between semantic knowledge and encyclopedic knowledge is not accepted in a framework known as Cognitive Linguistics (see Croft and Cruse 2004). This is the main reason why I am not employing that framework of description in the present chapter, even though metaphor is a central concept for cognitive linguists. Not recognising linguistic semantic knowledge as distinct from general (encyclopedic) information about the world makes it difficult to distinguish between literal and figurative meaning. Figurative usage can be inspirationally fresh, and it seems to me that it is worth asking how it differs from mundane language and how it is signalled and construed.

When figurative uses are recycled to the point of cliché, they frequently settle into the semantic system of the language as new senses for words. Metaphors based on the word *grain* 'seed of cereal' led to an additional sense for *grain*: 'small particle' – of sand, for example.

Although historical changes in word meanings are not covered in this book, it is useful to have a scheme that, in principle, could accommodate such processes.

Chapter 1 introduced (in Stage 1 of the three-stage model sketched there of how pragmatics connects to semantics) the idea of context-free semantic knowledge that people have simply because of knowing the language. In Stage 1 the meanings of words are **literal meanings**. Abstracted from contexts of use, they are suitable for re-use in many different situations, rather than only in re-enactments of the original contexts in which we met them. Literal meanings are encoded in the language system and underpin the entailment possibilities of sentences. According to the notion of compositionality (introduced in Chapters 1 and 2), the meanings of sentences derive from just the meanings of the component expressions and the way they have been put together.

In the process of explicature (Stage 2), context is applied to sentence meaning to disambiguate it and establish what the referring expressions refer to. If the only word meanings used in the explicature are literal meanings, then we have a **literal interpretation**.

The traditional term **figures of speech** covers various kinds of figurative – as distinct from literal – uses of language. Grant and Bauer (2004: 51) present a simple diagnostic test: constructions 'compositionally involving an untruth which can be reinterpreted pragmatically to understand the intended truth …' are figurative usages. Here is how their test applies to Example (5.1): having worked out whose face is referred to by the expression *My mother's face* (on the basis of contextual information, including who wrote the article containing that sentence), and taking *curdled* as an unaccusative verb encoding an accomplishment (terminology from Chapter 4), we arrive compositionally at a proposition about a process that affects the person's face to change it into a resulting state. This is a rather implausible meaning: the writer's mother's face was a liquid that thickened into sour lumps. According to Grant and Bauer's proposal, it is the unlikelihood of that being true that would motivate readers to prefer a figurative interpretation (such as the one I offered at the beginning of this chapter).

Grant and Bauer (2004: 50) admit that their test is too restrictive. It is not only falsity of a literal reading that motivates figurative interpretations. One of the examples cited by Stern (2000: 356) is *No man is an island* … It is clear from the rest of this Meditation of John Donne's (… *any man's death diminishes me, because I am involved in Mankind; And therefore never send to know for whom the bell tolls; It tolls for thee*) that *island* should be understood metaphorically: 'all people are interlinked'. It is not untruth that makes a literal interpretation of *No man is an island* unsatisfactory: it is self-evidently true that nobody is literally an island, and being so obvious is what makes that proposition hardly worth communicating. In some circumstances – for instance when reading poetry – a figurative interpretation might be the first preference, if one can be found. As always when interpreting what people say or write, one chooses among possibilities with the aim of finding a contextually appropriate reading.

I define a **figurative interpretation** as an explicature (a Stage 2 interpretation) that involves treating one or more words as if they had meanings different from their literal ones. Context is used not only as a foundation for inferring which referents are being talked about and which senses of ambiguous expressions are likely to be the intended ones, but also to decide whether any meanings should be replaced to yield figurative explicatures. The reason why a particular figurative interpretation is chosen as better than other interpretations that the listener or reader can think of may be that a literal interpretation is somehow deviant (untrue, too obvious, or empty of content, for instance); alternatively – or additionally – the context may be one that favours figurative usage. (Stage 3, implicature – also introduced in Chapter 1 – is a further constraint: the explicature – among the available ones – whether literal or figurative, that yields the most plausible implicatures will be preferred.)

Figures of speech should also be distinguished from **idioms** (introduced in Chapter 1). The difference is pithily put by Grant and Bauer (2004: 49): 'figures of speech can be interpreted according to general cognitive principles, while idioms have to be learnt.' In the rest of this chapter there will be illustrations of interpretation according to general pragmatic principles, and the principles will be taken up again, in a more theoretical way, in Chapter 8.

Also outside the category of figurative usage, as defined two paragraphs earlier, is the innovative creation of new words, because newly-minted words do not yet have established literal meanings. Though not figurative, such coinages are often imaginative, for example "NHS staff were *underwhelmed* by the government's proposals". The word *underwhelm* is on its way to becoming established in English, but the first time people encounter it, they tend to be surprised, most likely at the word-idiom *overwhelm* having been analysed (into *over* + *whelm*) to rationalise the construction of a contrasting word. The innovativeness of the humorous back formation makes the result more striking than the familiar word *unimpressed* would have been. (It was probably figurative usage that encouraged the historical meaning change from the Middle English word *hwelmen* 'turn upside down' to our word *overwhelm* 'overcome'.)

5.2 Irony, presuppositions and metonymy

5.2.1 Irony

In 2004, Halle Berry won an Oscar for acting, but in 2005 she pluckily attended an award ceremony to receive a Razzie – a golden raspberry – for "worst actress", in a different film. Collecting her Razzie, she said (5.2).[3]

(5.2)   "Oh, this is wonderful."

She also said 'If you aren't able to be a good loser you're not able to be a good winner'. A child who understood that the award was something of a humiliation might express surprise at (5.2), and it is conceivable that someone could attempt to explain things to the child along the lines of the traditional definition of irony: *She really means 'This is terrible'*. Such an explanation is of some help: the child has correctly detected the deviance of a celebrity claiming that it is wonderful to be humiliated, and is sensibly advised to treat the explicature of (5.2) as containing not the literal meaning of *wonderful* but the meaning of an antonym of that word, *terrible*. There is more to it, however.

Wilson and Sperber (2004: 622) summarise a proposal that they first made more than twenty years ago as 'verbal irony consists in echoing a tacitly attributed thought or utterance with a tacitly dissociative attitude'. Halle Berry was, perhaps ruefully, alluding to her 2004 triumph by saying something that would have been appropriate then. Implicatures (Stage 3) that the audience can draw from the fact of being reminded about her previous success and from deployment of a positive expression, *wonderful*, are that (having her record in memory as she talks) Berry is not dejected, and that (able to find a positive word now) she is a good loser.

Shakespeare's *Sonnet 130*, of which the first three lines and the closing couplet are quoted in (5.3),[4] fits Wilson and Sperber's account of irony (mentioned in the previous paragraph).

(5.3)   My mistress' eyes are nothing like the sun;
        Coral is far more red than her lips' red.
        If snow be white, why then her breasts are dun;
        …
        And yet, by heaven, I think my love as rare
        As any she belied with false compare.

There was a vogue for sonnets at the end of the sixteenth century. You could pay poets to compose sonnets of extravagant praise for a lover: eyes like the sun, coral lips, snow-white décolletage, perfume for breath and so on. Example (5.3) shows both the echoing and the dissociation that are the key components in Wilson and Sperber's definition of irony: Shakespeare echoes the standard sort of figurative usage of sonnets, but denies that it applies to the beloved he is writing about here. If you read the whole sonnet, you will perhaps agree that Shakespeare was gently sending up the business of sonneteering.

5.2.2 Presuppositions

Someone who knows nothing of the sonnet tradition – like the teenage me when I was first set to the reading of English literature – will very likely miss much in trying to understand *Sonnet 130*: in the last two lines of the sonnet, Shakespeare indicates that he likes the lady, but why then the list of specifications that she fails to meet; is he being cruel? **Intertextuality** is a term from literary criticism that covers the way in which texts connect with, allude to, depend upon and comment on the ideas and form of other texts (McArthur 1992: 525–6). Intertextuality is crucial for interpreting *Sonnet 130*: it recalls other sonnets and was written for readers familiar with sonnets and the figures of speech common in them.

More generally, utterances – whether figuratively or literally intended – are not made in a vacuum: when we interpret utterances, we use as background our best guesses about what the communicator assumes are the preconceptions and relevant information that we can bring to the comprehension task. Such presumed-to-be-shared beliefs that are taken for granted by the speaker or writer and are expected to be used for interpreting the message are called **presuppositions**. The notion of presupposition is explained more fully in Chapter 8, but an outline will be useful now.

Knowledge is sometimes defined as true belief. Presuppositions do not have to be true: communications may depend on mutual awareness of fictions and pretences, on ideologies, prejudices, national stereotypes that are false of many individuals, and so on. That is why presuppositions assumed to be shared between people communicating by means of language were said above to be beliefs, preconceptions and information, rather than knowledge.

Reference (Chapters 1 and 9) is founded on presuppositions about addressees' acquaintance – or unfamiliarity – with people, things, places, events and so forth. Much specific language knowledge also comes into play in interpreting utterances, for example that the process denoted by the English word *curdle* applies to liquids. (A figurative interpretation is preferable for (5.1) because this presupposition about curdling is not met: a person's face is not a liquid.) Pragmatic interpretation can also depend on cultural awareness of history, science, shopping practices, sonnet traditions, politeness conventions, award ceremonies and celebrities. For anything that humans talk or write about, there are almost always presuppositions to be retrieved from memory. Presuppositions are involved in formulating utterances and interpreting them. Only a fraction of what we store in memory is activated at a given time. It is only activated information – material currently being attended to in the language user's brain – that is available as presuppositions for the interpretation of an utterance in context.

Particularly in the case of planned speeches and literary works, the author will often indicate relevant presuppositions in the text itself: ideas the audience needs to orient to for understanding the text. Example (5.4) is part of a speech about civil liberties by Lord Mayhew, attacking proposals of the British government (the "executive") in March 2005.[5]

(5.4) "Throughout modern history, our sea defences against unfair executive power have been serially attacked by the threat of erosion. The executive, like the sea, will always come back."

The phrases 'like the sea' and 'will always come back' clarify how we should understand the metaphors in the first sentence of (5.4): *serially* alleges relentlessly recurring waves and they are beating against a sea wall, which is how *sea defences* should be understood (not, for instance, as a navy), and *erosion* is of the kind caused by the sea (not by rainwater run-off, for example).

The quotation in (5.5), from Shakespeare's *As You Like It*,[6] shows Jacques' metaphor of life as theatre being introduced by Duke Senior.

(5.5) Duke Senior: Thou seest we are not all alone unhappy.
                        This wide and universal theatre
                        Presents more woeful pageants than the scene
                        Wherein we play in.
        Jacques: All the world's a stage,
                        And all the men and women merely players.

Jacques' speech extends the metaphor over another twenty-five lines, but notice that Duke Senior's mention of *theatre*, *pageants*, *scene* and *play*[ing] has prepared the audience for a metaphorical take on *stage* and *players*. In turn, *All the world's a stage* from Jacques confirms that Duke Senior's *This wide and universal theatre* … is open to being construed as metaphorical, and is not (or not just) a literal comment on the situation being portrayed by the actors and the theatre in which they are performing.

5.2.3 Metonymy

(5.6) All hands on deck!

Particularly in the days of sailing ships, there was a lot of work for sailors to do with their hands. One of the several senses of *hand* has for a long time been 'sailor', but referring to sailors by means of the body-part word *hand*, as in (5.6), was probably figurative at some time in the past. When talking about metaphor (see Section 5.3, below), the term for a figuratively-used word (or phrase) is **vehicle**, but it is also useful in connection with metonymy. The vehicle "carries the figurative meaning". Before *hand* got 'sailor' as one of its literal meanings, it could be a vehicle for figuratively talking about sailors (or other skilled manual workers).

Traditional accounts of **metonymy** define it in terms of a person or object being referred to using as the vehicle a word whose literal denotation is somehow pertinently related. In my opinion, most of the clear cases rest on the *has*-relation (Chapter 3). For instance, countries have capital cities and the name of the capital can be used as a metonymic vehicle to talk about the country, as in *Moscow and Kiev certainly don't agree on everything* (instead of *Russia and Ukraine ...*). Another example is the use of *redcaps*, at least among the military, to refer to Royal Military Police. RMP uniform includes a cap with a red band: a prototype member of the RMP has one. All the examples of the *has*-relation in Chapter 3 were of wholes having parts, but it can now be seen that the relationship is less restricted: red caps are not parts of RMP personnel.[7]

The utterance quoted in (5.7) is what I take to have been a fresh metonym at the time of its use, not a dead one of long ago like (5.6). It was a comment by veteran singer Tom Jones regarding an intricately braided chain he was wearing during a 2002 interview[8] about his venture into hip-hop with Wyclef Jean.

(5.7) "When you're working with bling-blings, you've gotta wear bling-blings."

This was only three years after the 1999 introduction of the word *bling bling* in the lyrics of New Orleans rapper BG, to describe an ostentatious earring. The meaning soon firmed up as 'large, expensive, sparkling jewellery' such as worn by African American hip-hop artists. For some it now also denotes black music culture. In (5.7), at the end of the first clause, Tom Jones was using *bling-blings* as a metonym for hip-hop artists, who prototypically had (and displayed) bling blings.

To be good for the job, metonym vehicles must be distinctive properties of the people or objects referred to, in the way that having red cap(band)s is distinctive of RMPs. The vehicle must also be relevant in the context of utterance. *All noses on deck!* would probably fail to be understood figuratively in even roughly the same way as (5.6), despite prototypical sailors having noses. In a different context, *We need more noses on this trail* could be a way of demanding that extra tracker dogs be assigned to a police search. In a bookshop, the authors often count as distinctive features of books, which allows for a metonymy such as the section manager's request: *Put more feminist authors in this window*. But when photos are being taken for an interior design magazine, a different thing that a class of books has could be relevant: *Fill that bookshelf with hardbacks.*

The explicature (Stage 2) of *skinhead* could be 'potentially violent youth who has a shaven head'. The single word *skinhead* achieves savings compared to the eight-word elaboration, but metonymy also signals attitude. In working out implicatures (Stage 3), the listener has to wonder why attention is being drawn not to the whole, but to something that most of the individuals or items in question have. The speaker's attitude is seen in the fact that rather than the whole being of interest, it is a single salient possession that matters: hands to furl the sails, feminist authors of any kind to give an impression, skinheads apparently seen as interchangeable, any RMP the same unit of force as other wearers of the uniform. Metonymy is a salient common denominator figure of speech.

5.3 Metaphor

This section begins with metaphor and ends with a consideration of simile. (For the moment, it will suffice to say that similes differ from metaphors by containing words such as *like* or *as* to make a comparison explicit, for example *He eats like a horse*. However, a somewhat different account of them is going to be given later.)

On 15 February 2005, Ken Livingstone (the mayor of London) was reported[9] to have said the words quoted in (5.8), after refusing to withdraw remarks he had made the previous week that several newspapers and quite a few other people maintained he should apologise for.

(5.8) "I have been through several media firestorms ..."

I cited the precise date for (5.8) because it came only the day after widely-reported commemorative events in Germany of the firestorms caused by the bombing of Dresden sixty years earlier. Therefore, when he spoke, Livingstone could assume that *firestorms* would easily evoke information about the Dresden firestorms, as a presuppositional base for interpreting his metaphor. Stern's theory of metaphor has as one of its central proposals (2002: 114) that the metaphorical vehicle – *firestorms* in this case – points to contextually available presuppositions. Thus many people would have understood (5.8) as a claim by Livingstone that past media behaviour towards him had been intensely destructive, prone to spreading rapidly, drawing much else into the conflagration, but eventually burning out, and that he had survived such attacks before. An explicature of that kind would invite the implicatures that the media were repeating their previous behaviour and that he believed he would again survive.

The lengthy spelling out of what metaphorical use of the single word *firestorms* could convey illustrates, again, the "compression" made possible by figures of speech, especially metaphors. The role of pre-supposition in the interpretation of (5.8) exemplifies another feature of straightforward uses of metaphor: matters that may be relatively un-familiar to the addressees (particulars of Livingstone's conflicts with the media) are elucidated via a vehicle that they are presumed to know more about (having only one day earlier been offered descriptions of fire-storms). But there are also mind-taxing metaphors, notably in poetry, where the reader might not have the needed presuppositions, but is forced either to give up in bafflement or to consider hard what it could be that the poet presupposes about the vehicle that could yield a reasonable interpretation (Stern 2000: 118–20).

Metaphors have been said to be central to scientific theorising. They certainly facilitate explanation in the popularisation of science. See (5.9), from science writer Robert Kunzig.[10]

(5.9) "The Gulf Stream is not really a stream, then; it is merely the western edge of a giant spinning lens of water."

The Gulf Stream is a flow of warmish surface water in the North Atlantic, from roughly the Gulf of Mexico to Scotland. Two words used metaphorically in this sentence are of interest: *stream* and *lens*. The spin-ning lens image stimulates exploratory thought. A lens is shaped like a lentil. Apart from the shape, why does *lens* give us a good metaphor to use with water? You can see through a lens and through water. A lens refracts rays that pass through it. Likewise, a great lens-shaped disc of water, different in temperature and salinity from the surrounding water, can be detected by scientists because of the way it bends light and sound waves that slant through it. When something rotates, its centre moves least. Is there a region some distance east of the Gulf Stream where the ocean more or less stands still? Yes, there is: it is the Sargasso Sea. There was already a metaphorical use of *stream* in the name of the Mexico-to-Scotland ocean current, presenting it as a flow of water hemmed in by "banks" not of rock and earth but by other water. When Kunzig says that it "is not really a stream", he indicates that metaphors can be judged to be true or false and he rates this one as inaccurate, for instance because the east "bank" moves slowly in the same direction, instead of standing fixed.

Metaphor interpretation tends to be harder – and potentially more rewarding – than metonymy. In metonymy, the vehicle names the contextually significant aspect of the referent(s): the sailors' *hands*, the hiphop artists' *bling*, the *hard backs* (or *paper backs*) of books, and so on. However, when making sense of metaphor, an idea is pointed to and it is left to the addressee to find its salient features for a satisfactory interpretation. Proper name metaphors such as (5.10) support Stern's case. Proper names do not have conventional meanings that language users know from knowing the language, but useful ideas can be evoked by getting people to think of what they believe about the bearer of a name.

(5.10)   She's a Mary Robinson.

Out of context, *She's a Mary Robinson* could be intended either literally 'She is a person who has the name Mary Robinson' or metaphorically 'She is a person who is similar in some contextually relevant ways to the law professor Mary Robinson who was president of Ireland and, later, UN High Commissioner for Human Rights'. Stern's theory – which I am recounting selectively, informally and without detail – allows that the metaphorical process can optionally be made explicit with the word *metaphorically* (2000: 240). Below (5.11) is a real[11] example that illustrates this.

(5.11)   "He is a vast (metaphorically speaking) databank of information."

This was from BBC presenter Sarah Montague, writing about James Naughtie, a moderately bulky person. She was signalling that *vast* should not be taken literally as a comment on his physical size, but treated as a modifier within the vehicle phrase: readers were to do their interpretation by contemplating how the main features of a *vast databank of information* could help one form an impression of the nature of her colleague: that she rated him as extremely knowledgeable, efficient at supplying facts, etcetera. (She was perhaps also light-heartedly commenting on his bulk.)

5.3.1 Similes are metaphors too

The sentence in (5.12) exemplifies what would traditionally be called a **simile**, because it is figurative and hinges on the word *like*.

(5.12)   "The pursuit of absolute safety is like trying to get the bubbles out of wallpaper."

Get it? Michael Bywater, the author of this one,[12] provides more help by explaining in the next sentence that you 'Crush one danger and another pops up'. Stern (2000: 340) states that 'similes should be analyzed on the same model as metaphors'. The variant shown in (5.13) is undoubtedly a metaphor but it strikes me as equivalent, figuratively and communicatively, to (5.12).

(5.13)   The pursuit of absolute safety: it's trying to get the bubbles out of wallpaper.

Bywater's hint 'Crush one danger and another pops up' is just as useful for interpreting (5.13). The only clear difference appears to be that (5.13) is deviant on a literal interpretation: the pursuit of absolute safety is not literally the same activity as squashing bubbles under wallpaper.

Though metaphors – (5.13) for example – are often deviant, the cautious word *like* insulates corresponding similes from deviance, as in (5.12). For this reason linguists, philosophers and literary critics have often thought that analysis might be easier if the non-deviant ones were taken as basic. That is to say, it has been proposed that we can explain how metaphors work by saying that they are just similes with *like* erased. Lycan (2000: 213) calls this the "naive simile theory" of metaphor. It does not actually explain how the vehicle, which follows *like*, gets figuratively interpreted.

Stern (2000) does have an explanation for the figurative interpretation of the vehicle in a metaphor, as sketched at the beginning of the Overview in this chapter and in earlier parts of Section 5.3: context (or, as in (5.11), the overt signal *metaphorically*) guides addressees on whether to prefer a metaphorical interpretation. If they do, then the vehicle points to presupposed information they should think about and from which they should take salient, contextually-relevant features to replace the literal meaning of the vehicle for the purposes of explicature. Exactly the same considerations apply to similes: their figurative interpretations are handled by creative consideration of possibilities suggested by presuppositions pertaining to the vehicle. In Stern's scheme, deviance is nothing to worry about: it may be a cue that favours metaphorical interpretation, but – aside from that – it neither helps nor hinders metaphorical interpretation. Thus, instead of a naive simile theory of metaphor, we should regard similes as metaphors, which happen to contain *like* or some other explicit marker of similarity.

The sentence in (5.14a) has the form of a simile, but notice that it can be taken either figuratively, equivalent in meaning to the metaphorical use suggested by (5.14b), or literally, with the same meaning as (5.14c). The latter could be said about a person who, like the speaker's mother, perhaps worries about spilling salt or opening umbrellas indoors.

(5.14) a. She's like my mother.   (figurative or literal)
        b. She's a mother to me.   (figurative, a standard metaphor)
        c. She's similar to my mother. (literal)

Recalling that sentences which can be taken metaphorically can also sometimes be taken literally – (5.10) for instance – this is a further reason for regarding the difference between simile and metaphor as a superficial one.

Summary

The chapter has given a sketch of figurative interpretation in terms of two stages of pragmatics – explicature and implicature (which were introduced in Chapter 1). Semantically, words and sentences have literal meanings. A literal interpretation of an utterance in context is an explicature that involves only literal meanings. Figurative interpretation is explicature in which one or more literal meanings are replaced, for example by an antonym in some types of irony. Wilson and Sperber's more sophisticated account of irony was one illustration of how presuppositions – beliefs presumed to be shared – are the source for figurative alternatives to literal meanings. Stern's (2000) theory of metaphor was informally recounted, according to which vehicle expressions – ones that carry figurative meanings – are used rather in the manner of a deictic demonstrative (like the word *that*) to "point" out presuppositions for use in interpretation. Figurative interpretation is somewhat open-ended because different people come with different presuppositions and differ over what they regard as relevant in a given context. Similes were argued to be metaphors too. This chapter's introduction to presupposition is extended in Chapter 8.

Exercises

1. Consider again Example (5.1) *My mother's face curdled*, in the context stated for it. Being pointed to presuppositions about *curdling*, someone who thinks of *blood curdling* might next think of the proverbial saying *Blood is thicker than water*. Can you find a way of using this to elaborate on the interpretation offered in the text of the metaphor in (5.1)? Is there any end to the process of interpreting a metaphor?

2. Talking of a pair of garden birds in early summer: *They've got two*

hungry beaks to feed. What figure of speech is seen in the sentence in italics? What is the vehicle? What presupposition is needed to understand the example?

3. In Fiji, in the 1990s, I had to ask for an explanation of a metaphor that I could not understand even after I had been told that *tube light* meant 'fluorescent lamp': *He's a tube light.* Can you guess what it was supposed to convey? Whether you are confident of the correctness of your guess or rather uncertain, what did you need to think about in making a guess, or what kind of information did you lack?

4. Muhammad Ali, a notably agile, hard-hitting and also articulate former world heavyweight boxing champion, described his own fighting technique as "Dance like a butterfly, sting like a bee". Using the technical terms introduced in this chapter, and thinking carefully about it, try to identify the figures of speech he was using.

Recommendations for reading

Cruse (2000: ch. 11) is a thoughtful discussion of the topics in the present chapter. Lycan (2000: ch. 14) gives an accessible account of metaphor from the perspective of a philosopher of language. In Huddleston and Pullum (2002: 651–3, 682) there is an informative discussion of dead metaphors among English prepositional meanings. For a short survey of the roles of metaphor and metonymy in meaning changes that take place in the history of languages, see Traugott (2000), but be warned that it is not written for beginners.

Notes

1. In the *London Review of Books*, vol. 25, no. 12 (2003).

2. Readers familiar with Stern's (2000) book will see that not only is my account much sketchier than the original, but that I do not go along with his rejection of deviance as the basis for recognising that figurative interpretation is called for. Pragmatic deviance includes not just falsity but also other infelicities such as excessive obviousness. The deviance explanation does not force one into the uncomfortable position of accepting that figurative readings are explored only after failure to get a satisfactory interpretation based on literal meanings; simultaneous exploration of figurative and non-figurative possibilities is imaginable, and not implausible psycholinguistically.

3. Details from a BBC report by Helen Bushby, 22 February 2005, <http://news.bbc.co.uk/>.

4. Stanley Wells and Gary Taylor (eds) (1988), *The Oxford Shakespeare: the Complete Works*, Oxford: Clarendon Press.

5. Ben Russell, online edition of *The Independent*, 2 March 2005, <http://news.independent.co.uk/>.

6. Stanley Wells and Gary Taylor (eds) (1988), *The Oxford Shakespeare: the Complete Works*, Oxford: Clarendon Press.

7. There is a traditional label, *synecdoche*, specifically for the subspecies of metonymy in which the vehicle denotes a part of the whole that it figuratively represents.

8. Caroline Sullivan, *Guardian Unlimited*, 17 October 2002, <http://www.guardian.co.uk/>.

9. Chris Tryhorn, *Media Guardian*, <http://media.guardian.co.uk/>.

10. Robert Kunzig (2000), *Mapping the Deep: the Extraordinary Story of Ocean Science*, London: Sort of Books, p. 276.

11. From the *Today* Newsletter, 14 March 2005, <http://www.bbc.co.uk/radio4/today/newsletter/>.

12. From the online edition of *The Independent*, 1 December 2004, <http://news.independent.co.uk/>.

6 Tense and aspect

Overview

This chapter is about how English grammar allows us to locate events in time (**tense**), in relation to the time of speaking or writing, and about grammatical signals regarding the sender's notions of how an event is distributed in time (**aspect**); for instance, is it viewed as ongoing, or repeated, or characterised as compressed to a point?

Example (6.1), from an article[1] by Andrew O'Hagan, shows tense and aspect being used together to convey meaning.

(6.1)   When I told people I was spending time with farmers, they'd say: how can you stand it, they just complain all day and they've always got their hand out.

Anyone who knows English can understand the sentence. I would like to unpack some of what goes into understanding it. This is going to be a bit laborious, but is worth doing to reveal the level of intricacy there is in grammatical facets of communication connected with time.

Let us imagine ourselves at the time when Andrew O'Hagan wrote (6.1). *Told* is the **past simple** form of the verb *tell*. The first word in the two-part labels that I will use always represents tense, so *told* is a past tense form. The second component denotes aspect, and *simple* means that neither of the special aspectual meanings to be discussed later is involved. Other tenses and aspects are going to be introduced soon. The past simple indicates that he "told people ..." before the time when he wrote the material quoted in (6.1). Note that, although tense is marked on the verb, it is the whole event – or, more likely, series of events – described by the clause *I told people ...* that is located in the time before the time of writing.

Moving on in (6.1), *was spending* is in a form called **past progressive**. When tense is marked in a verb group, it goes on the first element in the sequence. The form *was* (in contrast to *am*) is what makes *was spending* past. **Progressive aspect** is marked by the combination of the auxiliary

BE (*be, am, is, are, was* or *were*) in front of the verb and the suffix -*ing* on the verb. Because *was spending* is a past form, we understand that the activity described by *I was spending time with farmers* was going on before the sentence was written. Presumably O'Hagan's original utterances in the tellings being reported on in (6.1) were something like "I have been spending time with farmers". Progressive aspect portrays an event (in this case, him spending time with farmers) as in progress – hence the name *progressive* – during the relevant period of time, but leaves open the matter of whether and when it ended.

Figure 6.1 diagrams the main time relationships in (6.1). Time is represented by the line running from left to right. The time of writing is represented as an interval on the time line. It is elastic. A writer or speaker can treat 'now' as shrunk to a point ('this instant') or as stretched to 'this minute/day/hour/week' etc.

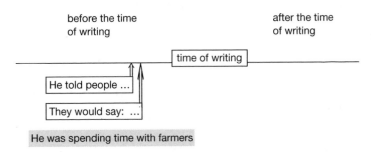

Figure 6.1 The main time relationships in Example (6.1)

The event marked by the past simple *told* is arrowed to a point on the time line because past simple encodes events as if they can be located precisely in time. For a clause denoting one of the goal-directed situation types described in Chapter 4 (achievements and accomplishments), it is the point of completion that is located in time by past simple. *Tell someone something* is an accomplishment, and the arrow marks the end of the telling. Actually, since the author did not write *When I once told a group of people that I was spending time with farmers*, we can infer that he told different people, individually or in groups, that he was spending time with farmers; so there should really be more than one arrow from the box containing the words 'He told people …' to separately locate on the time line each event in which he told a person, a pair or a group of people about his time with farmers.

The activity of O'Hagan's spending time with farmers is shown as a grey bar located generally before the time of writing, but not arrowed to a point in time, because that is what past progressive conveys: the event was ongoing before the time of utterance but its beginning and particularly its end are not in focus and might even have continued through the time of writing.

They'd say is a contracted version of *they would say*. *Would* is the past simple form of the modal auxiliary verb *will* (Chapter 7 has more on modal auxiliaries). There is no suffix in English to put on to verbs as an indicator of futurity. *Will* is the main grammatical device for signalling future time in English. In this case it marks the event described by the clause *they'd say* ... as future. What can be the motive for the author using the past tense form of a future-marking auxiliary? The start of an answer is that he is describing events completed before the time of writing, which justifies the past tense.

The events were the ones in which people said (rather derogatory) things about farmers. The first word in (6.1), *when*, links the events in which O'Hagan told people how he had been occupying some of his time to the corresponding responses from the same people. His use of a marker of futurity indicates that the responses were located towards the future from the past points in time of the tellings. Each of the responses from people is not merely in the past from the time of writing; it is futurewards (towards the right in Figure 6.1) from each corresponding event in which he had told them of his visits to farmers. Because of what we know about how statements and responses are timed in conversation, the responses can pragmatically be assumed to have occurred soon after people heard that he had been spending time with farmers.

The forms for the verb groups in the two clauses *how can you stand it, they just complain all day* are **present simple**. The time benchmark(s) against which events are located as past, present and future switch(es) now to the time(s) when the people said what they said about farmers (given after the colon in (6.1) as purported examples of the sort of thing that was said).

Present simple can signal different things, not just times coinciding with the time of utterance. In *how can you stand it* the question is how O'Hagan could habitually tolerate the company of complaining farmers. English does not have a grammatical marker of habitual aspect. Habituality has to come out of a pragmatic interpretation of present simple (for instance, *They sell cannabis in special cafés in Amsterdam*) or past simple (for instance, *Coleridge drank laudanum* – not just once; he took the drug for years from 1801); or indeed of other forms, as will be seen in Section 6.2.1. By using the present simple *They just complain all day* to represent what the people said, O'Hagan indicates that he understood that they regarded complaining as habitual behaviour from farmers.

The verb group *have ... got*, in *they've always got their hand out*, is in a form known as **present perfect**. It is present in tense. (For instance, *They've got their hands out an hour ago* is ungrammatical because of having a time adverbial, *an hour ago*, that does not include the time of utterance.) However, it is used to talk about the time-of-utterance consequences of earlier events. The people who spoke to O'Hagan were claiming that you were always faced (metaphorically) with the begging hand of a farmer, the farmers having previously got their hands into that position.

6.1 Tense

The first element in the two-part labels indicates tense and the second indicates aspect. Nine different combinations are set out in Table 6.1. Tense is the main topic for the rest of Section 6.1. Aspect is discussed in Section 6.2.

Table 6.1 Two-part labels for tense–aspect combinations, with examples

	past tense	*present tense*	*future tense*
simple aspect	**past simple** *saw*	**present simple** *see*	**future simple** *will see*
progressive aspect	**past progressive** *was/were seeing*	**present progressive** *am/is/are seeing*	**future progressive** *will be seeing*
perfect aspect	**past perfect** *had seen*	**present perfect** *have/has seen*	**future perfect** *will have seen*

6.1.1 Preliminaries

The locations in time of the points or intervals being spoken or written about are worked out pragmatically, in the process of explicature (the second of the three stages of interpretation introduced in Section 1.1.2 of Chapter 1). Tense has to be explicated in relation to the time of utterance, which makes it a deictic feature of language (see Chapters 1 and 5). In straightforward cases, present tense indicates that the sender portrays the situation as 'in a time interval including the time of utterance', past means 'before the time of utterance' and future 'after the time of utterance'. Estimating the length of relevant time intervals and – for past and future – how long before or after the time of utterance is also a pragmatic matter.

There is not a one-to-one match between the tense and aspect forms and the meanings signalled by those forms. The forms that encode tense and aspect are the explicit markers listed below, or they are indicated by default through the **unmarked** forms of verbs (*see, look, can,* for instance).

auxiliary verbs: WILL, HAVE, BE
irregular forms of verbs, for example *saw, seen, thought, blew, blown, is, am, are, was, cut, would*
and the following **inflectional** suffixes:
  past tense, usually written *-ed*
  present tense, when the subject is singular non-sender and non-addressee, usually written *-s*, for example *goes, sees*
  progressive *-ing*, for example *am singing, was emerging*
  past participle *-(e)n* or *-ed*, for example *has seen, have helped*

The range of time meanings that are in practice carried by these forms will now be illustrated.

6.1.2 Present, Past and Future

Instances where the tense called present is used with reference to events and states that occur or exist in a period of time that includes the time of utterance are shown in (6.2). We could tag *now* on to the end of any of the three sentences.

(6.2) a. He drives for goal. (said by a sports commentator)
      b. That dog is happy.
      c. It's wagging its tail.

Present forms are also used for timeless truths, as in (6.3). Someone who says one of these is not making a restricted claim about what happens *now, today* or *this year*. The adverb *always* could be put in front of the verb in (6.3a) and, redundantly (because the quantifier *every* already signifies a maximum), in front of the verb in (6.3b). *Always* fits the specification of being 'a period of time that includes the time of utterance', but uses such as (6.3a, b) go beyond an intuitive idea of what the label present tense might cover.

(6.3) a. At sea level, water boils at 100°C.
      b. Every dark cloud has a silver lining.

In (6.4) *arrive* and *am* are present tense forms, but *next year* and *next Wednesday* are semantically future.

(6.4) a. You arrive in Australia in time for the Melbourne Cup next year.
      b. Next Wednesday I am examining in Newcastle.

Here the present tense forms signal the future. Looking at a travel itinerary, (6.4a) would be a reasonable thing to say. And (6.4b) can be imagined as uttered on the basis of a diary entry. As suggested by mention of an itinerary and a diary, this usage seems most natural when the future event is already scheduled.

The examples in (6.5) show past tense in its basic use for communications about events and states located in time before the time of utterance. The adverbials *at 7 o'clock this morning* and *yesterday* come before the time of utterance, and the times that they denote do not include the time of utterance.

(6.5)   a.   We ate at 7 o'clock this morning.
        b.   I heard it on a bulletin yesterday.

The examples in (6.6) illustrate two well-known divergences between location in time before the time of utterance and the tense forms used.

(6.6)   a.   They were watching TV when suddenly a runaway truck crashes through their living room wall.
        b.   If we introduced proportional representation, there'd be more coalition governments.

The "historic present" (6.6a) is a way of describing a past event vividly but using a present tense form to do so (*crashes* in the example). The first clause in (6.6b) is conditional. *Introduced* is a past form, but the clause puts forward a possibility rather than locating it in the time before utterance. Possibilities are either in the future or not on the time line at all.

Prediction is the characteristic function of the modal auxiliary verb *will*, as in (6.7a, b).

(6.7)   a.   Lemon juice will remove that stain.
        b.   A small rise in sea-level and Kiribati will disappear under the Pacific.
        c.   You'll get a chance in the coffee break tomorrow morning.
        d.   He's going to stay at home and look after the kids.
        e.   I am going to work.

Because predictions are forward-looking, *will* has come to be the nearest thing in English to a grammatical mark of future time, as in (6.7c). *Will* is not the only way to mark futurity, however. The examples in (6.4) have already shown present simple and present progressive forms used for this purpose. Example (6.7d) illustrates another stratagem for indicating the future: *going to* + verb. Physical motion to a place need not be involved. Thus, (6.7e) is ambiguous between a physical motion interpretation and a future reading: 'I am on my way to my place of work' or 'I intend to work'.

A person who notices children playing on the parapet of a bridge and fears that an accident is about to happen can say (6.8a) or (6.8b).

(6.8) a. Someone's going to fall into the water soon.
b. Someone will fall into the water soon.
c. ?Someone falls into the water soon.

This shows that *going to* + verb is fine for any sort of prediction, just like the auxiliary *will* in 6.8b. However, (6.8c) with present simple *falls* would be odd in this situation, though it would be usable if the event had been scheduled, for example in the script of street theatre performers acting as children on the bridge parapet (compare this with (6.4a), also present simple).

Not only is the future marked in a variety of ways; the examples in (6.9) show that *will* is also used for timeless truths, like the present simple in (6.3).

(6.9) a. A diamond will cut glass.
b. Water will always find its own level.

6.1.3 Tense and adverbials

Past, present and future (relative to the time of utterance) have links with various deictic adverbials as shown in Table 6.2.

Table 6.2 The compatibility of some deictic adverbials with past, present and future time

past time	*present time*	*future time*
then	*now*	*then*
last year	*at present*	*next year*
last Bastille Day	*nowadays*	*tomorrow*
yesterday		*in forty-five minutes from now*
	today, this week, this year	

The tense forms called present simple and present progressive can be used with adverbials such as *in forty-five minutes from now*, as in (6.10a–c), but the events are in the future, so that set of adverbials is shown only in the future time column of Table 6.2.

(6.10) a. Mark Lawson is here in forty-five minutes. (BBC Radio 4 continuity announcer, saying who can be heard three-quarters of an hour later.)
  b. She lectures in Milton Keynes tomorrow.
  c. He's visiting Scotland next year.

Some deictic adverbials are compatible with all three times, exemplified in Table 6.2 by *today*, *this week* and *this year*. This kind of adverbial motivates part of the definition given earlier for basic present tense: 'in a period of time that includes the time of utterance'. It cannot be just 'at the time of utterance' because *today*, *this week* and *this year* denote periods too long to count as 'the time of utterance'. *Last year*, *next year* and the other items from the past-only and future-only cells of Table 6.2 exclude the time of utterance, but the versatile adverbials of the *today* set include not only the time of utterance but also either times prior to the moment of utterance or times after the moment of utterance, or both.

6.2 Aspect

Tense is about inflectional pointers to the position of events relative to the time of utterance. Tense is deictic; aspect is not deictic. Once you have thought yourself into the present, past or future: **aspect** is about grammatical resources for encoding the time profiles of states and events within an interval of time. Some examples will indicate what is meant by time profiles: even if it takes time to play out, an event can be imagined as compressed into an instant (and then it could be one-off or repeated); or we can mentally stretch events and concern ourselves only with their middle stages; or we can concentrate on culminations; and there are many other possibilities in the languages of the world. Section 6.2.1 examines the distinction between habitual aspect and "single-event" aspect. The two subsections after that are on two kinds of aspect explicitly marked in the grammar of English: progressive in 6.2.2 and perfect in 6.2.3.

6.2.1 Habituality and simple aspect

The adverb *nowadays* triggers **habitual** interpretations of present tense clauses, as in (6.11). The situation types of the clauses are given in parentheses, according to the scheme set out in Chapter 4.

(6.11) a. She loves music nowadays. (state)
  b. He drinks decaffeinated coffee nowadays. (activity)

c. Little Maurice brushes his teeth by himself nowadays. (accomplishment)
d. The clown pops the balloon nowadays. (achievement)

It is clear that all four sentences are about habitual matters: evidence of her loving music recurs nowadays; there are recurring instances of him drinking decaffeinated coffee, and of Little Maurice brushing his teeth unaided; and (6.11d) tells us that the balloon popping is now regularly done by the clown.

Habitual interpretations are available even without *nowadays*. Table 6.3 gives examples that will be discussed in the following order: past tense and future tense examples first; then a different generalisation that has to be made with regard to states; finally the interpretation of present tense examples without *nowadays*.

Table 6.3 A range of sentences which all have habitual as a possible interpretation

past simple	*present simple*	*future simple*
She loved music.	She loves music.	She will love music.
He drank decaffeinated coffee.	He drinks decaffeinated coffee.	He will drink coffee.
Little Maurice brushed his teeth by himself.	Little Maurice brushes his teeth by himself.	Little Maurice will brush his teeth by himself.
The clown popped the balloon.	The clown pops the balloon.	The clown will pop the balloon.

The past tense sentence *He drank decaffeinated coffee* clearly can be a description of a single event, for example it could be used to tell us what Carl had after last night's meal. However, and this is the point I want to make here, it can also be interpreted as a statement about Carl's past coffee-drinking habits. It can be taken to mean the same as *He drank decaffeinated coffee in those days*. (A **habitual** interpretation is forced by the phrase *in those days*, the past time equivalent of *nowadays*. *Used to* is another trigger of past habitual readings.) Even without using *in those days* – and though there are single-event readings available as alternatives – habitual is a possibility for all four sentences in the past tense column. For example, (*In those days*) *the clown popped the balloon* (*at the climax of each show*), *but that had to stop when the accountant insisted that just saying "bang" was good enough*. All four sentences in the future column can also sustain a habitual interpretation, for instance that, when he is a bit older, Little Maurice will regularly brush his teeth without help, and (now that the accountant has moved to a managerial post elsewhere) the clown will in future performances again pop the balloon at the end of each show.

Next, notice that the sentences denoting states – the sentences in the top row of Table 6.3 – not merely can be interpreted as habitual, they have to be. *She loved music* cannot mean there was a single event in which she did some music loving, like Carl once drinking a cup of decaffeinated coffee after dinner. Rather, it means that 'she habitually loved music'. *She will love music* means 'she will habitually love music', and *She loves music* also admits only the habitual interpretation. This is because of the nature of states.

Now consider the present simple examples in Table 6.3 (other than the state sentence just discussed): an activity (*He drinks decaffeinated coffee*), an accomplishment (*Little Maurice brushes his teeth by himself*) and an achievement (*The clown pops the balloon*). A single-event interpretation is available for each of these, but it is not the preferred interpretation. **Habitual** is the strongly preferred reading for present simple (Miller 2002: 148). Imagine yourself watching a children's show with a child and seeing a clown pop a balloon. Surely – instead of using present simple – you would say to the child 'Look, the clown's popping the balloon' (using a present progressive form)? Likewise for the other two, to describe a single event happening before you, it is more natural to say 'He is drinking decaffeinated coffee' or 'Little Maurice is brushing his teeth'. Progressive aspect is the topic of Section 6.2.2, below.

To summarise: all twelve of the simple aspect sentences in Table 6.3 allow a habitual interpretation, and this is the only interpretation available for the three state-denoting clauses in the top row. The other nine are open to both habitual and single-event interpretations. For present simple forms, the habitual interpretation is preferred even when a single-event reading is available (though broadcast commentating is an exception; see (6.2a)). Habitual interpretations can be made obligatory by means of certain adverbials: *in those days* (with past tense), *nowadays* or *these days* (with present tense) and *in future* (with future tense).

Thus it seems that the English simple aspect forms are semantically indifferent between the single-event and habitual interpretations. To understand which is intended on a given occasion, we rely on context of utterance and other items in the construction (as when *nowadays* or *used to* marks habituality).

6.2.2 Progressive aspect

Progressive aspect is marked by BE+Verb-*ing*. Semantically, it down-plays the onset and ignores the end of an event, focusing instead on its middle phase(s), presenting it as an ongoing activity. This is a way of portraying an event as drawn out in time. Particularly at the beginning of a narrative, the background to other events is often stated in a clause with progressive aspect, as in (6.12), the first sentence of a novel by Michael Ondaatje.[2]

(6.12)   When the team reached the site at five-thirty in the morning, one or two family members would be waiting for them.

The waiting that constitutes the background is expressed by a pro-gressive form *would be waiting*, in the second clause of (6.12). It was an ongoing vigil by family members at the site of a forensic exhumation. The forensic science team's arrival is expressed through a past simple form (*reached*), portraying it as a punctuation that occurs, each day, within the continuing vigil. (The situation type of *the team reached the site* is an achievement. In context, it has to be given the interpretation habitual – they came there day after day – though each day's arrival was a single event.)

Progressive aspect can be used to mentally extend even a short event like the departure of a bus into an ongoing activity (another of the aspectual types introduced in Chapter 4), making it a possible setting for other events, as in (6.13), where we might guess that the speaker wants the addressee to hurry in order fit an event, such as boarding the bus, into the normally brief transition (an achievement) of the bus leaving.

(6.13)   Hurry, the bus is leaving.

That progressive aspect disregards the end of an event is clearly seen in an effect that it has on the entailments with situations of the accom-plishment type (see Chapter 4). The a & b examples in (6.14–6.16) entail that the goal was reached. However the c examples, with past progressive, do not have that entailment; it is left open whether the building came down, the napkin got folded or the contract was finished. (*Ditto* avoids retyping of each entailed – or not entailed – sentence.)

(6.14)   a.   The firm demolished the building.
                                    ⇒ The building came down.
         b.   The firm has demolished the building.
                                    ⇒   ditto
         c.   The firm was demolishing the building.
                                    does not entail   ditto

(6.15)   a.   The waiter folded a napkin.

⇒ The napkin was folded.

b.   The waiter has folded a napkin.

⇒   ditto

c.   The waiter was folding a napkin

does not entail   ditto

(6.16)   a.   They drew up a contract.

⇒ The contract was drawn up.

b.   They have drawn up a contract.

⇒   ditto

c.   They were drawing up a contract.

does not entail   ditto

As noted in Chapter 4, many of the verbs that encode states reject progressive aspect. This can be seen in the ill-formedness of (6.17a).

(6.17)   a.   *Who is knowing Danish?
         b.   Your keys are lying at the bottom of the swimming pool.
         c.   Full fathom five thy father lies. (Shakespeare: *The Tempest.*)

When it is possible to use progressive aspect with a state-denoting verb, the effect is sometimes what Cruse (2000: 279) has called "provisionality", as seen in the comparison of (6.17b) with (6.17c). The keys will probably be retrieved fairly soon, unlike Prospero's remains. The explanation for this consequence of apparently converting a state into an activity is probably that activities are typically less long-lasting than states.

6.2.3 Perfect aspect

In English, it is the combination of the auxiliary HAVE (*have, has* or *had*) in front of the past participle form of a verb that marks what is called **perfect aspect**. (*Perfect* is a widely used traditional term; we are stuck with it. It does not have any connotation of "exactly right" or "ideal"!)

The perfect is used to indicate occurrences in the aftermath of an event or state. The **aftermath** is the time – however long it may be – during which the event or state seems to continue to have consequences. For example, if someone is grinning on her way back from getting her examination results, a friend can say 'Look, she has passed'. The present perfect form *has passed* portrays the happy student as in the aftermath of passing – still affected by passing. (The passing happened earlier, when she and the examiners did their work. As long as records and memories last, there is a sense in which she will continue to be in the aftermath of passing that exam.) This is in line with the account that Quirk et al. (1985: 193) give for two common features of present perfect meaning: 'the relevant time zone leads up to the present' and 'the result of the action still obtains at the present time'.

One reason for signalling that we are in something's aftermath is to indicate completion of an accomplishment or achievement (see Chapter 4). The b examples of (6.14–6.16), above, illustrate that in the period following an accomplishment there is an entailment that the event has culminated. If the relevant present perfect sentence is true, then we know that the processes of taking the building down, folding a napkin or drawing up a contract were completed. The examples in (6.18) have an achievement verb *start*.

(6.18)	a.	The rain started.	⇒	A switch from not raining to raining occurred.
	b.	The rain has started.	⇒	We are in the aftermath of a switch from not raining to raining.
	c.	The rain was starting.	does not entail	There was a switch from not raining to raining.

There might not seem to be any significance to the difference between the entailments that I have written for (6.18a) and (6.18b). But there is a point: an event described by (6.18a) could have been followed by a switch back to not raining, or by any number of stops and starts. In contrast to this, the obvious interpretation of (6.18b) is that it is still raining at the time of speaking. What counts as aftermath is a matter of human judgement. If (6.18b) was spoken by a scientist who had predicted that climate change would bring the possibility of rain to some desert place where it had never rained, it might be used to report signs of rain having fallen – for example runnels made in the sand by water – even if the field trip that found evidence of rain was made in dry weather. This interpretation of (6.18b) is habitual (see Section 6.2.1): that bit of desert has changed its habits and become one where rain can now be expected to fall from time to time.

If you look back to (6.15a, b), you will see that a similar distinction can be made there: the past simple merely indicates that, at some time, the folding of a napkin was completed (and it might or might not subsequently have been unfolded; or unfolded, refolded and unfolded and so on), whereas *The waiter has folded a napkin* means that we are in the aftermath of completion of the folding of the napkin and it is probably currently in a folded state (though habituality is possible too: one can perhaps see from the waiter's general expertise that he is someone who has often folded a napkin).

Using the present perfect to depict a situation as in the aftermath of an event can be a way of indicating that it has a bearing on the present. Example (6.19) was a sequence of two utterances, spoken to me by a person for whom English was a foreign language.

(6.19) a. Did you hear what happened to a Japanese airplane?
      b. ?The pilot has lost control of it.

I put a query mark, indicating semantic oddity, in front of (6.19b) because the aircraft had crashed into a mountain the previous day, with the loss of all on board. I would only have used present perfect marking in the second sentence if there was still a chance, at the time of utterance, of the pilot regaining control. The plane having been destroyed, we were in the history, not merely the aftermath, of the pilot losing control of it.

Many linguists have noted that present perfect forms tend not to accept past time adverbial modifiers, as illustrated in (6.20a).

(6.20) a. *I have arrived yesterday.
      b. *They go there recently.
      c. They went there recently.
      d. They have been there recently.
      e. They have been there since 1999.

Klein (1992) has pointed out that the present perfect unexpectedly accepts members of a small class of past time adverbials, including *recently*. Examples (6.20b, c), using present simple *go* and past simple *went*, confirm that *recently* behaves as a past time adverb. Example (6.20d) shows it comfortable with a present perfect. And (6.20e) shows that the same is true for a preposition phrase with *since*. This is because reference to the time of utterance is included in the meaning of these deictic expressions: *recently* 'a short time prior to the time of utterance' and *since 1999* 'in the time between 1999 and the time of utterance'.

Although I said that aspect does not locate events in time – that is what tense does – it has to be admitted that perfect aspect does locate events relative to a time in their aftermath. From a present perfect, like *The rain has started* (6.18b), we can infer that the event happened before the time of utterance – even if only a moment before. That would appear to mean that present perfect is deictic: explicated with reference to the time of utterance. This is a reason why it is sometimes called "perfect tense", as it is in Huddleston and Pullum's authoritative grammar of English (2002).

I attribute the deictic connection with utterance time to the present tense (*have* rather than *had*) in present perfect. This raises the question of what the effect is of using past tense *had* with perfect aspect. Below, (6.21) includes a past perfect form (*had sent*).

(6.21) a. When he phoned I had already sent the email.
   b. When he phoned I had sent the email.

With *already* as a cue, (6.21a) clearly places the telephone call in the aftermath of the dispatch of the email. If (6.21a) was used for real communication, context should enable the addressee to locate the telephoning in time, for instance (6.21a) might be in response to having just been told "He said he would phone you first thing today to ask you not to send the email". In this case, the simple past (*phoned*) deictically points to a location in time before the time of utterance, and the past perfect *had sent* indicates a sending time before that. Even without *already*, (6.21b) can be understood in the same way.

It would probably take more scene-setting than there is room for here, to persuade you that (6.21b) could also be used appropriately to describe certain situations in which the phoning and the sending of the email were simultaneous. On that interpretation, it is equivalent to a past simple (*sent*): *When he phoned I sent the email*, which would make it a type of tense rather than an aspect. This is getting well beyond introductory level. If you would like to pursue the issue further, see Huddleston and Pullum (2002: 146).

Summary

Tense is deictic. It locates events in relation to the time of utterance: present (unmarked or with an -*s* suffix), suffixed past and the variously marked future. Time adverbials help reveal the mapping between tense forms and time.

Aspect is about the time profile of events. The grammatically marked forms in English are: progressive (ongoing without attention to ending) and perfect (we are in the aftermath of the event – or, for past perfect, we are talking about a time in the aftermath). Habitual aspect is not grammatically marked in English, but is readily available and, when one is trying to make sense of tense and aspect, is an essential interpretation to distinguish.

There are interactions between the topics discussed in this chapter and the situation types described in Chapter 4.

Exercises

1. Table 6.2 presents various kinds of deictic adverbial showing the different times – relative to utterance time – that they are compatible with. Which group does *recently* belong in? And where does *soon* belong? You will need to make up sentences and scenarios for past, present and future tense and try them for compatibility with *recently* and *soon*.

2. With reference to aspect and to situation types (introduced in Chapter 4), discuss the difference in meaning between *Arthur's a tyrant* and *Arthur's being a tyrant*.

3. *A tobacco company told the Czech government that they had saved many millions of dollars because people were dying early.* Think of the sentence in italics as part of a newspaper report (and note that the pronoun *they* refers to the Czech government). Identify the combinations of tense and aspect used in the sentence and draw a diagram similar to Figure 6.1 to represent the relative timing of the events. Position 'time of report' on a time line. Then indicate the positions when the tobacco company told the Czech government something, when the government saved many millions of dollars and when people died early.

4. Sentence (a) illustrates BE *to Verb* as a rather formal way of marking the future. A tutor could write it on an exercise handout. When 11 May comes, the tutor could say (b) to remind the class about (a). Sentence (b) embeds a future tense within the past; w*ere* is a past tense form and BE *to Verb* is, as illustrated in (a), a way of marking future.

   (a) On 11 May you are to submit a written solution to this exercise.
   (b) You were to submit written solutions today.

Now try to find some less formal ways of embedding a future in the past. Imagine that your friend offered yesterday to bring a copy today of a particular novel, but now admits "Sorry, I remembered promising to get something for you, but at home I just couldn't think what it was". To remind your friend, you could use a 'future in the past' form: past because the offer was made yesterday; future because lending you the book was at that time set in the future. Suggest one or two reasonable completions for (c), but they must involve a form of future marking with past tense on it.

   (c) You said you _____ bring me that book called *White Teeth*.

Also, how might the request – corresponding to (a) – have been worded?

Recommendations for reading

Trask (1993) is a good first resort for looking up terms like *tense, aspect, progressive* and *perfect* that may be unfamiliar. Chapter 13 in Miller (2002) is a short, clear introduction to the meanings associated with tense and aspect. Kearns (2000: ch. 7) provides an excellently accessible and systematic account of English tense and aspect. Cruse (2000) and Saeed (2003) have good discussions too. Worthwhile generalisations, as well as many interesting details, are available via the index entries for *tense* and *aspect* in Huddleston and Pullum (2002) and Quirk et al. (1985).

Notes

1. 'The end of British farming', *London Review of Books*, vol. 23 (2001).

2. Michael Ondaatje (2000), *Anil's Ghost*, London: Bloomsbury.

7 Modality, scope and quantification

Overview

Modality is the term for a cluster of meanings centred on the notions of necessity and possibility: what must be (7.1a) or what merely might be (7.1b).

(7.1) a. This has to be a joke.
       b. The letter said the students might go there.

There are interesting interactions between modality and negation. For instance, the two sentences in (7.2a, b) have nearly the same meaning,[1] suggesting that the expressions of modality *have to* and *must* are nearly synonymous. But the related negative sentences are sharply different in meaning: (7.2c) is a prohibition, but in Standard English (7.2d) indicates that there is no necessity to report the matter.

(7.2) a. You must report it.
       b. You have to report it.
       c. You mustn't report it.
       d. You don't have to report it.

The difference depends on (1) whether the obligation encoded by *must* or *have to* holds with regard to a negative state of affairs, as in (7.2c) – *not* reporting it is 'a must', or (2) whether the obligation is itself negated, as in (7.2d) – there's no 'have to' about reporting it. Differences of this kind can be understood as arising when different parts of sentences are affected by operations such as negation and the marking of modality. This is called **relative scope**, the second major topic of the chapter.

Relative scope is also needed for understanding quantificational meanings. **Quantifiers** are words such as *all*, *some* and *most*. They constitute the third main topic in the chapter. There is an intrinsic connection between quantifiers and modality: what 'must be' is expected under *all* circumstances, and if a situation is possible in *some* circumstances, then it 'may be'.

7.1 Modality

To put it very generally, a clause characterises a situation. Modality is the label given to the meanings signalled by the italicised expressions in (7.3). This family of meanings includes obligations to make a situation come about (7.3a), indications of whether or not it is permissible (7.3b), or feasible (7.3c). Also included are signals as to how confident the speaker is regarding knowledge of the situation: whether, in the light of available evidence, the proposition seems certain to be true (7.3d) or probably true (7.3e) or merely possibly so (7.3f).

(7.3) a. You *must* apologise.
    b. You *can* come in now.
    c. She's not *able to* see you until Tuesday.
    d. Acting like that, he *must* be a Martian.
    e. With an Open sign on the door, there *ought to* be someone inside.
    f. Martians *could* be green.

The main carriers of modality are a set of auxiliary verbs called **modals**: *will, would, can, could, may, might, shall, should, must* and *ought to*. Modality is encoded in various other expressions too, such as *possibly, probably, have (got) to, need to* and *be able to*.

7.1.1 Modal verbs and tense

A distinction was made in Chapter 6 between tense forms and time. It is relevant here again. The modal verbs *would, could, might* and *should* are past tense forms, but the examples in (7.4) show that past forms of modal verbs often do not mark past time. The requests in (7.4a–7.4c) are more tentative and polite than those in (7.4d), but none of them is semantically about the past. Also, the (7.4a) sentences have almost the same meaning as those in (7.4d) where the modals are not past tense forms.

(7.4) a. Would/Could you help me tomorrow?
    b. Might you be free to help me tomorrow?
    c. Should you have the time tomorrow, please help me then.
    d. Will/Can you help me tomorrow?

Past tense forms of the modals, particularly *would* and *could*, do sometimes have reference to past time, as in (7.5a, b).

(7.5) a. Previously we would meet every New Year, but not anymore.
    b. Two years ago she could swim fifty lengths, but not anymore.

It was pointed out in Chapter 6 that, although the modal *will* can signal futurity, it can also be used for predictions and timeless truths such as *A diamond will cut glass*. Marking of modality is in some respects complementary to marking for tense. English syntax often forces us to choose whether a clause will have tense in it or modality instead. In an analysis of text samples totalling 40 million words – a representative range of British and North American written and spoken text types – it was found that modals were used in about 15 per cent of clauses that could have them (Biber et al. 1999: 456). Clauses with tense but no marking for modality are the default pattern. Exercise 1, at the end of this chapter, is about the relative strength of ordinary tensed clauses and ones that are modally marked.

7.1.2 Deontic and epistemic modality

Expressions of modality exhibit an intriguing spectrum of partially similar meanings. The modal auxiliaries are also among the most frequently used verbs in English: six of the top twenty English verbs are modals: *will, would, can, could, may* and *should*, each of them averaging more than 1,000 occurrences per million words of running text (Leech et al. 2001: 282). Whole books have been written about English modals and modality, for example Palmer (1990). My aims here are to present a sample of the principal issues that make modality interesting and to illustrate the basic distinctions and terminology of the area.

Two philosophical terms, *epistemic* and *deontic*, have regularly been used to label two main classes of modality.

Epistemic interpretations have to do with knowledge and understanding. Markers of epistemic modality are understood as qualifications proffered by speakers or writers (or from someone they are reporting) regarding the level of certainty of a proposition's truth. Modally unmarked sentences, like the (a) examples in (7.6–7.9), form a background against which epistemic modality, seen in the (b) examples, contrasts.

(7.6) a. The whole hillside is slipping down into the valley.
      b. The whole hillside could be slipping down into the valley.

(7.7) a. They meet in the centre court final tomorrow.
      b. They may meet in the centre court final tomorrow.

(7.8) a. Jessica went by motorbike.
      b. Jessica probably went by motorbike.

(7.9) a. The car was travelling very fast, so it came unstuck at the bend.
      b. The car must have been travelling very fast because it came unstuck at the bend.

Modally unqualified statements are found in live commentary (as in 7.6a; imagine this coming from a news reporter watching a landslip happening), when speakers are talking about events on fixed schedules (7.7a), in other cases when they feel that they have reliable information about what happened (7.8a), and for eyewitness testimony (7.9a).

Modality comes in different strengths. A gradient from weak to strong can be seen in the modally marked (b) examples (7.6b–7.9b). Because of *could*, someone who produces (7.6b) is likely to be understood as conceding that the possibility of the hillside slipping down into the valley is not ruled out by available evidence. The presence of *may* in (7.7b) is likely to convey that a meeting between the players in question, in the centre court final the next day, is compatible with some available information. Use of *probably* in (7.8b) signals that the speaker or writer regards the available evidence as not just compatible with Jessica having gone by motorbike, but that the balance of evidence points towards this having been her mode of travel. *Must* (7.9b) is a mark of strong modality: a speaker or writer who says this is vouching that all the available evidence leads to the conclusion that the car was going very fast.

Deontic interpretations of modality relate to constraints grounded in society: duty, morality, laws, rules. Deontic modality lets language users express their attitudes (or relay the attitudes of others) as to whether a proposition relates to an obligatory situation or permissible one, or somewhere in between. See (7.10a–d).

(7.10) a. You can ride my bike anytime you like.
        b. The consul could have been more helpful.
        c. You should send him an email.
        d. Tax forms must be submitted by the end of September.

Example (7.10a) illustrates a common way of giving permission (even if some people assert that it is better, or even mandatory, to use *may* for this purpose): using *can* (or *may*), the utterer offers no objection to the addressee riding the bike. *Could* contributes to a presumption behind (7.10b): that the consul was not very helpful. Additionally – and this is the deontic modality part of the meaning – *could* conveys a judgement that it would have been preferable if the consul had been more helpful. *Should* makes (7.10c) a statement that the desirable course of action is for an email to be sent to 'him'. With *must*, (7.10d) conveys an obligation regarding tax returns.

It turns out that the same expressions are often interpretable in two ways: as marking either epistemic or deontic modality. The (a) examples in (7.11–7.17) are likely to be interpreted epistemically (degree of certainty offered by evidence) and the (b) examples favour a deontic interpretation (along the permission–obligation dimension). The expressions of modality are in italics.

(7.11) a. *Might* you have put the ticket in your jacket pocket?
   b. *Might* I have another piece of cake, please?

(7.12) a. It *may* be dark by the time we've finished.
   b. OK, we'll permit it: you *may* copy these two diagrams.

(7.13) a. Prime numbers *can* be adjacent: 1, 2, 3.
   b. The pigeons *can* have this bread.

(7.14) a. The tide *should* be turning now; I looked up the times before we came here.
   b. You *should* try harder.

(7.15) a. The tide *ought to* be turning now; I looked up the times earlier today.
   b. You *ought to* try harder.

(7.16) a. Warmer summers *must* be a sign of global warming.
   b. The treaty says carbon dioxide emissions *must* be reduced.

(7.17) a. At 87 metres this *has (got) to* be one of tallest trees in the world.
   b. He *has (got) to* be more careful or he'll break the crockery.

Please, seen in (7.11b), is optionally present in requests. Requests are deontic. Note that *please* cannot really be put into the epistemic (a) examples in (7.11a–7.17a): for instance, ?*Prime numbers can be adjacent please: 1, 2, 3* seems weird. If the addition is acceptable at all, it changes the character of the sentence, into one that is understood deontically, for instance *Warmer summers must please be a sign of global warming* sounds like someone with a vested interest in this proposition praying that its truth will be confirmed or accepted. The deontic examples (7.14b–7.17b) readily accommodate *please* without changing into something different: for example *You ought to try harder please* is just a more polite version of (7.15b). Interrogatives closely related to (7.12b) and (7.13b) would accept *please*: *May I copy this please?* and *Can the pigeons please have this?*

The double meanings illustrated in (7.11–7.17) are more interesting than ordinary cases of ambiguous words, such as the adjective *light* meaning either 'bright' or 'not heavy', or the noun *bank* denoting either financial institutions or the land borders of lakes and rivers. With modality there is a sustained parallel. We would seem to be missing generalisations if we just listed the different meanings: *may* 'possibly' or 'permitted', *should* 'likely, according to how things normally go' or 'desirable, according to normal rules of conduct'. A way of accounting for the related meanings is explored in Section 7.1.3 below.

7.1.3 Core modal meanings

(7.18) a. *She expected the coffee to be strong*, she'd tasted that blend before.
       b. She told the waiter that *she expected the coffee to be strong* and would not accept it otherwise.

Context influences the interpretation of modality. This is illustrated by (7.18a), which is epistemic, a moderately strong expression of conviction about how reality would turn out, and (7.18b), which is deontic, a moderately strong demand about how she wanted it to be. The italicised clause is the same, but coupled with mention of experience from which evidence could have been gained (in 7.18a) the interpretation concerns degree of certainty of knowledge, while mention of a waiter and a sanction (in 7.18b) makes us take the clause as a reported demand. The markers of modality in the earlier examples of this chapter were auxiliary verbs or similar (such as *have got to*) and the adverb *probably*, but *expect* in (7.18) is a main verb. A different word class was chosen to make the point that the epistemic–deontic ambiguity is fairly general.

At the beginning of this chapter modality was introduced as having to do with necessity and possibility. The notions of **necessity** and **possibility** are interlinked. Either can be defined in terms of the other, as shown in (7.19–7.21):

- it is not possible to dodge whatever is necessarily true (see 7.19a)
- possible situations are ones that are not necessarily impossible (7.20a)
- if it is impossible for something to be true, then it has to be untrue (7.21a).

P stands for any proposition and the double-headed equivalence arrow represents **paraphrase** (sameness of sentence meaning), a term introduced in Chapter 2. The double-headed arrow is a reminder that entailment between paraphrases goes in both directions.

(7.19) a. P is necessarily true ⇔ It is not possible for P to be untrue.
       b. necessarily P ⇔ not possibly not P

(7.20) a. It is possible that P is true ⇔ It is not necessarily so that P is untrue.
       b. possibly P ⇔ not necessarily not P

(7.21) a. It is impossible for P to be true ⇔ P is necessarily untrue
       b. not possibly P ⇔ necessarily not P

The abbreviated versions of these paraphrases given as (b) in (7.19–20) are in a format that will be useful later, in Section 7.2. A way to understand them is to deal with the material on each side of ⇔ separately. For instance, the second half of (7.19b) can be understood by thinking: P means 'the proposition P is true'; *not* P means that 'P is not true' (or 'P is untrue'); *possibly not* P means 'it is possible that P is untrue' and *not possibly not* P means 'it is not possible that P is untrue'. Bracketing will be added in 7.2, to mark the steps, but at this stage bracketing might make things harder to grasp.

What does it mean to say that a proposition is necessarily true? An example is that the result is an even number whenever a whole number is multiplied by two. The way arithmetic has been set up ensures that that proposition (amongst others) is always true – that it is necessarily true. If the previous few paragraphs are hard to understand, try putting *for sure* in place of *necessarily*.

Modality is often used for communicating about matters that, unlike arithmetic, have not been systematised. In such cases, necessity is relative to the context as it is understood by the speaker and hearer(s) involved in a communication. In ordinary communications, speakers and writers present a proposition as necessarily true – something that *must* be – if it is the unavoidable consequence of everything that they, at the moment of speaking, assume to be both true and relevant to the case in hand. And a proposition is regarded as possibly true if some information currently salient in the attention of the communicator and assumed to be true and relevant is compatible with the proposition.

There is justification for the cautious talk, in the previous paragraph, about information being assumed to be true and relevant. Humans are not perfect computers that run through all imaginable scenarios. In everyday communication, people generally take into account only those aspects of reality that immediately occur to them as relevant and that they believe will be readily accessible to their addressees. The addressees come into the story because they have to be able to interpret the message in context by accessing the assumptions that the speaker has started from. But it should also be noted that an addressee who trusts the speaker in regard to a particular utterance with a marker of modality in it could just accept what is being said without checking the supporting information. For example, *It may be dark by the time we've finished* (7.12a) could simply be accepted if the speaker is someone familiar with the task and known to keep accurate track of time. (On the other hand, the addressee could choose to probe what the propositions are that support the assertion and, if confirmatory evidence cannot easily be found, could fairly ask a question along the lines of "Why do you think that?" The onus is then on the speaker to offer some justification.)

Chapter 5 introduced the notion of a set of **presuppositions**: propositions that form the context in the light of which an utterance is uttered, and which the sender regards as available to be used by the addressee(s) to interpret it. Such a set of assumed-to-be-relevant propositions could be far smaller than the set of propositions that exhaustive research might establish as having relevance to the communication. The presuppositions are simply what the sender relies on at the time of utterance and assumes can be readily accessed by the addressee(s).

Epistemic modality gets used when the contextually relevant presuppositions are not sufficient to establish the truth of the proposition being communicated. If there was enough information to decide the truth of the matter, then it would be expressed baldly without recourse to modality (see Exercise 1). Epistemic marking signals that the speaker or writer is going beyond the available evidence and making inferences regarding what the actual situation was, currently is, or will be.[2]

Have to is one of the ways that English has for encoding necessity. And *may* is a way of encoding possibility. Re-using two earlier examples, (7.1a) and (7.7b), their meanings can now be stated as in (7.22a, b).

(7.22) a. *This has to be a joke.* 'All the presuppositions that I take into account here, necessarily lead me to conclude that 'this' is (to be) a joke'.

  b. *They may meet in the centre court final tomorrow.* 'In at least one plausible elaboration of the presuppositions taken into account here, tomorrow's state of affairs has them meeting in the centre court final'.

Put differently, (7.22b) is 'there is at least one plausible scenario in which they meet in the centre court tomorrow; so – accepting that this is not the only plausible development of the relevant context – such a meeting is not necessarily ruled out'. *Ruled out* is a negative expression, which means that 'not necessarily ruled out' is a case of the negated negative analysis of 'possibly P' given in (7.20b): 'not necessarily not P'.

Both of the example sentences in (7.22a) and (7.22b) can be taken as either epistemic or deontic. Example (7.22b) – then numbered (7.7b) – was presented earlier as an example of a sentence with epistemic modality, but there are imaginable situations in which it could have deontic modality. Epistemic interpretations arise when the presuppositions are propositions assumed to be facts: common knowledge, or propositions that have recently been accepted in the conversation or that are made obvious by sights, sounds and so on available to be experienced in the context of utterance. Deontic interpretations arise when preferences, wishes, requirements or recommendations form the contextual presuppositions. Examples (7.23a–d) offer imaginary scenarios for the two sentences just discussed.

(7.23)   a.   A sixteen-year-old who has grown 25 per cent in the past year opens a present from a family friend who has not seen him recently. It is a garment. He measures it against himself and it is clear that he'll never fit into it. He says "This has to be a joke". (Epistemic)

   b.   TV producer explaining to an actor that she wants humour in a scene: "This has to be a joke". (Deontic)

   c.   Someone who takes an interest in tennis tournaments is asked about the prospects of two players, currently in the semi-finals. The reply is "They may meet in the centre court final tomorrow". ('They' could both win their current matches, so their facing each other the next day in the final is not ruled out. Epistemic.)

   d.   In a fantasy story, an all-powerful manipulator is asked to make a match take place, and consents, adding specifics of where and when: "They may meet in the centre court final tomorrow". (Deontic)

In passing, it is worth noting that pragmatic interpretations often have multiple layers. In the setting of (7.23a), it is unlikely that the family friend who sent the undersized item of clothing to the teenager meant it as a joke. For the receiver to pretend that all the evidence points to the gift being intended humorously is a way of making a joke out of what would otherwise be a present that flopped.

This approach to the epistemic–deontic difference is parallel to what was suggested in Chapter 6 for the single-event and habitual interpretations of simple aspect forms. In each case the distinction is pragmatic: a context-dependent overlay on a semantic core that is indifferent to the distinction.

The selection of contextual information taken as relevant can be influenced by the nature of the sentence itself (see Biber et al. 1999: 485–6). There is a tendency – no more than a tendency – for epistemic sentences to have non-human subjects and state verbs, something illustrated in two earlier examples (with the subject and main verbs underlined): *It may be dark by the time we've finished* (7.12a); *At 87 metres this has (got) to be one of tallest trees in the world* (7.17a). And there is a tendency – again just a tendency – for deontics to have human subjects and activity or other non-state verbs, for example: … *you may copy these two diagrams* (7.12b); *You should try harder* (7.14b). It makes sense that human subjects should predominate in sentences that favour deontic interpretations. It is people, rather than inanimates and animals, who are conscious of and guided by the preferences, wishes, advice and rules that constitute the foundation of deontic modality. It is also people's actions, rather than the states they happen to be in, that are most open to influence through permissions, demands and counselling.

Table 7.1 proposes core meanings for some important markers of modality in English.[3] To make it easier to focus on semantic similarities and differences between the markers, think of each of them in the same sentence frame and consider only epistemic interpretations. A sentence frame that would do is *It ___ be true*, as a response to *Is that true?* The proposition that *that* refers to is represented in the table by *P*.

Table 7.1 Core semantics of some markers of modality in English

marker of modality in the frame P ___ be true	meaning	type of propositions presupposed
must *has to* *will*	P is true in all plausible scenarios based on the presupposition	factual propositions
should *ought to*	P is true in all plausible scenarios based on the presuppositions	norms
may *might*	at least one plausible scenario based on the presuppositions does not rule out P	factual propositions
can	no plausible scenarios based on the presuppositions rule out P	factual propositions

For deontic interpretations the third column of Table 7.1 would have presuppositions relating to preferences and requirements instead of factual propositions. A frame such as *You ___ go; that's what the manager said* can be used to check the details. In the case of *should*, the label 'norms' covers schedules and averages for epistemics (see 7.24a, b) and conventions of conduct for deontics (see 7.24c).

(7.24) a. There should be a train at 10.20, according to that timetable (but perhaps it's not running today).
    b. We shouldn't get snow in May, in a normal year (but exceptions do happen).
    c. The people who didn't cook should wash the dishes (but I'll let you off this time).

    d. ?There must be a train at 10.20, but perhaps it's not running today.

    e. ?The people who didn't cook must wash the dishes, but I'll let you off this time.

Should is a necessity modal, like *must*, but not as strong: exceptions to claims with *should* are coherent, as seen in the bracketed continuations of (7.24a–c), but attempting to do the same with *must* (7.24d, e) is problematic; and probably only acceptable if *must* is understood ironically.

The meanings proposed in Table 7.1 make *must*, *have to* and *will* synonymous; likewise the pair *should* and *ought to*; and *may* and *might*. The table does not show various restrictions on use, notably:

- *Must* is hardly ever used for epistemic claims about the future; *will* is used instead.
- *Might* is generally weaker than *may*, past tense somehow distancing the possibility.
- Although *can't* clearly has both epistemic and deontic uses, *can* is sometimes not usable for epistemic modality; for example, epistemic *can* is peculiar in the suggested frame: *?It can be true.*

Table 7.1 makes *may* a superordinate for *can*. *May* is generally substitutable for *can* (its hyponym – the sense relation of hyponymy was introduced in Chapter 3) with some loss in precision but no other large switch in meaning, in the same way that it is generally possible to substitute *animal* for *dog*. Examples are: *You may/can ride my bike* (7.10a), *Prime numbers may/can be adjacent* (7.13a) and *The pigeons may/can have this bread* (7.13b). However, this does not work when *can* denotes "ability", as in (7.4d) *Can you help me tomorrow?* Putting *may* in place of *can* in (7.4d) yields *May you help me tomorrow?* which is perhaps a prayer, but hardly an alternative way to request help. Another example where *may* is not a suitable replacement for "ability" *can* is *There's no trace of mist; I can see all the way across to Jura.* This is the kind of evidence that has led some linguists to recognise a separate "ability" meaning of *can*, one that is sometimes taken to be a sub-meaning of what is called dynamic modality. It is said that the constraints encoded in **dynamic modality** originate inside the person (or animal or machine) referred to by the subject noun phrase of the sentence, thus contrasting with the social constraints that underlie deontic modality and the inferential constraints that epistemic modality is based on. I regard "dynamic modality" as a subspecies of epistemic modality.

7.2 Relative scope

The basic idea was introduced in Chapter 1, in connection with the ambiguous word *unlockable*. Part of the issue was whether *un-* has as its **scope** – which is to say the material that it applies to – the verb *lock* or the adjective *lockable*. Questions of relative scope arise when there are two **operators** – items that have scope – in the same expression. With two operators we can get different meanings depending on which operator includes the other within its scope.

Interesting things happen when a marker of modality interacts with negation. Consider deontic interpretations of the sentences in (7.25).

(7.25)   a. You mustn't provide a receipt.
         b. You don't have to provide a receipt.
         c. You must provide a receipt.
         d. You have to provide a receipt.

Deontic interpretations are the obvious ones here: advice or demands, for instance concerning an application for a refund of money spent. Sentences (7.25a, b) are sharply different in meaning, but the affirmative sentences (c, d) that would seem to correspond respectively to (a, b) are very similar in meaning. How can removal of *n't* (and the auxiliary *do* that carries it in 7.25b) affect the two sentences differently?

The difference between (7.25a) and (7.25b) is that the (a) sentence indicates that it is necessary for a negative state of affairs to hold (necessity includes the negation within its scope), while the (b) sentence negates a necessity (negation has scope over the necessity). Analytic statements about relative scope can be hard to grasp. A conventional notation that is helpful is used in (7.26), and is explained immediately below the example.

(7.26)   a. necessarily (not (you provide a receipt))
         b. not (necessarily (you provide a receipt))
         c. necessarily (you provide a receipt)

Each operator is written to the left of a pair of brackets and the material inside the brackets represents the scope of the operator. The representation in (7.26a) reflects the relative scope of (7.25a)'s arrangement of operators, and (7.26b) represents the scope relations of (7.25b). Note that the components in (7.26a, b) are the same; relative scope is the only difference. Working from the innermost brackets outwards, (7.26a) has a proposition 'you provide a receipt' that is negated: 'you are not to provide a receipt'; that negative specification constitutes the scope of the necessity operator; it is that negative state of affairs that the sentence characterises as one that is necessary, that must be achieved. (Perhaps the speaker doesn't want a fraud to be traceable!) On the other hand (7.26b), from the inside outwards, is about you providing a receipt, provision of a receipt being necessary and then, because of the *not* on the outermost brackets, that necessity being cancelled.

Now (7.26c) represents the meaning of (7.25c, d). To show the negation of a clause, put whatever represents it in brackets and add *not* to the left. So the negation of (7.26c) is (7.26b), which in turn represents (7.25b) *You don't have to provide a receipt. Don't have to*, by getting the negation to the left of the marker of necessity *have to*, signals that the negation includes necessity within its scope. (Actually the fact that *don't* is higher in the verb phrase than *have to* matters more than left-to-right order.)

Now consider epistemic interpretations of *must* and *have to*, as illustrated in (7.27). Think of these as suggested explanations for why some people have not turned up at an event. If they are people who usually come to such an event, are – as far as is known – not otherwise occupied and are assumed to have no problems over transport and so on, then the explanation is very probably that the invitation did not reach them.

(7.27)   a.   They mustn't have received the invitation.
         b.   They can't have received the invitation.
         c.   necessarily (not (they received the invitation))

Probably more users of English employ (7.27b) than (7.27a) for the epistemic meaning outlined just above. However, (7.27a) – whether with *mustn't* or *must not* – is becoming more widespread (Miller 2002: 140). It is clear that – for those who accept (7.27a) epistemically – (7.27c) is the meaning it carries (exactly parallel to 7.25a being represented by 7.26a). How, though, does (7.27b) manage to express the meaning (7.27c), the same meaning that (7.27a) has for those who accept it with an epistemic interpretation? There is an overt difference between (7.27a) and (7.27b). One has *mustn't* where the other has *can't*. The two sentences are otherwise the same. *Must* and *can* are different in meaning (see Table 7.1), so we might expect *mustn't* and *can't* to be different in meaning; so shouldn't (7.27a, b) have different meanings?

The paradox (that *can't* and *mustn't* have the same meaning even though *can* and *must* differ in meaning) disappears when it is realised that *can* generally falls within the scope of a negative operator attached to it – in the words *can't* and *cannot*. A reasonable paraphrase for (7.27b) is (7.28a) *It is not possible that they received the invitation*, with *not* in a higher clause and to the left of *possible*. Please think carefully about this: (7.27b) is not a paraphrase of the much less confident speculation 'possible … not' given below in (7.28b). The latter has the same meaning as the sentence with *may* given as (7.28c). The scope relations are informally indicated for the first three sentences in (7.28).

(7.28) a. *It is not possible that they received the invitation.*
              not (possibly (they received the invitation))
        b. *It is possible that they have not received the invitation.*
              possibly (not (they received the invitation))
        c. *They may not have received the invitation.*
              possibly (not (they received the invitation))
        d. not possibly P ⇔ necessarily not P

An equivalence between necessity and possibility that was given in (7.21b) is repeated in (7.28d). This makes the meaning represented by the expression with brackets in (7.28a) equivalent to that given for an earlier example, (7.27c). This comes down to *mustn't* and *can't* having the same meaning – as they do in (7.27a, b) – even though the unnegated *must* and *can* are different in meaning! Examples (7.27a, b) are paraphrases because it is a feature of *can't* that its negation has the widest scope – is on the outermost brackets – whereas with *mustn't* the negation comes within the scope of the modality. Exercises 4 and 5, at the end of the chapter, are on the relative scope of modality and negation.

The meanings given for modals in Table 7.1, above, make use of the expressions *all*, *at least one* and *no*. The next section looks at the latter sort of expression. They are known as **quantifiers** and the kind of meaning they convey is called **quantification**.

7.3 Quantification

Apparently there used to be vegetarian tigers in Mysore; so the populace was unworried about them walking down the street in the Nizam's annual parade. How about corgis? Are any of them vegetarian? I don't know the answer, but the question is about how many individuals – corgis in this case – there are in the intersection of the set of all corgis with the set of all vegetarians. The two ovals in Figure 7.1 represent the two sets. The letter *I*, for *intersection*, has been written into the region of overlap. If there are any vegetarian corgis, then they belong in this intersection. (An intersection of sets is itself a set.)

Some possible answers to the question of whether any corgis are vegetarian are shown in (7.29). The quantifiers are in italics.

(7.29) a. *No* corgis are vegetarian. $| \, C \cap V \, | = 0$
        b. *Several* corgis are vegetarian. $2 < \, | \, C \cap V \, | < 10$
        c. *At least three* corgis are vegetarian. $2 < \, | \, C \cap V \, |$

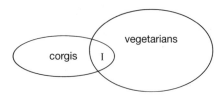

Figure 7.1 Corgis and vegetarians. *I* labels the intersection of the two sets, $C \cap V$

    d.   *Some* corgis are vegetarian. $1 < \mid C \cap V \mid$
    e.   *At least one* corgi is a vegetarian. $0 < \mid C \cap V \mid$

The quantified sentences in (7.29) are true or false depending on the number of individuals in the intersection.[4] Each sentence is true if, and only if, the set-theoretical specification written to its right is met. The notation '$C \cap V$' stands for the intersection of C and V, the set of corgi vegetarians or vegetarian corgis (if there are any such). Enclosing the label of a set within a pair of vertical lines is a way of representing the number of elements in the set, its **cardinality**; for example, with C standing for the set of all corgis, $\mid C \mid$ is the total number of corgis that there are. For the sentence with *no corgis* as the subject noun phrase (7.29a) to be true, the intersection must be empty; it must have no elements in it, which is to say that $\mid C \cap V \mid$ has a cardinality equal to zero.

With the quantifier *several* (7.29b) the intersection contains more than two elements (more than two vegetarian corgis) and – to accord with my intuitions – fewer than ten. With *at least three* as the quantifier (7.29c) the minimum number in the intersection is the same ('greater than two' = 'at least three'), but no upper bound is placed on the size of the intersection of corgis and vegetarians. For the *some* ... version of the sentence (7.29d) there have to be two or more in the intersection ('greater than one' = 'two or more'). A small change gives us the set-theoretical truth condition for *At least one* ... (7.29e). Because they are tied to just the cardinality of a set, quantifiers of the kind exemplified in (7.29) are called **cardinal quantifiers**.

If a thorough worldwide census of corgi eating habits was conducted and it turned out that there was only one vegetarian corgi, this finding about the intersection could be reported as *A corgi* (or *One corgi* or *Some corgi*, the latter with a singular noun) *is a vegetarian*. The underlined words are also cardinal quantifiers, $\mid C \cap V \mid = 1$.

Sentences with cardinal quantifiers, such as those in (7.29), have a kind of symmetry that they would not have with certain other quantifiers: the nouns can exchange positions without truth or falsity being affected. Thus *No vegetarians are corgis* expresses the same proposition as (7.29a):

| C ∩ V | = | V ∩ C | = 0. It will be true as long as the facts make (7.29a) true, and false under the same circumstances as (7.29a) is false. Similarly for *Several/at least three/some vegetarians are corgis* and *At least one vegetarian is a corgi.*

7.3.1 Proportional quantifiers

The sentences in (7.30) have what are called **proportional quantifiers** (italicised). These do not exhibit the symmetry found with cardinal quantifiers. *Most meat eaters are corgis* is clearly different in meaning from the sentence in (7.30a). Think about it. And, while (7.30b) is probably false, reversing the nouns – *Less than half the world's meat eaters are corgis* – yields a sentence that is probably true. Switching (7.30c) to *Few vegetarians are corgis* does not state the case nearly strongly enough: hardly any of them are corgis!

(7.30) a. *Most* corgis are meat eaters. | C ∩ M | > | C – M |
      b. *Less than half* the world's corgis are meat eaters.
                                   | C ∩ M | < | C – M |
      c. *Few* corgis are vegetarian. | C ∩ V | << | C – V |

In the set-theoretical formulations to the right of the sentences in (7.30), *M* labels the set of all meat eaters and, as before, *C* is the set of all corgis. Figure 7.2 should make it easier to understand what is being claimed about the meanings of the quantifiers in (7.30a, b).

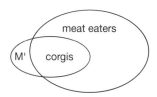

Figure 7.2 Corgis and meat eaters. *M'* labels a subset of corgis that are not meat eaters, C – M

The corgis in the part of the oval that bulges out on the left in Figure 7.2 are not included in the set of meat eaters. The bulge is the set of corgis minus the (large) subset of meat eaters amongst them: C – M. The meat-eating corgis, as in Figure 7.1, are in the intersection of corgis and meat eaters: C ∩ M. The specification given in (7.30a) for *Most corgis are meat eaters* is simply that the number of meat-eating corgis | C ∩ M | is greater than the number of corgis who do not eat meat | C – M |. Another way of putting this is to say that more than half of the members of the corgi set are meat eaters. The sentence in (7.30b) is probably false. It would be true if, and only if, the balance went the other way and there were fewer corgis in the intersection with meat eaters than $\mid C - M \mid$. With *few* (7.30c, and you might find it useful to look back to Figure 7.1) truth requires the intersection to be quite a lot smaller (doubled 'less than' sign: $<<$) than $\mid C - M \mid$.

The truth of the sentences in (7.30) depends on how the totality of corgis is split between an intersection and a remainder, hence the name ***proportional*** **quantifier**. This is different from cardinal quantifiers (7.29), where only the number in the intersection needs to be taken into account; the number of corgis in the bulge on the left in Figure 7.1 has no bearing on the truth of cardinally quantified sentences.

Two more sentences with proportional quantifiers (italicised) are given in (7.31). The symbol $\subseteq$ stands for 'is a subset of'. The set-theoretical truth condition for both is that corgis be a subset of meat eaters. It is obvious that these sentences do not show the symmetry of the sentences in (7.29): *Every meat eater is a corgi* and *All meat eaters are corgis* are both obviously false, whereas the sentences in (7.31) might, just possibly, be true.

(7.31) a. *Every* corgi is a meat eater. $\quad C \subseteq M$
        b. *All* corgis are meat eaters. $\quad C \subseteq M$

How does this involve comparison between an intersection and a remainder set, as seen with the proportionally quantified sentences in (7.30)? Think of the corgi oval moving to the right in Figure 7.2 until the $C - M$ remainder, labelled M' in the figure, has vanished. That is what it means for C to be a subset of M. If all corgis are meat eaters and if the meat eater set is larger than the corgi set, then corgis would be a proper subset of meat eaters, $C \subset M$ (which, incidentally, is the condition for hyponymy; see Chapter 3).

Though the same set-theoretical specification is given for *all* and *every* on the right in (7.31), these two quantifiers are not identical in meaning. *Every* is a **distributive quantifier**, so that, for instance, *Every corgi at the dog show was worth more than £1,000*, would mean that if there were ten of them, the total was over £10,000. *All*, however, is ambiguous between a **collective** and distributive reading: if it is true that *All the corgis at the show were worth more than £1,000*, then that figure could be the value per dog or could be the total for all of them. *Each* is another distributive quantifier. Like *every* and *all*, it is specified in terms of a subset relationship, $C \subseteq M$, just like the quantifiers in (7.31). There is thus more to the meanings of these quantifiers than is covered by their set-theoretical properties.

Earlier in this chapter, in Table 7.1, three quantifiers were used as components in explanations of modal meaning. These quantifiers are repeated in (7.32), in a more general form than the sentences about corgis, with the modality markers that they contributed to shown in parentheses.

(7.32) a. All As are Bs. $A \subseteq B$ (*must, has to, will,*
                                                              should, ought to)
        c. At least one A is a B. $0 < |\, A \cap B \,|$ (*may, might*)
        b. No As are Bs. $|\, A \cap B \,| = 0$ (*can*)

Like negation and markers of modality, quantifiers are operators with scope. The quantifiers considered in this chapter are syntactically located in noun phrases, but they have clauses as their scope. Clauses express propositions; so the quantifiers are propositional operators. When two quantifiers, or a quantifier and negation, are present, there can be differences in meaning attributable to relative scope. Consideration of a few examples will give the flavour of this. Think of the sentences in (7.33) as reports back after a problematic visit to the library. Italics have been used for operators with scope. Informal bracketed indications of relative scope are shown to the right of each sentence, along the same general lines as in Section 7.2.

(7.33) a. *None* of the books was available.   As for every book (not
                                                 (it was available))
        b. *All* the books were *not* available. Not (as for every book
                                                 (it was available))
                                            or As for every book (not
                                                 (it was available))
        c. *Not all* of the books were available. Not (as for every book
                                                 (it was available))

Unlike in the corgis examples, we are not talking here about the full set of books in the world. Almost certainly not about the whole stock of a particular library, but about a contextually recoverable set of books. Use of *the* before *books* is a pragmatic indicator to the listener: 'With a minimal amount of thinking you'll be able to work out which set of books I am referring to'. Perhaps this is a student talking to the university teacher who recommended a set of six books for reading.

It is easy enough to interpret the combination of quantification and negation in (7.33a), because the two operators are pre-packaged in a single word (*none*) with the quantifier having wider scope than the negation. The majority of people using sentences like (7.33b) give intonational prominence to the quantifier *all*, with a sharp pitch inflection, perhaps greater loudness and maybe slightly more length to the vowel.

This is a signal in English that an item falls within the scope of negation, as shown in the first of the bracketings for this sentence, which is also the meaning of the unambiguous (7.33c). The meaning can be built up by starting with the operator more deeply buried in brackets: think what it means for all, or every one, of the relevant set of books to be available; consider the effect of negating that situation; if even one of the books was not available, then that is a situation in which it is not so that 'all the books are available'. Without intonational prominence on *all*, (7.33b) in principle has the alternative meaning shown for it. Looking back to the set-theoretic formulation in 7.32a, this is: 'the entire set of books in question is a subset of the unavailable ones'. However, this meaning of (7.33b) is not often in play because there is an unambiguous way of conveying it, namely (7.33a). Pragmatically, listeners are likely to reason that a speaker who said (7.33b) could not have meant what is encoded by (7.33a) because that would then have been the obvious way to say it.

In (7.34) sentences are presented that have two quantifiers (italicised) in them.

(7.34)   a.   *Each* student borrowed *a* book
               As for every student (there was a book (the student borrowed it))
         b.   *A* student borrowed *each* of the books.
               There was a student (as for every book (the student borrowed it))
         or   As for every book (there was a student (the student borrowed it))

It is an encoded feature of the meaning of *each* that it is generally taken to have wider scope when it occurs with another quantifier, so that the bracketing shown to the right of (7.34a) is practically the only scope pattern for it: start inside the brackets; think of a student borrowing a book; then think of each student in turn doing that, so there were as many books borrowed as the number of student borrowers. However, (7.34b) illustrates another factor regarding the decoding of relative scope: quantifiers in subject noun phrases tend to have wider scope. This favours the first interpretation: just one student borrowing book after book. In (7.34a) the tendency for the subject's quantifier to have wide scope reinforces the bias favouring wide scope for *each*. But in (7.34b) *each*, in the object noun phrase, is pitted against the quantifier on the subject. Neither tendency wins out conclusively and (7.34b) is ambiguous, with an alternative book-focused meaning: book after book was borrowed, each one by a student, and it is not said how many students did the borrowing.

Summary

Must, should, can't and similar expressions encode modality. Markers of modality are interpreted either in relation to the demands and preferences of people, or in relation to evidence. With interpretations of the first kind (called deontic), *You must* ... communicates that the speaker demands that you ...; *You can't* ... that the speaker disallows it, and so on. Interpreted in a context where the issue is the sender's degree of certainty about inferences from evidence (epistemic modality), *It must* ... conveys strong conviction about the likelihood of something being true, *It should* ... that the proposition is expected to be true if things unfold in an average sort of way, and so on. Necessity and possibility are fundamental concepts in modality, and elucidating them involved consideration of quantifiers, such as *all* and *some* (the second topic of the chapter), because – for example – what is necessarily true pertains all the time; and what holds some of the time is possible. The chapter also covered relative scope: the interactions between modality markers, negation and quantifiers when more than one of them is involved in the meaning of a proposition.

Exercises

1. There are differences in strength between modal verbs when they are used to indicate how certain a speaker is about a conclusion. What about using no modal verb at all; how strong is that? Here is a situation to think about. Edward has seen crowds streaming into a department store and says either *There might be a sale on* or *There's a sale on* or *There must be a sale on*. Rank these three in terms of how confident Edward seems to be that there is indeed a sale on in the store. Comment on what we can infer about speakers' knowledge of a situation as soon as they use a modal verb in talking about it.

2. Think about possible interpretations of the modality in the five sentences below. Can they be understood as deontic, epistemic, both or neither? Give a reason for each answer.

They must be made from buckwheat.
We must get up early tomorrow.
The email needn't have been sent.
I can hear you now.
They might or might not make it.
You better apologise.

3. Propose alternative scenarios for each of the following three sentences that could lead to their being interpreted (a) epistemically and (b) deontically.

> Guests may check in between 3 pm and midnight.
> You must be a musician.
> There should be a hallmark.

4. In terms of relative scope, *can't P* means 'not (possibly P)', deontically as well as epistemically. The same holds for *cannot P*. What about *may not* (or *mayn't*, if this reduced form is acceptable to you)? *They may not have an invitation* can be understood either deontically ('I forbid them having an invitation') or epistemically ('Perhaps they do not have an invitation'). What is the scope of negation relative to the scope of modality for these two interpretations?

5. Heard on the radio once: "Which category of witness may | not be named in court?" There was a sharp intonational break after *may*, marked here by the vertical line. It was clear from the context that the question was about unusual circumstances when a court would consent to a witness having the protection of anonymity. For this meaning, what are the relative scopes of modality and negation? To keep things manageable, answer with respect to the sentence *The witness may | not be named.*

6. In example (7.30c) in the chapter, *few* was introduced as a proportional quantifier: *Few corgis are vegetarian* is true provided the proportion of vegetarian corgis is small, in comparison to the number who are non-vegetarian. However, *few* is an ambiguous quantifier. It can also serve as a cardinal quantifier, as when someone who has been asked whether there are many boats in the harbour replies: "No, there are few boats there today". If possible, write the set theoretic specification for this sentence's truth conditions. If that is too hard, explain in words the meaning of *few* when it is a cardinal quantifier.

7. *In this part of the factory, one machine tests each product.* The underlined clause is ambiguous in terms of relative scope. State the two possible meanings clearly.

Recommendations for reading

Kearns (2000) provides clear explanations, at greater length and with much more rigour, of all the topics covered in this chapter. Huddleston and Pullum (2002) contains a substantial survey of modality, with many persuasive examples and a useful treatment of quantifiers too. Van der Auwera and Plungian (1998) try to map out the ways that the encoding of modality can and can't change in the history of a language. If you are studying Old English, this might be an interesting paper to look at.

Notes

1. The small difference in meaning is that the source of authority for (7.2a) is probably the speaker, but for (7.2b) is more likely to be someone else or a regulation.

2. The notion of relevant context and the role suggested for it in the text makes this a very loosely stated variant of Sperber and Wilson's (1995) Relevance Theory. The idea of modality indicating inferences from relevant context's incomplete information to an actual past, present or future situation is an informal invocation of the notion of possible worlds (see Swart 1998: 212–14, for a concise account). The term *possible world* has been avoided in the body of the chapter largely because its *possible* is different from the possibility operator of modal logic, which figures informally in (7.19–7.21), and explaining the difference would take more space than can be afforded here.

3. The idea for *should* in Table 7.1 came from Papafragou (2000); *must, may* and *can* are loosely based on Groefsema's (1995) analysis.

4. Much of what is said about quantifiers in Section 7.3 is a reduced and informal version of Generalised Quantifier Theory. See Keenan (1996) and Swart (1998: ch. 8).

8 Pragmatics

Overview

Up to now this book has concentrated on **semantics** – abstract knowledge of word and sentence meaning – though pragmatics was introduced in Chapter 1, as the study of how senders and addressees, in acts of communication, rely on context to elaborate on literal meaning. Pragmatics has been appealed to, for instance in Chapter 5's account of figurative interpretation and in parts of Chapters 6 and 7. It is now time, however, to deal in more detail with the main concepts and principles of pragmatics. This is done in Chapters 8 and 9.

A cluster of theoretical proposals is outlined here that have been developed by linguists and philosophers, for understanding how additional meanings arise when speakers and writers put language to use in context, and for classifying such meanings. Based mainly on proposals by three philosophers – J. L. Austin, H. P. Grice and J. R. Searle – the framework has come into existence over the past forty years and is still actively under development. However, it is the ideas that are going to be described now, rather than their history.[1]

One of the basic ideas in pragmatics is, as Levinson (2000: 29) puts it: 'inference is cheap, articulation expensive'. Language users save themselves breath, writing and keyboard effort by producing utterances that deliberately rely on context, allowing receivers to infer information beyond what is laboriously explicit in the signal. Example (8.1) is from a real conversation and it will be used for basic orientation to the three main topics of this chapter. A told B that, on her trip overseas, she had spent some time in hospital. B showed sympathetic interest, which led to the following exchange.

(8.1)   A: "I was bitten by something in Berlin Zoo." B: "Was it an insect?"
        A: "Yes."

How did B guess that it was an insect? (I have confident intuitions here because I was B.) A's use of the word *something* was an important semantic clue. *Thing* is a high-level superordinate covering many differ-ent more specific words (hyponyms, see Chapter 3): *lawnmower, shoe, key, tiger, penguin* and so forth.

At least on a first attempt at making sense of what A had said, B could rule out inanimate objects: familiarity with things in the world (encyclo-pedic knowledge, Chapters 1 and 3) indicates that they do not have the mouth parts required for the acts denoted by the verb *bite*, though metaphorical interpretations can be imagined, especially for a lawn-mower. But was the *something* a tiger, a penguin or some other creature? In Section 8.1, implicature, a type of pragmatic reasoning investigated by H. P. Grice will be explained. Amongst other things, it enables us to see why a relatively uninformative utterance, like "I was bitten by some-thing", when more informative alternatives are at hand (such as *I was bitten by a tiger* or *I was bitten by a giraffe*), systematically invites an inference that the speaker is not in a position to make one of the more informative possible statements, probably because of not knowing. The starting point for the pragmatic inference that A did not know exactly what had bitten her is semantic: alternatives encoded in the language (*thing* and its hyponyms).

Another item of encyclopedic knowledge was involved in the prag-matic interpretation of (8.1): the animals in zoos are usually labelled – for the benefit of those who, for instance, might not recognise an aardvark by its heavy tail or a peccary by its downward pointing tusks. If A did not know what had bitten her, it probably was not one of the animals officially on display. (Further encyclopedic knowledge that could have con-tributed is the likelihood of an animal bite leaving a visible scar.) If it was not one of the resident animals, then what? An enraged zookeeper or feral child? No, a human biter would have been referred to as *someone* (another instance where semantic distinctions – *someone* as against *something* – are the basis for pragmatic reasoning). There were not many other possi-bilities; hm – perhaps it was an insect? And, yes, that proved to be so.

Assumptions that speakers and writers make about the background to communication are dealt with in Section 8.2, on presuppositions. In (8.1), after A had used the expression *something* to talk about what bit her, the biter could be treated as a presupposed item of background information and could be referred to using the pronoun *it*, as when B asked "Was it an insect?". (Chapter 9 has more on the role of presuppositions in connect-ing utterances to previous discourse.)

Section 8.3 is about speech acts. Two different kinds of speech act occur in (8.1): A's statements and B's question. To make a statement is to propose an update to the shared background: 'add to what you know about me that something bit me in Berlin Zoo'; and, in context, A's eventual "yes" conveyed that she endorsed adding to that knowledge that it was an insect. B's *yes-no* question bore differently on the background information: 'I could add to what I know about you that the thing which bit you was an insect; I'd like an indication as to whether that would be true or false'. There are other kinds of speech act too – many of them: advice, threats, apologies and so on.

8.1 Conversational implicature

Conversational implicatures are inferences that depend on the existence of norms for the use of language, such as the widespread agreement that communicators should aim to tell the truth. (It is for historical reasons that *conversational* is part of the label. Implicatures arise as much in other speech genres and in writing as they do in conversation; so they are often just called *implicatures*.) Speakers, writers and addressees assume that everyone engaged in communication knows and accepts the communicational norms. This general acceptance is an important starting point for inferences, even if individuals are sometimes unable to meet the standards or occasionally cheat (for instance, by telling lies). Chapter 5 has already shown that apparent violations of the norm of truthfulness (referred to below as the "quality maxim") can invite metaphorical interpretation, as when a reader finds a way to reconcile the real-world unlikelihood of someone's face curdling with an assumption that Jenny Diski aimed to make a true statement when she wrote 'my mother's face curdled'.

The inferences called implicatures are ever-present in language use, but, unlike entailments, they are not guarantees. In (8.1) I could have been wrong in my guess – an implicature – that A did not know quite what had bitten her in the zoo, or over the further implicature that it was an insect that had bitten her.

Grice (1975 and elsewhere) identified some of the communicational norms and showed how they are involved in the reasoning that makes it possible for utterances to convey rather more than is literally encoded in the underlying sentences. He proposed that four "maxims" – listed and glossed in (8.2) – could be regarded as the basis for co-operative communication.

(8.2) **Quality** – try to be truthful when communicating.
      Quantity – give appropriate amounts of information, not too little and not too much.
      Manner – utterances should be clear: brief, orderly and not obscure.[2]

Relevance[3] – contributions should be relevant to the assumed current goals of the people involved.

A **maxim** is a pithy piece of widely-applicable advice, for instance Polonius' precept to Laertes 'Give every man thine ear but few thy voice' (Shakespeare, *Hamlet*; not one of Grice's maxims). Grice's maxims play an as-if role: he was not putting forward the maxims as advice on how to talk; he was saying that communication proceeds as if speakers are generally guided by these maxims.

Imagine that person X makes the statement in (8.3a) to person Y. Two of several different subsequent things that Y might say are shown in (8.3b, c), one a response to X, the other a statement to someone else. These two possibilities are of interest because both are relatable to the maxim of quality.

(8.3) a. X to Y: "The Greens will get more votes in the next election."
      b. Y to X: "What's the evidence for that?"
      c. Y to Z: "X believes that, come election time, the Greens will get more votes."

Notation

X uttering "U" +> 'i' stands for: language user X producing utterance U **implicates** proposition i

(This notation is borrowed from Levinson 2000. Recall from Chapter 1 that, when it seems useful to mark distinctions, utterances are enclosed in double quotes, and meanings in single quotes.)

Example: X uttering "The Greens will get more votes" +> 'X believes that the Greens will get more votes'

Later in this chapter a slightly different symbol +< (my own invention) is used to represent **presupposition**. A reminder: the symbol ⇒ (introduced in Chapter 1) stands for entailment.

People use utterances to communicate. It is speakers and writers who implicate or (to anticipate the other two main topics of this chapter) presuppose and perform speech acts. But it will often be a useful shorthand to say that utterances, or the underlying sentences, or the words in them, carry implicatures (or presuppose various things, or constitute speech acts), so I will sometimes put the implicature symbol +> (or the presupposition symbol +<) between an expression and a meaning (see Stalnaker 1999: 7).

The naturalness of the sequence (8.3a, b) shows that the quality maxim is indeed a factor in communication. General agreement that communication is supposed to be truthful leads to an inference – an implicature – that speakers have justifications for what they assert; otherwise how could they hope to fulfil the quality requirement? In many situations an interlocutor is free to ask about the supporting evidence, and (8.3b) is one way of doing that. The evidence that X cites need not come from statistical analysis of political poll data. It could be based on what a few people at the hairdresser's said. (It is another matter, outside the scope of semantics and pragmatics, whether Y will rate X's reason(s) as persuasive.)

In (8.3c) Y can, quite naturally, report to someone else, Z, what X said as something that X believes, even though X did not say in (8.3a) "It is my belief that ..." This, too, is an implicature deriving from the maxim of quality. Truthfulness is the norm, so speakers making statements should express only propositions that they themselves believe. Thus, in the absence of indications that X was drugged up, talking ironically or telling a joke, it is a fair assumption that X believed the proposition carried by the statement in (8.3a).

In (8.4) Levinson's notation is used to show, in a generalised way, the two quality-maxim implicatures that were exemplified in (8.3).

(8.4) X stating "U" +> 'X has evidence for the proposition expressed by the utterance U'
X stating "U" +> 'X believes the proposition expressed by the utterance U'

What the kind of uttering called *stating* amounts to will be examined, along with other speech acts, in Section 8.3. Examples of implicatures grounded in the other maxims of (8.2) are discussed next.

8.1.1 Implicatures from the quantity maxim

An implicature relating to the low end of the quantity maxim – giving too little information – is illustrated in (8.5).

(8.5) a. "Are you from America?"
b. "No" followed by silence +> 'I am not willing to talk to you any further'

In Japan, (8.5a) is a fairly common conversation opener addressed to me. The rude implicature is the reason why I have never stopped with the simple answer in (8.5b). "No" would be true, but insufficient; so I go on to say where I am from.

It is not the case that an unadorned "No" is always rude. The preamble in (8.6) puts the words of (8.5) into a different context, one where the implicature from an unelaborated "No" does not arise.

(8.6) a. "That is an interesting accent. Let me guess where you are from. Are you from America?"
 b. "No".

After (8.6b) the guessing game can continue without offence given or taken. Implicatures depend on context, which is why they belong in a chapter on pragmatics.

There are sets of words that can be ranked according to informativeness (for instance *excellent > good > OK*, used in an example in Chapter 1). Such scales support one-way entailment, as in (8.7), where the scale items are identified by being printed in italics.

(8.7) It was *excellent* ⇒ It was *good* ⇒ It was *OK*
 We brought *three* spare mugs ⇒ We brought *two* spare mugs ⇒ We brought *a* spare mug
 There was an *earthquake* ⇒ There was an *earth tremor*
 I *know* that we've met before ⇒ I *believe* that we've met before
 He *hates* being corrected ⇒ He *dislikes* being corrected
 You are allowed to ask for cereal *and* fruit juice ⇒ You are allowed to ask for cereal *or* fruit juice

Scales like these regularly invite quantity-maxim implicatures going in the reverse direction of the entailment arrows. Implicatures arrived at in this way are always negative. See (8.8).

(8.8) We brought a spare mug +> 'We did not bring more than one spare mug'
 There was an earth tremor +> 'It was not violent enough to be called an earthquake'
 I believe ... +> 'I'm not certain enough to say that I know ...'
 He dislikes ... +> 'It would be too strong to say that he hates being corrected'
 (First line of breakfast menu:) CEREAL OR FRUIT JUICE +> 'You mustn't choose both cereal and fruit juice'

The possibility of cancellation without contradiction, as in (8.9), confirms their status as implicatures rather than entailments.

(8.9) We brought a spare mug, or perhaps even two or three of them.
 I believe we've met before; in fact I'm certain of it.
 He dislikes being corrected; as a matter of fact he hates it.
 Waiter (brushing aside an implicature from the menu's CEREAL

OR FRUIT JUICE): "You'd like both cereal and fruit juice – not a problem."

Implicatures can derive from the other end of the quantity maxim – avoid giving too much information – as illustrated in (8.10).

(8.10)   A: "Can anyone use this car park?"
         B: "It's for customers of the supermarket." +> 'No'

If the car park was for the use of everyone, then that would include the supermarket's customers and there would be no need to mention them; so B's utterance appears to offer superfluous information. An assumption that B is abiding by the quantity maxim – and therefore not giving more information than needed – invites an implicature that it is necessary to specify supermarket customers – it is for them and not for other motorists, which amounts to an informative negative answer to A's question.

Two features of implicature can be observed in (8.10). Firstly, implicatures provide ways of communicating indirectly, and indirectness can be employed for politeness. B's answer is polite, whereas just saying "No" would have been rude (see the discussion of (8.5)). Secondly, being based on an implicature – rather than an entailment – the 'no' meaning conveyed by B's answer is not guaranteed to be true; it could be overridden, for instance, by B adding "but when it's only half full, like today, we never make an issue over anyone else parking here".

8.1.2 Implicatures from manner

The sentences in (8.11) illustrate a distinction mentioned in Chapter 4, between direct causation (a) and indirect causation (b).

(8.11)   a.   Helen switched the lights off.
         b.   Helen caused the lights to go off. +> 'She did it in an unusual way'

Part of Grice's maxim of manner (see 8.2) makes brevity a goal. The indirect causative (8.11b) is longer than the direct causative (8.11a). Both sentences entail that the lights went off. The normal way to make lights go off is to operate the switch. Levinson (2000: 136) summarises the effect of departing from the manner norms as follows: 'What is said in an abnormal way indicates an abnormal situation ...' Unusual ways of putting out the lights include overloading the circuits by starting up a pottery kiln, or singing a high enough note to shatter the bulbs. However, as with all implicatures, it is merely a reasoned guess that Helen did not switch them off in the usual way: *Helen caused the lights to go off by flicking the switch in the normal way* is not a contradiction. (Why would anyone want to use a sentence like that? Maybe it could be an explanation to someone who was surprised at the lights going out, had not seen Helen flick the switch and was suggesting that a poltergeist might have been responsible.)

According to the maxim of manner, our speech (and written utterances) should also be orderly. What this means can be illustrated with the examples in (8.12).

(8.12)   a.   We sold our car and bought a tandem bicycle.
             +> 'Car sale before buying of tandem'
             +> 'Car sale led to buying of tandem'
         b.   We bought a tandem bicycle and sold our car.
             +> 'Tandem bought before car was sold'
             +> 'Tandem purchase had car sale as a consequence'
         c.   You asked what happened last summer: we sold our car and bought a tandem bicycle. The two transactions came through on the same day, but they were unrelated; we'd begun separate negotiations for them weeks beforehand.
         d.   We didn't buy a tandem and sell the car – we wouldn't have been able to afford to do that; we sold the car and then bought the tandem.
         e.   Her name is Moira and his name is Jon.

In (8.12a, b) *and* seems to mean 'and then', or even 'and consequently', but (8.12c) is evidence that these additional interpretations are implicatures, not inherent aspects of the meaning of *and*. Implicatures can be cancelled without contradiction and that is what could be done by the long-winded supplements that turn (8.12a) into (8.12c). Examples (8.12a, b) could simply be accounts of two events that occurred in any of three possible sequences: car sale before tandem purchase, tandem purchase before car sale, or simultaneous sale of car and buying of the tandem, but they are likely to have the implicatures shown to the right of +>. The reason is that the assumption that utterers are orderly when they recount events invites listeners or readers to assume that if two events are presented in a particular order – without markers of sequence (like *before, first, then* and *after*) being used – then the utterance ordering directly reflects the order of the events. Encyclopedic knowledge – selling a car could raise the money for buying a tandem, or ownership of a tandem bicycle could help people realise that they do not need a car – is the basis for the further implicatures about consequence or causality.

The word *didn't* in (8.12d) denies an implicated order. The possibility of denying the implicature testifies to the reality of that implicature.

Example (8.12e) shows that when the clauses linked by *and* appear to describe states (see Chapter 4), which have continuing existence rather than being located at points in time (see Chapter 6), then *and* conveys minimal linkage of two propositions, without implicating ordering or consequence. *Her name is Moira and his name is Jon* seems interchangeable with *His name is Jon and her name is Moira*. Exercise 5 at the end of the chapter is meant to help consolidate the points just made about (8.12d, e).

An advantage of having a two-component account of meaning (semantics plus pragmatics) has been illustrated with the analysis of *and*. Attempting to explain the meaning of *and* purely in terms of semantics would demand that *and* be recognised as three ways ambiguous, with the meanings '&', '& then' and '& consequently'. To account for which one of the three appears in a particular sentence, we would still probably need to invoke context and encyclopedic knowledge. With a promising theory of pragmatics, like Grice's, the semantics can be kept simple: *and* just means '&'[4] and interpretation in context yields the meaning overtones as implicatures.

8.1.3 Implicatures from relevance

Grice's relevance maxim lays down that contributions should be relevant to the assumed current goals of the interlocutors (see 8.2). "What's the date?" can reasonably be answered "Early nineteenth century" if the questioner is interested in something that you know to be a relic from Napoleonic times, but "Early twenty-first century" would be a joke response when your friend asks "What's the date?" while filling in a form at the bank. How considerations of relevance can help make sense of a conversational turn is illustrated in (8.13).

(8.13)   A: (Picking up a book from a display in a bookshop) "Have you read *Long Walk to Freedom?*"
　　　　 B: "I find autobiographies fascinating." +> '*Long Walk to Freedom* is an autobiography'
　　　　　　　　　　　　　　　　　　　　　　　　　 +> 'Yes, I have read it'

A asked about *Long Walk to Freedom*. B talks about autobiographies. A asked whether B had read the book. B talks about what she finds fascinating. One might think that B had ignored the question, but the conversation can be read as co-operative and coherent by trying to work out how B's contribution could be relevant to A's question. If the book is an autobiography, then B has not switched topics. Asked about a book that you have read, it is customary to offer an evaluation. If *Long Walk to Freedom* is an autobiography then, by saying that she finds autobiographies fascinating, B could be taken as evaluating it. And maybe her knowing that the book is autobiographical came from reading it. These guesses relevantly link B's utterance to A's question, so it is worth running with them. They are only implicatures, however, which means they could be wrong: B would not be speaking contradictorily if she extended her utterance to cancel one of the implicatures as follows "I find autobiographies fascinating, but I haven't read that one yet." It is even imaginable that, if B (mistakenly) thinks that *Long Walk to Freedom* is not an autobiography, she could say "I find autobiographies fascinating; so they are the only books I tend to read; I'm not into Chinese history."

Relevance is regularly the basis for disambiguation at the pragmatic level of **explicature** (see Chapter 1). In an art gallery a *painter* is much more likely to be an artist than a person who applied colour to the walls and woodwork of the building, but it is the other way round when the current concern is home renovation. (In each case the context-based inference could be wrong, because the gallery itself has to have been painted and paintings can be hung in houses.) In Chapter 1, the example of contexts disambiguating *That was the last bus*, according to whether *last* meant either 'final' or 'most recent', depended on assuming that the sender of a text message and the driver of a bus would make their utterances relevant to their addressees' concerns.

Relevance also explains the way "Thank you" can be used to cut short a turn from a caller phoning in to a radio programme. How – the caller is supposed to wonder – have thanks suddenly become relevant? Oh, the anchor person is acting as if I have had my say, because that would make thanks relevant. It then depends on whether the caller is compliant enough to take the hint or so hard-boiled as to ignore it. Frequently-used short cuts tend to become established paths, so this use of *Thank you* is now largely conventional.

8.1.4 General points about implicature

Do we need all four maxims? There appears to be some overlap among them. Utterances that invite consideration in terms of the high end of the quantity maxim, like the parking attendant's response in (8.10), are also usually longer or contain more difficult words, which takes them into the ambit of the manner maxim.

In (8.12a, b) the 'consequence' implicatures connecting tandem purchase and car sale could be explained via the maxim of relevance. Contributions should be relevant at the point where they occur in conversations. Uttering the clause that comes before *and* in (8.12a, b) creates context for the clause that follows *and*. Addressees will expect the second clause to be relevant to the first clause and will use their encyclopedic knowledge of the various motives for and merits of car and tandem owning to try to work out a connection.

It is reasonable to wonder whether relevance might not encompass the other maxims: what is false (quality failure) is probably irrelevant for understanding what is going on in communication; relevance might subsume the quantity maxim because too little information could be thought of as not enough to ensure relevance, and too much as cluttered with irrelevant extras; and we could regard utterances constructed in an unhelpful manner as at risk of not working because their relevance might not be grasped.

However, there is a difference in character between cases typically covered by Grice's relevance maxim and the others, especially in the contrast between relevance- and quantity-maxim implicatures which depend on scales, like the examples in (8.8). These latter are systematically calculable: a negative proposition is derived by backing up through the entailments that establish the scale: *We brought four mugs* entails ($\Rightarrow$) *We brought three mugs*, which entails *We brought two mugs*; so uttering "We brought 2 mugs" implicates ($+>$) 'We did not bring three or more mugs'. In comparison with this straightforward calculability, implicatures based on relevance make random demands on the addressee's ingenuity, as suggested by the formulations in (8.14).

(8.14)   (In a bank:) "What's the date?" $+>$ 'The day of the month is what I am asking about?'
(Talking about home renovation:) "… painter" $+>$ '… person who applies protective and decorative paint coatings'
(On a radio phone-in:) "Thank you" $+>$ 'You should stop talking'

With recourse to encyclopedic knowledge, the hearer or reader has to come up with guesses that will make relevant sense of an utterance in its context.

Grice's system has been the inspiration for much other work, but the overlaps and differences mentioned above have encouraged theorists to attempt revision. Two different reworkings will be mentioned here, but not pursued because that would take us beyond introductory level. The name of Sperber and Wilson's "Relevance Theory" (1995) indicates their direction: they propose one scheme to cover all kinds of implicature. For them relevance is not a maxim; instead they explore the mental processes that go into maximising the useful information we get from utterances while minimising the interpretive effort that is put in. Horn (1984) and, more recently, Levinson (2000) have taken a different tack, concentrating on implicatures of the quantity and manner kind – ones that depend more on semantic distinctions encoded in the language than on encyclopedic knowledge – and trying to specify in detail how they are calculated.

8.2 Presuppositions

Chapter 5 introduced **presuppositions**, the shared background assumptions that are taken for granted when we communicate. These are important in pragmatics because (as will be shown in Chapter 9) they are essential to the construction of connected discourse. Shared background presuppositions are also the obvious starting point for a reader or listener wondering what the author of a message might regard as relevant (see Section 8.1.3, above). People who know each other well can build up quite accurate impressions of what assumptions are shared between them, but it is harder to be aware of which aspects of that information the other person is thinking about at any point in a communicative interaction; and for communications between strangers it is even harder to know what is presupposed. **Presupposition** is also employed more specifically as the term for a particular kind of inference to be set out in this section. Inferences in this class are of interest here because they are an important way for speakers and writers to give hints, in the process of making each utterance, as to what assumptions they are currently taking for granted.

If, having missed out on the first distribution of dessert, you are asked "Would you like some more dessert?" you cannot really answer with a simple "Yes, please" or "No, thank you". The problem is that *more* indicates that the questioner presupposes you have already had some. Both answers would pick up and preserve part of the question: "Yes, please (I would like some more)" and "No, thank you (I would not like any more)". That means that *more* is still in there pointing to the same false presupposition that you have already had some dessert.

The pronoun gender distinction of English (*she–he, her–him, hers–his*) is presuppositional. This is illustrated in the exchange between A and B in (8.15). The presuppositions are on the right, following the symbol +<. (This symbol is meant to be easy to remember: the material on the left can be appropriately added to contexts in which the proposition to the right is true.)

(8.15) A: "Where is the head of department's office? I want to speak to
            him." +< 'The HoD is male'
        B: "She is female." +< 'The HoD is female'

What is presupposed is background information. It is not asserted, so it does not count as the overtly presented information carried by an utterance. B's response "She is female" carries the meaning 'female' twice, but the utterance is not unnecessarily repetitive. This is because the word *female* is the part that encodes the asserted gender information, whereas in the word *she* that same information is presupposed; it is merely the basis for the appropriate choice of a pronoun to refer to this particular head of department. (B could have merely said firmly "Her". This form of response approaches the problem in a different way, not by asserting the needed information, but by correctively offering a word that the enquirer should have used.)

8.2.1 Presupposition distinguished from entailment

A selection of further examples appears in (8.16–8.18).

(8.16) Hana forgot to post the letter.
Hana remembered
(/did not forget)
to post the letter.
Did Hana forget to
post the letter?

+< 'Hana was supposed to post it'

(8.17) Dick has begun to do a share of the chores.
Dick hasn't begun to do a share of the chores.
Has Dick begun to do a share of the chores?

+< 'He didn't previously do …'

(8.18) The medicine has cured her uncle.
The medicine hasn't cured her uncle.
Has the medicine cured her uncle?

+< 'Her uncle was ill'

Being triggered by particular words in the examples (*forget, begin, cure*) and syntactic patterns (as will be illustrated later), presuppositions are akin to the encoded-in-the-language meanings that characterise semantics. But they are different too. (8.16–8.18) were written out as triples to highlight a distinguishing feature: **presuppositions** are not affected by negation of the asserted part of a sentence, and questioning the main drift of a sentence leaves the presuppositions intact too. Survival in this way is symptomatic of presuppositions being information that is assumed to be true. By way of contrast, (8.19) shows that entailments do not, in general, survive negation.

(8.19)   a.   The medicine has cured her uncle. ⇒ 'Her uncle is well'
        b.   ~~The medicine hasn't cured her uncle. ⇒ 'Her uncle is well'~~

Scoring through indicates that there is no entailment in (8.19b).

Presuppositions are different from entailments in another respect. They can be cancelled, as illustrated in (8.20), a fact that makes it clear that they are pragmatic. When this happens, communication is in danger of being derailed, and a warning to that effect is usually signalled by increased pitch on the stressed syllable of the presupposition trigger, for example on the *get*-syllable of *forget*, or the *mem*-syllable of *remember*. In the examples of (8.20) the extra height is shown by raising the v that marks the expected fall-rise contour.

(8.20)   Hana didn't for^{v}get to post the letter; she didn't even know it
        needed to go.
        Hana didn't re^{v}member to post the letter; she didn't even know it
        needed to go.
        He hasn't be^{v}gun to do a share of the chores; he's been doing his
        share for years.
        The medicine hasn't ^{v}cured her uncle; he never was ill; you must
        be thinking of someone else.
        The medicine has ^{v}cured her uncle; he was just pretending to be
        ill and when he heard what sort of medicine they were planning
        to give him he got up and declared himself well.

Being a presupposition trigger is not a rare quirk. There are plenty of them. Put *stopped doing* in place of *begun to do* in (8.17) and note that the presupposition is now that 'he previously did do …' **Restitutive** *again*, employed in Chapter 4 in the tests for distinguishing verb-based situation types, triggers a presupposition about a state or activity having existed before. The quantifier *both* presupposes that there are just two entities being spoken about; and so on.

Factive predicates are a class of verbs – including *regret, matter, realise* and *explain* – and adjectives – like *(be) odd, sorry, aware* – that have been extensively studied as presupposition triggers (see Huddleston and Pullum 2002: 1,004–11). These predicates introduce a clause that the speaker or writer, in normal communication, presumes to be true. A sample of factive predicates is given in (8.21–8.23).

(8.21)   It matters that they lied to us. ⎫
        It doesn't matter that they ⎪
        lied to us.   ⎬   +< 'They lied to us'
        Does it matter that they   ⎪
        lied to us?   ⎭

(8.22) You should have explained
        that your train was late.
        You didn't explain that your   } +< 'Your train was late'
        train was late.
        Should you explain that your
        train was late?

(8.23) She's sorry that the Olympics
        are over.
        She's not sorry that the   } +< 'The Olympics are over'
        Olympics are over.
        Is she sorry that the Olympics
        are over?

For comparison with the above, a non-factive predicate (*prove*) is shown in (8.24).

(8.24) a. It proves that they lied to us. ⇒ 'They lied to us'
        b. ~~It doesn't prove that they lied to us. ⇒ 'They lied to us'~~
        c. ~~It doesn't prove that they lied to us. +< 'They lied to us'~~
        d. ~~Does it prove that they lied to us? +< 'They lied to us'~~

With *proves*, the proposition 'They lied to us' is entailed in (8.24a), but – as expected for an entailment – the entailment falls away when the sentence is negated (8.24b). The inference on the right of (8.24a) does not count as a presupposition because it is not maintained under negation or questioning (8.24c, d).

There are syntactic constructions that trigger presuppositions too. Relative clauses,[5] such as *that Admin sent us* in (8.25), exemplify this.

(8.25) The email that Admin sent us
        said Thursday.
        The email that Admin sent us   } +< 'Admin sent us an email'
        didn't say Thursday.
        Did the email that Admin sent
        us say Thursday?

Time clauses with past reference, like *when we were in Monterrey*, also trigger presuppositions. The sentence *I loved you when we were in Monterrey* presupposes that 'We were in Monterrey'. If one or more of the people referred to by means of *We* were never in Monterrey, then this presupposition is not met and trying to use the sentence in that context is likely to lead to puzzlement: "What are you on about. I've never been to Monterrey. Who did you go there with?"

8.2.2 The tell test

A presupposition triggered by a word or construction in a sentence is supposed to be background information assumed to be already known by the addressee, so it does not count as having been communicated. This was illustrated in (8.15) where the double occurrence of the meaning 'female', in "She is female", does not comes across as pleonastic. The verb *tell* provides a test for presuppositions. Using *tell* to report gleaning information from someone when that information was presupposed is misleading. Some examples are given in (8.26), with initial query marks signalling that they are inappropriate ways of passing on information inferred as presuppositions. Their example numbers in earlier occurrences are noted on the right. A more acceptable way of retailing the information is shown as the third member of each triple.

(8.26) A to B: ... Head of Department ... I want to speak to him. +<
'The HoD is male' (8.15)
?B to C: A told me our Head of Department is male.
better: B to C: A just assumed that our Head of Department would be male.

A to B: Dick has begun to do a share of the chores. +< 'He didn't previously do a share of the chores' (8.17)
?B to C: A told me that Dick did not previously do a share of the chores.
better: B to C: I gathered from what A said that Dick did not previously do a share of the chores.

A to B: It matters that they lied to us. +< 'They lied to us' (8.21)
?B to C: A told me that they had lied to us.
better: B to C: From the way A spoke it seems she believes that they lied to us.

Another example is shown in (8.27), based on *both* indicating a presupposition that two entities are being referred to.

(8.27) Soldier about to pat someone down:
"Put both your hands on the wall, up here." +< 'You have two hands'
?Pattee to someone else: "The soldier told me I had two hands."

In the next section presupposition will be seen to be part of the foundation for the acts that we perform when we use language.

8.3 Speech acts

J. R. Searle, in his elaboration of work by J. L. Austin, established *speech acts*[6] as the term for what is going to be discussed in this section (see Searle 1975, 1979).

What is the point of talking, typing or writing to other people? Stating – passing on facts that will be news to our addressees – is indeed an important function of language, but it is not the only one. There are straightforward, almost non-technical ways of describing people's linguistic interactions: *She's giving the players a warning, They're greeting the visitors, I'm using this email to apply for an extension, That man is telling them what he saw, The letter confirms your appointment.* These basic units of linguistic interaction – such as give a warning to, greet, apply for, tell what, confirm an appointment – (the acts, not the labels) are called **speech acts**.

A sample of speech acts is listed in (8.28). Austin (1962), who founded the modern study of speech acts, reckoned that this sort of list could be extended to several hundred.

(8.28) a. statement: "I lived in Edinburgh for five years."
      b. order: "Pay this bill immediately."
      c. question: "Where are you from?"
      d. prohibition: "No right turn"
      e. greeting: "Hello."
      f. invitation: "Help yourself."
      g. felicitation: "Happy New Year!"
      h. (grudging) apology: "I hereby apologise as required by the magistrate."

Speech acts can be done in writing, not only in speaking; the New Year wish in (8.28g), for instance, would be equally appropriate printed in a card or spoken. The utterances on the right in (8.28) are each based on single sentences. The sentence is the level of language that speech acts are tied to (Verschueren 1999: 131), which means that an average ceremonial speech or political speech is not a speech act, but a sequence of speech acts.

8.3.1 Syntax and words that indicate speech act type

The speech acts in (8.28a–c) were put at the head of the list because they represent the default uses for three of the main patterns according to which English sentences are constructed (for an explanation of sentence types, see Miller 2002: 27–9). A declarative sentence construction, as in

(8.28a), is likely to be the vehicle for a **statement** unless factors in the context suggest otherwise (as when that example conveys an offer to locate Corstorphine, after people who do not know Edinburgh have expressed exasperation at not being able to find the hill and suburb of that name on a map of the city). **Orders** are the speech acts carried by utterances based on imperative sentences, as in (8.28b), unless context indicates that it is advice, from your best friend for instance. Interrogative constructions, like the one in (8.28c), have **questioning** as their central use, but context can lead to them being interpreted as other speech acts reminders, for instance "Have you confirmed your flight?", or requests "Could you hold the door open for a moment?"

When a sentence type is used in the performance of speech acts different from their default kind, we have what are called **indirect speech acts** (Verschueren 1999: 25). An example of this is (8.29).

(8.29)   "Could you put the lid on that one to your right?"

This was said to me while I was cooking, by someone working a couple of metres away, talking about another saucepan on the cooker I was working at. I said "OK" and put the lid on the pan to my right. The sentence type is interrogative, making a question the default speech act type, but it would have been uncooperative to take the utterance as simply a question, say "Yes, I could (my arm's long enough and I'm strong enough)" and do nothing more; so, of course, I treated it as a request. Searle (1975) showed how a general account can be given, in terms of implicature (Section 8.1), of the way this question came to be treated as an indirect request, as follows:

She appears to be asking whether I am capable of putting a lid on to a pan. It is so obvious that I could, that that surely can't be what she's wanting to know; so how could such a question be relevant? Well, if she's thinking of requesting that I cover the pan, then a precondition would be that I am capable of doing so; and her pretending that anything even a tiny bit inconvenient for me could count as incapacity would offer me a polite way out of acceding to such a request, or even a way in which she – if it seems that I might have grounds for refusing the request – could give up the idea of making the request. Yes, that would fit; so, why don't I short-circuit the process and, without even waiting for the request, treat the preliminary query as if it was a request and put the lid on the pan to my right?

That is certainly long-winded, but it is coherent and does explain why it is possible to respond to both the direct speech act and the indirect one: I could have said "Yes, I can, I'm not as busy I look; so OK, I'll do it." But, perhaps through similar reasoning having been gone through by large numbers of English speakers, the form *Could you ...?* has become an idiomatic way of making a polite request, just as *Why not ...?* is an idiomatic way of making a suggestion.

Particular words can contribute to identifying the kind of speech act being performed: for example the word *promise* may figure in speech acts of promising and *sorry* may figure in apologies. They do not determine the kind of speech act because there are many ways of using words: "I promise to make you regret this" is a threat rather than a promise. We can ask people who say "We were sorry that we hurt his feelings" whether or not they apologised, because the quoted utterance could be just a description of the right frame of mind for a sincere apology, not necessarily an actual apology. It really does depend on context too. "I promise to be there" could count as a threat rather than a promise if the addressee would be intimidated by the speaker's presence in the place referred to, and so on.

Language is the only general way of carrying out the kinds of acts illustrated in (8.28), though it must be admitted that some could be performed without language, as when (compared to 8.28d–f) a street sign indicates that right turns are prohibited, or someone smiles 'hello', or gestures a 'help yourself' invitation. The act is done in the actual transmission of the linguistic signal itself. When the addressee reads or hears (8.28h) in a real-life context, that is the apology happening. Notice how *hereby* in (8.28h) is deictic (see Chapter 1): the word *hereby* is used to point to the utterance itself as the apology. If someone writes to me "This is to wish you a happy New Year", *this* is another example of discourse deixis, pointing to that particular written utterance itself as the felicitation.

8.3.2 Content and force in speech acts

Entailment, which is foundational in semantics, is defined in terms of truth: under conditions that make S1 true, S2 must be true (Chapter 1). Truth is vital for the speech acts known as statements, but can be peripheral to other speech acts. This is illustrated by (8.30 – 8.31), a real example. I fumed when I read (8.30) at the top of an electricity bill.

(8.30) PAY THIS BILL IMMEDIATELY

Issuing a uncompromising order like that only three days into the quarter seemed outrageous. The sentence *Pay this bill immediately* is an **imperative** construction and, as noted above, the default speech act borne by an imperative is an order. It was not an issue of truth that bothered me. I did not think "Liars!". Then I looked at more of the bill and calmed down, because what I had seen was only the first clause of an offer, given in full in (8.31), and an offer is a different speech act from an order.

(8.31) PAY THIS BILL IMMEDIATELY AND RECEIVE A £2.50 PROMPT PAYMENT DISCOUNT

Most speech acts have **content**: propositions carried by the speech act, presupposed by it or in some other way involved. In (8.30) the content is a proposition about the addressee settling a bill very soon; (8.31) has the same proposition and another one about the addressee getting a discount. I understood the shared proposition as being presented differently: in (8.30) as something I was being coerced into doing, but in (8.31) as a condition for me receiving a discount.

There is a cover term, **force**, for the characteristics that differentiate speech acts from one another. Force is mainly about the different ways the content propositions are involved in speech acts. All of the speech acts in (8.32) include the same content 'someone won two gold medals'. I will abbreviate that proposition to 'sw2gm'. Notice how it figures differently according to the force of a range of speech acts.

(8.32) a. "Someone won two gold medals" – a statement expressing commitment to the truth of 'sw2gm' and doing so on the assumption that the addressee does not already know that 'sw2gm'.

b. "Who won two gold medals?" – a question presupposing 'sw2gm' and wanting to know the identity of the winner, to get a more explicit proposition.

c. "Who won two gold medals?" – praise from the champion's mother, presupposing 'sw2gm' and giving the champion a chance to relish thinking or saying "I did".

d. "Who won two gold medals?" – a boast from the champion, presupposing 'sw2gm' and ready to smirk as the audience realise they are in the presence of the someone who w2gm.

e. "Be the one who wins two gold medals!" – an order from an athlete's coach, demanding that the athlete make it true that she is the someone in 'sw2gm'.

Schemes have been devised to group speech acts into a limited number of categories according to the main features of their force. Sorting the many different types of speech acts into categories raises the hope of discerning a system amid all the variety. Searle (see 1979) proposed a set of five categories. Two of them will be mentioned here to give an idea of the approach:

Expressives – for example thanking, condoling, congratulating and apologising – are used to express a psychological state (gratitude for thanks, sympathy for condolences, pleasure for congratulations, regret for apologies) about a presupposed proposition. The proposition concerns: something done by the addressee in the case of thanks and congratulations (to the advantage of the utterer for thanks, to the credit of the addressee for congratulations), a death in the case of condolences, a wrong deed by the speaker in the case of apologies.

Directives – for example ordering, demanding, requesting – convey a proposition about a future act of the addressee that the speaker desires, and the point is to try to get the addressee to commit to making the proposition true.

The pragmatic study of speech acts feeds back into semantics because, among the thousands of word meanings that need to be described in semantics, there are hundreds of speech act verbs (*thank, congratulate, tell, assert, ask, demand, excommunicate* and so on). A good understanding of the speech act characteristics of these verbs and how they differ (for example, that *assert* is a hyponym of (*to*) *state*, meaning 'state strongly') is useful for describing their meanings.

That content (the propositional meaning focused on by semantics) is distinct from force (the distinctive ways in which content is involved in speech acts) can be seen from the fact that they can be separately negated, as shown in (8.33).

(8.33)   I tell you the ball wasn't in; it was out. (negated content)
         I'm not telling you the ball was in; I'm asking you whether it was. (negated force)

As part of performing the sentence-level speech acts discussed in this section, senders have to do acts of **referring**. To refer, they have to judiciously use expressions like "they", "your right", "this bill" and "the ball" in relation to what can be seen, heard or safely presupposed in context, to pick out for their addressees the things, places, people, events, times, or whatever, that are being spoken or written about. Before the addressees understand what is being referred to in an utterance, they do not fully know what the content of that utterance is. Recall the three-stage account of utterance interpretation outlined in Chapter 1. Contextual disambiguation of ambiguous words (see Section 8.1.3, above) and the working out of reference is done at the stage of explicature, where propositional content is determined.

Summary

Pragmatics is about the use of utterances in context, about how we manage to convey more than is literally encoded by the semantics of sentences. The extra and different meanings inferable as conversational implicatures save production effort. Pragmatics builds on what is semantically encoded in the language. For instance the scale of modal verbs *must* > *should* > *may* allows a speaker who says "Fred may leave" to implicate that there is no obligation on Fred to leave. Presupposition is a pervasive feature of communication. There are words, like *again*, that act as presupposition triggers (this one signalling that the speaker or writer believes that the state or event referred to was instantiated before), and some syntactic constructions (for instance, relative clauses) act as presupposition triggers too. Notations were introduced for implicature (+>) and presupposition (+<). In Chapter 9 it will be seen that the coherence of discourse depends on us fitting our utterances to the presupposed background.

Also introduced in this chapter were speech acts: conventional acts that we perform with language – like telling, requesting, asking, greeting, advising, betting and challenging. Most speech acts have propositional content. The main differences between different speech acts concerns the way their content is involved: for instance, is it presented as an updating of presuppositions; as a desired change to the presupposed background; or as a presupposed proposition over which we are expressing regret, gratitude, or whatever? Indirect speech acts – as when "Tell me your name" is used not as an order but as a question – are ones that do not stick to the three main default correlations with sentence type (stating with declarative sentences, ordering with imperative sentences, and questioning with interrogative sentences). The forces of indirect speech acts can be understood as implicatures, though some become established as idioms.

Referring is a pragmatic act too, using noun phrases in context to let your addressee know which people, things, or whatever, you are communicating about.

Exercises

1. A: "Who's that?" B: "It's me." In this exchange, B's response could seem to be unhelpful. *Me* is a normal way for speakers to refer to themselves, so it appears not to tell A anything that is not obvious when someone is speaking from the other side of a door, or by telephone: 'The one who is here speaking is the speaker of this utterance'! What is it that B probably

manages to communicate? Which of Grice's maxims is involved in interpreting the utterance? Explain how. Why would someone choose to talk like this, instead of saying, for example "My name is Yann Lumsden" or "I am your wife"?

2. What are the first three words doing in "The truth is: continued growth is unsustainable"? We are expected to speak truthfully anyway, so why use that claim to lead into a statement? Presumably the speaker is inviting serious attention by explicitly orienting to what pragmatic theorists know as Grice's quality maxim: 'Perhaps you think I sometimes bluff, I assure you that what I am about to say is true'. Which maxims are invoked by the following two different ways of making a similar emphatic statement about unsustainability? (The idea for this exercise comes from Grundy 2000: 79.)

> Continued growth is unsustainable and that's all there is to it.
> Let me make this clear, continued growth is unsustainable.

3. A: "Where are the sociolinguistics books kept?" B: "I don't know, but psycholinguistics is at that end of the shelf." B's utterance probably implicates 'Perhaps sociolinguistics books are there too'. Explain, with reference to Grice's maxims, how this implicature might arise.

4. According to a report in the *Guardian Weekly*, 10–16 December 2004, the Plain English Campaign's Foot in Mouth award for 2004 went to Boris Johnson's *I could not fail to disagree with you less*. Which of Grice's maxims did Johnson violate? Try to find a simpler way of expressing the same proposition? Speculate on why he phrased the remark in this way.

5. Example (8.12d) illustrated denial of an implicature about order. It might have been said in response to "I hear you bought a tandem and sold your car". Using (8.12d) as a model, attempt to construct for (8.12e) a parallel denial of an order implicature. Does it provide a convincing reason for believing that there is an implicature of order conveyed by (8.12e)?

6. If you hear someone say "It seeped into the basement" you can infer, amongst other things, that the stuff referred by means of "it" was a fluid substance (that is, a liquid or gas). You can also infer that, whatever it was, it entered the basement slowly. One of these inferences is a presupposition and the other is an entailment. Which is which? Give reasons for your answers.

7. Using the notions of speech acts and presupposition, give a brief description of the wording of this notice seen in a bus: "Thank you for not smoking. MAXIMUM FINE £100". (In the same frame there was a picture of a cigarette with a slash through it, inside a mandatory-prohibition red circle.)

8. For each of the following , name the kind of direct speech act that is the default for the sentence type noted in brackets, and say what indirect speech act the example would probably be used to perform.

   a. (interrogative:) Can't you stop talking?
   b. (imperative:)   Help yourself to milk and sugar.
   c. (interrogative:) Have you heard: our team's leading 18 to 15?
   d. (declarative:)   You have my sympathy.
   e. (imperative:)   Don't imagine that entailment and implicature are the same thing.
   f. (imperative:)   Accept my profound condolences.
   g. (interrogative:) Have I ever let you down?
   h. (declarative:)   I recommend that you keep a copy of the letter.

9. A: "Do you like Brooke Shields?" B (after a puzzled pause): "What are they?" What is illustrated about the use of proper names by A's failed attempt (which I overheard) to refer to the actress Brooke Shields?

Recommendations for reading

Grundy's (2000) introductory pragmatics book is accessible and has lots of examples. Verschueren (1999) is a wide-ranging and interesting survey of pragmatic theory. An easy introduction to philosophical accounts of implicature, presupposition and speech acts is given by Lycan's (2000: chs 12 and 13). Chapter 11 of Kearns (2000) is a rigorous and detailed, but very readable, treatment of implicature. Saeed (2003: ch. 8) is a good account of speech acts. An excellent outline intonation and its pragmatic effects can be found in Roach (2000: ch. 15). The basics of Relevance Theory, mentioned in Section 8.1.4, are well explained by Blakemore (1992); see also Wilson and Sperber's (2004) handbook article.

Notes

1. For original work by these authors, see Austin 1962, Searle 1979, and Grice 1989.

2. Grice's manner maxim also said 'avoid ambiguity'. I believe that – except in punning mode and when carefully checking written material – language users

are generally not much aware of the multiple ambiguities in their output, and (as will be illustrated later) considerations of relevance generally enable addressees to work out which way to explicate ambiguous input.

3. Grice's label for this maxim was *relation*, but later writers have usually called it *relevance*.

4. A straightforward account of the meaning '&' can be given in terms of truth: a pair of clauses linked by & is true if each of the linked clauses is separately true, but false if one or the other or both of the separate clauses is false. Look under the heading *truth tables* in any book that introduces logical semantics, such as Kearns (2000).

5. Strictly, it is restrictive, or identifying, relative clauses that are presupposition triggers. See Huddleston and Pullum (2002) for details on relative clauses. There is some discussion of relative clauses in Miller (2002: ch. 6).

6. To be precise over terminology, I should be talking about **illocutionary acts** (IAs), one of about three general categories of speech act. However, because linguists have focused their speech act research almost exclusively on IAs, I will go along with other writers and use the label *speech act* as if it meant IA.

9 Connecting utterances to the background

Overview

Connected utterances make up a **discourse**, for instance a conversation is a discourse; a TV interview is a discourse; a letter that I write to a friend is a discourse; a whole book could be a discourse, to the extent that writer and reader keep track of the connections. This chapter concentrates on one aspect of the pragmatics of discourse: how our utterances are adapted to connect to the current interests and existing knowledge of addressees. The adaptations include **focal stress** (as in the contrast between "Meg's a SCOT" and "MEG's a Scot" – where the capitals indicate syllables pronounced with stronger stress); definiteness, often seen in the choice among determiners, for example *the* versus *a*; and distinct syntactic patterns (such as *It's Mary who is Scottish* and *Mary is Scottish*).

The chapter's aims are limited to making the matters mentioned in the paragraph above intelligible and – I trust – interesting. Discourse pragmatics is a wide field, so a selective approach is necessary.

It is communicatively counterproductive to enter a room where people are having a conversation and, taking no interest in what they are saying, blurt out whatever it is you want to tell them. The point of talking or writing is to try to update the presuppositions shared between sender and addressee(s), an idea introduced in Chapters 5 and 8. Rationally, someone hoping to do that needs to make assumptions about where the discourse is currently at and then shape any contribution so that it will fit the presupposed background. Assumptions about addressees' background knowledge and interests are based on: all humans sharing some things (the earth, sun and moon, capacity for pain and love, and so on); norms in a given culture (for instance, about what is edible); the fact that someone has opted into a discourse (as with me assuming that readers of this book are interested in meaning); any past experience with the addressees; and, very importantly, what has already been transacted in the current discourse (things recently said and written, by all who have had chances to contribute to the discourse). What is pre-supposed is part of context. Remembering that pragmatics is the study of meaning in relation to context, the issues to be discussed here belong under the heading *pragmatics.*

9.1 Definiteness

Definiteness in noun phrases is a significant aspect of the grammar of English and will be used as a starting point here. If you are not already familiar with this notion, then the lists in Table 9.1 may be of some help. (Do not feel overwhelmed by the list; only the determiners *a* and *the* are going to be used much.)

Table 9.1 A selection of indefinite and definite forms

indefinite	*definite*
	proper names *Aberdeen, Zoroaster*
determiners *a, an, some, another, several,* *most, no, enough, any* absence of a determiner when head noun is plural *_cities worth visiting,* *_famous people*	determiners *the, this, that, these, those, its,* *their, her, his, your, my, our*
indefinite pronouns *something, someone, somebody,* *anything, anyone, anybody*	personal pronouns *it, they, them, she, her, he, his,* *you, I, me, we, us*

The definite article *the* signals 'this reference is constrained: I am referring to something that you know about'. One class of example is (9.1), which might be spoken by someone phoning from the other side of town.

(9.1)   Go and have a look outside, there's a weird green glow in the sky.

In a common way of thinking about it, the same sky is outside almost everywhere, so the phone caller can expect the receiver of the call to know about the sky; and that is what makes immediate definite reference appropriate. The sky is a topic. A **topic** 'is what the utterance is primarily about' (Huddleston and Pullum 2002: 236). As I will use the term, the topic is not the new information presented in an utterance – for example, it is not the weird green glow in (9.1). Instead, topics are entities easily accessible in the presupposed background, like the sky. For a topic there should not be any need to run a preparatory check: "If I were to say *sky*, would you know which one I was talking about?"

A different and more common pattern can be seen in (9.2), excerpted from a recipe.[1] Intervening material has been omitted, but the sequence of these fragments is the same as in the original.

(9.2)   675 g fresh green beans
  ½ l vegetable oil
  Trim the beans and cut them into ... 4-cm lengths.
  Heat the oil in a wok over a medium-high flame.
  Fry the beans ... until the skins just begin to crinkle ...
  Turn off the heat under the wok.

There is a tendency here – highlighted in (9.3) – for *the* to be used only from second reference onwards. (An exception to this generalisation will be discussed quite soon.)

(9.3)   *first reference*   *subsequent reference*
  675 g fresh green beans the beans, them, the beans
  ½ l vegetable oil   the oil
  a wok   the wok
  a medium-high flame   the heat

The first two lines of data in (9.3) illustrate a feature of recipes: the list of ingredients puts some things into the mind of the reader – makes them into topics – and after that definite reference is appropriate whenever the author wants to refer to the same items, which might by then already be gathered on a kitchen worktop. However, the next two lines of data show that an ingredients list is not the only way to establish a topic, to get something into the background knowledge of a discourse.

The expressions *a wok* and *the wok* refer to the same wok. The expression *the oil* refers to the same half litre of vegetable oil mentioned among the ingredients. The last line of (9.3) illustrates an important point about topics. They are entities in the knowledge base that an addressee consults and modifies in the course of understanding a discourse. The topics are not the words themselves. The expression *the heat* does not contain any of the words in *a medium-high flame*, but it constitutes a second reference to the same topic. It is not an actual instance of burning gas that is the topic here, because a recipe can be understood without starting work in a kitchen. On reading *the heat*, the definite article cues the reader to search through the developing mental representation of ideas relevant to this particular discourse, looking for something already in there that could be referred to by that expression.

The line *Fry the beans … until the skins just begin to crinkle…*, in (9.2), contains an exception to the generalisation illustrated in (9.3). This is the first reference in the recipe to any sort of skin, but it comes with *the* as its determiner, a signal to the reader 'you already know about these particular skins'. Bean skins are not ubiquitous like the sky. It is because prototype beans have skins – and the beans are, at this point, already a topic – that it is possible to treat the skins as a topic, part of the background for understanding the utterance. As noted in Chapter 3, the *has-*relation is a basis for use of *the* for first reference to parts provided the relevant whole is already a topic. Thus we can talk about *the brakes* whenever vehicles belong to the shared background, because prototype vehicles have brakes. (Unicycles are non-prototypical and do not have brakes.) Perishable foods in supermarkets have sell-by dates; so someone asked to buy a carton of milk can be reminded in the same breath to check *the sell-by date.* In our prototype conception of an electrical appliance, it will have an instruction manual, which justifies saying *Why not look in the manual?* once the appliance acquires topic status, for example from someone saying *I can't make this thing work.*

The examples in (9.2–9.3) showed new referents being brought into a discourse by means of indefinite expressions like *a wok* and *675 g fresh green beans.* Indefinite marking (here: determiner *a* or – with a plural head noun *beans* – no determiner) is a signal to the addressee: 'I don't believe you have already got a referent for this one in the mental file you have opened for this discourse'. An indefinite reference invites the addressee to set up a representation for a referent, in other words to start treating it as a topic.

9.2 Clefts and passives

The syntactic patterns that are about to be discussed come in paraphrase sets (that is to say, sets of mutually entailing sentences; see Chapter 2), ones that, at the semantic level, have the same meaning. Yet they differ in their capacity for connecting with the presuppositional background. With definiteness, above, the issue was the addressee's awareness of referents, such as a particular wok. In this section and the following ones, propositional knowledge is also in play.

9.2.1 Pseudo-clefts

In June 2004 a hot rock fell out of the sky, went through the roof of a house in New Zealand and bounced off the sofa, leaving a big dent. Any of the sentences in (9.4) could accurately describe the rock hitting the sofa.

(9.4) a.   What hit the sofa was the meteorite.
     b.   What the meteorite hit was the sofa.
     c.   The meteorite hit the sofa.

(Use of *the* with both *meteorite* and *sofa* is deliberate, to make both of them topics here and keep definiteness out of the picture.) Each of the sentences in (9.4) entails each of the others; so all three are paraphrases of one another. Furthermore all of them have the same speech act potential (see Chapter 8) and, in the absence of special reasons to the contrary, they would most likely be used to make statements. Example (9.4c) shows the basic, unmarked, transitive (see Chapter 4) clause pattern of English. **Unmarked** means that it is a "default" pattern, the normal one. The sentence pattern in (9.4a, b) is called **pseudo-cleft** and has three distinguishing characteristics:

- a *wh*-clause with (in the technical sense of argument explained in Chapter 4) an unspecified argument (*what hit the sofa* is not explicit about the subject, and *what the meteorite hit* lacks detail regarding the object)
- a noun phrase that supplies the missing details for the unspecified argument in the *wh*-clause (*the meteorite* in 9.4a, *the sofa* in 9.4b)
- BE is the main verb (appearing as *was* in 9.4a, b).

The *wh*-clauses relate to presupposed propositions, ones that can be inferred from both an affirmative and a negative version of the pseudo-cleft sentence, as spelt out in (9.5). (Recall that $\Rightarrow$ represents entailment and +> stands for implicature. At (9.8–9.10) below, there is a discussion of the difference.)

(9.5) a.   What hit the sofa was the meteorite $\Rightarrow$ Something hit the sofa
     a'   What hit the sofa wasn't the meteorite +> Something hit the sofa
     a"   "They say something hit the sofa." "Yes, what hit the sofa was the meteorite."
     a[?]   ?"They say something hit the sofa." "Yes, what the meteorite hit was the sofa."
     b.   What the meteorite hit was the sofa $\Rightarrow$ The meteorite hit something
     b'   What the meteorite hit wasn't the sofa +> The meteorite hit something
     b"   "I heard that the meteorite hit something." "Yes, what the meteorite hit was the sofa."
     b[?]   ?"I heard that the meteorite hit something." "Yes, what hit the sofa was the meteorite."

The double-primed exchanges (9.5a", b") are natural, even if the responses are a bit ponderous. This shows that the pseudo-clefts are appropriate when the information that the addressee already has ('They say …' or 'I heard …') matches the presuppositions (9.5a, a', b, b') associated with each pseudo-cleft. But, as seen in (9.5a², b²), these pseudo-clefts are inappropriate as responses in a background that does not fit with their presuppositions. (The query marks draw attention to the awkwardness of these as two-person mini-discourses. There is nothing problematic with the individual turns considered in isolation.)

In (9.5a, a') an affirmative sentence and the corresponding negative sentence both allow the same inference, which makes that inference a presupposition. Using the notation introduced in Chapter 8, *What hit the sofa was the meteorite* +< *Something hit the sofa*. The same is true of (9.5b, b'): the clause on the right *The meteorite hit something* is presupposed. And, where we get similar inferences later – in (9.8) and (9.12) – the clauses inferable from both an affirmative and the corresponding negative are presuppositions.

Thus the *wh*-clause of a pseudo-cleft identifies a presupposition, which should be old information, already known to the addressee. If it is not, then that particular sentence will not be a suitable one to use. The presuppositions are propositions with unspecified variables, *something* in (9.5a, a', b, b'). An appropriate pseudo-cleft – one that matches the presupposition – does two things: by means of its *wh*-clause it indicates the presupposition and it presents a noun phrase as the value of the variable (specific detail in place of the indefinite *something* in the present examples). This noun phrase carries the **new** information provided by the utterer of a pseudo-cleft.

The unmarked sentence in (9.4c) *The meteorite hit the sofa* could replace either of the pseudo-cleft sentences in the two-turn conversations (9.5a", b"). See (9.6a, b).

(9.6) a. "They say something hit the sofa." "Yes, the MEteorite hit the sofa."
   b. "I heard that the meteorite hit something." "Yes, the meteorite hit the SOfa."
   c. "They say something hit the sofa." "Yes, the sofa was hit by the meteorite."

The responses in (9.6a, b) are very likely to exhibit stress differences – marked by the capitalised syllables *ME* and *SO*. These will be discussed in Section 9.3 on *Focal stress*. Passive sentences, such as the response in (9.6c), will be discussed later too.

9.2.2 It-clefts

(9.7) a. It was her grandma who took Judy to the Potter film.
      b. It was Judy who her grandma took to the Potter film.
      c. It was the Potter film that her grandma took Judy to.

It-clefts highlight a noun phrase, often in order to contrast it with another. For instance, (9.7a) is an *it*-cleft when used to convey 'In spite of what you might think, the person who took Judy to the film was her grandmother, not her aunt'. (If you have been worrying whether *her* refers to Judy or to someone else, note that English simply does not make this clear; so it is not worth worrying about. I have been thinking of *her* as *Judy*, but it makes no difference to the structure and use of these *it*-clefts.)

It-clefts have similar distinguishing traits to the ones listed earlier for pseudo-clefts:

- a clause with an unspecified argument (*who took Judy to the Potter film* does not provide details about the subject, though *who* suggests a human subject, rather than, say, the no. 12 bus; *who her grandma took to the Potter film* does not specify the object; and *that her grandma took Judy to* has a gap after the preposition *to*)
- a noun phrase that specifies the missing argument (*her grandma*, *Judy* and *the Potter film* in, respectively (9.7a–c))
- BE is the main verb (*was* in (9.7))
- *It* is the grammatical subject.

As with pseudo-clefts, the clause with the unspecified variable is presupposed, which is to say that its truth can be inferred from the *it*-cleft in both its affirmative and negative form. The presuppositions are propositions but, again, to represent them in the form of sentences it is necessary to put an indefinite pronoun (*someone* or *something*) in place of the missing argument. See (9.8).

(9.8) a. It was her grandma who took Judy to the Potter film
          ⇒ Someone took Judy to the Potter film
      a' It was not her grandma who took Judy to the Potter film
          +> Someone took Judy to the Potter film
      b. It was Judy who her grandma took to the Potter film
          ⇒ Her grandma took someone to the Potter film
      b' It was not Judy who her grandma took to the Potter film
          +> Her grandma took someone to the Potter film
      c. It was the Potter film that her grandma took Judy to
          ⇒ Her grandma took Judy to something
      c' It was not the Potter film that her grandma took Judy to
          +> Her grandma took Judy to something

The inferences in (9.8a, b, c) are entailments. Unless the sentence on the right is true, the entailing sentence on the left in each case cannot be true, as shown by the fact that (9.9a–c) are contradictions.

(9.9) a. *It was her grandma who took Judy to the Potter film, but no-one took Judy there.

      b. *It was Judy who her grandma took to the Potter film, but her grandma took no-one there.

      c. *It was the Potter film that her grandma took Judy to, but her grandma didn't take her to anything.

However, the implicatures in (9.8a', b', c') are inferences which are normally available, but can be avoided in a pinch: (9.10a', b', c') are not contradictory.

(9.10) a' It was not her grandma who took Judy to the Potter film; no-one took Judy there.

      b' It was not Judy who her grandma took to the Potter film; her grandma took no-one there.

      c' It was not the Potter film that her grandma took Judy to; Judy wasn't taken to anything.

Sentences like those in (9.10) are usable when someone is demonstrating substantial confusion over the facts – perhaps because of difficult handwriting, or noise or inattention in speech – during earlier steps in the discourse. In situations where reasonable communication is taking place, speakers and writers would use the *it*-clefts in (9.8) only when the corresponding presuppositions on the right hold true. For example, (9.8a) could be used to reply to "Who took Judy to the Potter film? Her aunt?" because the first of these questions also presupposes 'Someone took Judy to the Potter film'.

9.2.3 Passives

(9.11) a. The conspirators liked the scheme.

      b. The scheme was liked by the conspirators.

      c. (9.11a $\Rightarrow$ 9.11b) & (9.11b $\Rightarrow$ 9.11a)

Sentence (9.11b) is of a type called **passive**. Grammarians call the unmarked transitive type of clause (9.11a) **active**, when contrasting them with passive clauses (see Miller 2002: 26). A passive is longer than the corresponding active. This is because passives are marked by a greater number of grammatical morphemes (BE – showing up as *was* in (9.11b) – the preposition *by* and, for some verbs, a past participle form). By contrast actives have fewer "markings", which is a reason for calling them *unmarked*. Another difference is that the arguments (the conspirators and the scheme) that appear as grammatical subject and object are interchanged between active and passive. However, corresponding actives and passives are mutually entailing, as noted in 9.11c, which means that they are semantically equivalent, or paraphrases.

The existence of a construction that allows exchange between the subject and object positions plays a role in the meshing of new information with presupposed background information. There is a tendency – not an invariable rule – in English, and perhaps in all languages, for utterances to present old information ahead of new information (Huddleston and Pullum 2002: 1372). Intuitively this is reasonable: start with knowledge the addressee is presupposed to have, use a topic expression to indicate which bit of that knowledge you want to build on, then present the new information. Thus if the addressee is assumed already to know about the conspirators but not about the scheme, (9.11a) will be preferred, while (9.11b) might be chosen if the addressee is thought to know about the scheme but not about the conspirators.

Another tendency in English usage is one that favours the subject slot for references to animate beings, as in (9.11a) (see Biber et al. 1999: 378). Hearing or reading a relatively more marked form, the addressee should consider whether this may have been done for a reason, and such consideration – often largely unconscious – can, as indicated in Chapter 8, help in making sense of a communication. So, an addressee faced with (9.11b), a passive that furthermore goes against the animate-subject norm, should wonder what motivated the extra effort. Why was *the scheme* put in subject position? Perhaps to make it an obvious topic, a crucial link with the background to the discourse. And that might help the addressee find a recent memory representation of something that might have been spoken about as *a plot*.

It is worth asking what (9.11b) presents as new, given that *the conspirators* – with its definite article – might also refer to a topic. It could be the establishment of a link between two topics: 'you're interested in the scheme; you know about the conspirators; I'm telling you that the former was liked by the latter'.

In speech, (9.11b) would normally be uttered with one syllable more prominent than the others, and the location within the sentence of that stressed syllable influences what it presupposes. The typical position for this focal stress is near the end of a clause (see Huddleston and Pullum 2002: 1372). The kind of presupposition relevant in this chapter is shown on the right in (9.12a, a'), when *conspirators* is the word containing the stressed syllable.

(9.12) a. The scheme was liked by the conSPIrators ⇒ Someone liked the scheme.

    a' The scheme wasn't liked by the conSPIrators +> Someone liked the scheme.

    a" "Who liked the scheme?" "The scheme was liked by the conSPIrators."

    a² ?"What did the conspirators like?" "The scheme was liked by the conSPIrators."

Think of *someone* in the presupposition of (9.12a, a') as not restricted to just one person, but encompassing 'some people' too. The questions in the last two lines of the example indicate that the questioner is pre-supposing in (9.12a") that 'Someone liked the scheme' (which matches the presupposition of the passive stressed as shown), but in (9.12a²) as presupposing 'The conspirators liked something'. With the stress on the indicated syllable (9.12a") is a plausible question-and-response sequence, but (9.12a²) is unnatural.

Thus one function of passives – the only one discussed here – is to put an argument into subject position, a basic slot for topics. A quick look will now be taken at another way of moving material into and out of topic and new information positions.

Chapter 2 introduced the sense relation of converseness that holds between some pairs of words. As a reminder, (9.13) illustrates a converse pair of verbs, *like* and *please*.

(9.13) a. The conspirators liked the scheme.

    b. The scheme pleased the conspirators.

    c. (9.13a ⇒ 9.13b) & (9.13b ⇒ 9.13a)

Notice the overall similarity between (9.11) and (9.13): interchange of arguments when (a) is compared to (b), going along with differences in the verb (*liked* – *was liked by*, *liked* – *pleased*), while semantic equivalence is preserved (c). Actives and their corresponding passives are **syntactic converses**. The similarity between syntactic converseness, as in (9.11), and lexical converseness, as in (9.13), is further illustrated by the sentences in (9.14), which are all mutually entailing.

(9.14) a. The conspirators liked the scheme.

    b. The scheme was liked by the conspirators.

    c. The scheme pleased the conspirators.

    d. The conspirators were pleased by the scheme. (or *at* or *with*)

There are not all that many pairs of converse verbs; so the alternative to the passive that *like* and *please* offer is not generally available.

In (9.15) some other sentence patterns are illustrated that facilitate the presentation of new information in relation to background by making it possible to move phrases around in sentences without affecting the semantics.

(9.15) To the Potter film, her grandma took Judy.
Judy, her grandma took to the Potter film.
The Potter film, her grandma took Judy to it.
Her grandma, she took Judy to the Potter film.
Took her to the Potter film, Judy, did her grandma.

Huddleston and Pullum (2002: 1366) list more such structures and provide labels for them.

9.3 Focal stress

The intonation of spoken English generally gives extra weight to one syllable in a stretch that often coincides with a clause. A syllable is a unit of pronunciation, but the kind of stress under discussion is associated with syntactic units, occurring in unmarked cases on the rightmost word of a phrase (Giegerich 1992: 252–4), usually a content word. **Focal stress**,[2] then, is syntactically-located intonational prominence doing semantic or pragmatic signalling work. There were glimpses in Chapter 7 of a semantic role for focal stress, in demarcating the scope of negation, modals and quantifiers. The present section gives a sketch of its use as a signal of new or contrastive information in pragmatics. (Each English word has its own stress profile, as seen in the difference between *conSPIrator*, *conspiraTOrial*. If a word is going to carry focal stress, then which syllable within the word will be the one that is stressed is determined at the word level. (There is an introduction to English word stress patterns in McMahon 2002: 119–23.)

An unremarkable two-turn conversation is given in (9.16), to show how focal stress marks new information.

(9.16) A: "Did you come by BUS?" B: "I came by TRAIN."

A's focal stress indicates that the means of transport ('by bus') is the nub of the query: new information being offered for verification – B's arrival probably being what has made it alright to presuppose 'You came by some means'. The focal stress in the reply is used to say that a different kind of transport was used.

The display in (9.17), suggested to me by Swart and Hoop (2000: 123), presents a more complicated set of possibilities, to illustrate how focal stress ties in with syntax.

(9.17) a. Could you   [email   [her   [new   BOSS?]]]
        b. No, but I could   email   her   new   SECretary.
        c. No, but I could   email   her   uniVERsity.
        d. No, but I could   email   MEEna.
        e. No, but I could   GO there.

The request in (9.17a) has focal stress on the last word. The different imaginable responses in (9.17b–e) show that what is taken as new could be just the referent of *boss*, as in (9.17b), or any of the different phrases that *boss* is the final word of. The square brackets in the first line make the point that these phrases are nested one inside another. The response in (9.17d), to take one example, treats the request as presenting the phrase *her new BOSS* as new information, signalled by having focal stress on its last word. And, if that is what is new, the presupposed residue is 'you could email someone', which makes *I could email MEEna* an appropriate response, one that takes what is presupposed and supplies an argument that fits in as object of the verb *to email*.

Compare (9.18) with (9.16). In (9.18a) the question's focal stress is on *you*. Three different appropriate replies are given in (9.18b–d).

(9.18) a. A: "Did YOU come by coach?"
        b. B: "**I** came by TRAIN." (where both *I* and *TRAIN* have focal stress)
        c. B: "I came by TRAIN".
        d. B: "LORna came by coach."

The speaker and addressee are often automatically treated as part of the background (because it is difficult to have a conversation without them), in which case *I* and *you* do not carry focal stress. However, (9.18a) and (9.18b) are examples where they can carry stress naturally, to indicate contrast. The question (9.18a) presupposes 'one or more came by coach', but the focally stressed *you* in (9.18a) suggests an additional presupposition 'you perhaps came by coach and I didn't think you would'. The stressed *I* in (9.18b) conveys 'I emphatically distinguish myself from the possibility you are apparently thinking of' and the second focally stressed item in (9.18b) points to train travel as new information going against the questioner's presupposition of coach travel as a possibility. (Yes, it can happen that there are two focally stressed items in one clause, though this is unusual.)

Example (9.18c) ignores the questioner's apparent surprise at the possibility of the interlocutor having come by coach and simply provides information that contradicts the 'you perhaps came by coach' part of the presupposition. It is a neutral sort of response that lacks the crowing overtones of (9.18b). Example (9.18d) does not directly answer the question. Focal stress on *Lorna* supplies an argument to substitute for the variable 'one or more' in the 'one or more came by coach' part of (9.18a)'s presuppositional background. The questioner has to infer, via the maxim of quantity (discussed in Chapter 8), that if the speaker of (9.18d) thinks it is enough of an answer, then *Lorna* must be the only mutual acquaintance who came by coach. So (9.18d) implicates that the speaker did not come by coach.

Summary

This chapter has been an introductory survey of structures and devices (definiteness, two kinds of cleft sentence, passives and focus) in English that indicate:

- what the communicator is presupposing about the background information against which the addressee interprets the utterance
- and which part of the message is presented as new.

There is more complexity to the subject than this introduction has suggested. The distinctions made in the chapter between background, topics within the background and new information are too coarse. For instance, a "reminder" like *There's your future to think about* uses a structure (existential *There's ...*) that is specialised for introducing new items of information – such as 'a weird green glow' in (9.1) – but *your future* is definite, which marks it as relating to known background information, and it is hard to imagine non-infant interlocutors who have never thought about their future. Probably at least two different kinds of background information need to be distinguished, depending on how recently or prominently they have figured in the discourse.

Also not discussed in the chapter are interactions between stress and construction type. If the grammatical subject position of a passive presents a topic (information assumed to be already known), how is a spoken passive interpreted when the subject carries focal stress, marking it as new? (The quick answer is that such passives are presuppositionally ambiguous.)

Chapter 7 had some examples that showed focal stress doing semantic work, implying that it can affect entailments, which would make focal stress different from what has been claimed in this chapter about passivisation and clefting having no semantic effect. The relevant cases usually involve the scope of operators (what is affected by negation, quantifiers and *only* etc.). Passivisation and *it*-clefts can show such effects too. See Rooth (1996) and Swart and Hoop (2000) for discussion.

Clearly, there is more to say on the matters covered in this book. I hope you will think on and read further about the ways in which language encodes semantic distinctions and how people put the semantics to work in the pragmatics of communication.

Exercises

1. The only time I met the poet Hamish Henderson, it was unexpected and I asked "Are you THE Hamish Henderson?" His modest answer was that he was trying to stay in the top 100. Using the technical terms *definite* and *topic*, explain briefly what was going on in this exchange.

2. Why is there no need for a preparatory introduction of topic before giving the following warnings: *Keep your head down* and *Mind the step*, where the underlined phrases are definite?

3. Pseudo-clefts can be inverted, for example *The meteorite was what hit the sofa*. Compare this with the example discussed in the chapter *What hit the sofa was the meteorite*. Is the presupposition the same or different? (Hint: start by trying to find a proposition that is both entailed by *The meteorite was what hit the sofa* and implicated by *The meteorite wasn't what hit the sofa*. That is to say: find out what it presupposes.)

4. Tom says that, as he remembers it, "It was the ATlas that Lucy borrowed". Tom is wrong. You are clear about who borrowed what: (a) Mary borrowed the atlas and (b) Lucy borrowed the dictionary. Indicate how to correct Tom by filling in the following to make a complete sentence:

"No, you're wrong: _____".

Which of the scenarios, (a) or (b), does your completion relate to? How does this fit with the presupposition pattern of *it*-clefts discussed in the chapter?

5. According to the second half of (9.11c), *The scheme was liked by the conspirators* entails 'The conspirators liked the scheme', but according to the first line of (9.12) *The scheme was liked by the conSPIrators* entails 'Someone liked the scheme'.

It is a fact that *The scheme was liked by the conSPIrators* also entails 'The conspirators liked the scheme'. Study these examples and the surrounding text and identify the reason why the less informative entailment 'someone ...' was cited in (9.12). Do not just say that it is because of stress on the syllable *SPI*; that is a side issue in this exercise. Try, instead, to understand the logic of what was said about these examples.

6. Example (9.18) had a question *Did YOU come by coach?* Amongst other things, it presupposes 'one or more came by coach'. What different presupposition is indicated by *Was it YOU who came by coach?* (a question based on an *it*-cleft)? There isn't an answer to look up in the chapter. Think about circumstances under which the *it*-cleft question would feel more appropriate.

Recommendations for reading

A comprehensive and readable account is given in Huddleston and Pullum's (2002) chapter on information packaging, ch. 16. If you would like to know more about theories in this area, then Swart and Hoop (2000) is an excellent and up-to-date survey. It is accessibly written but, even so, parts of it are quite hard. Rooth (1996) concentrates on focal stress. His article contains difficult technical material, but also lots of interesting examples.

Notes

1. Madhur Jaffrey (1983), *Eastern Vegetarian Cooking*, London: Jonathan Cape, p. 18.

2. I use the label *focal stress* simply because it makes it easier to remember that it is a kind of stress. In linguistics, the term *focus* is more common for the same thing; less common alternatives are *sentence stress* and *tonic*.

Suggested answers to the exercises

Chapter 1

1. *Arriving* denotes a change from not *being in/at* a place to *being in/at* it. *Leaving* denotes the reverse transition: from *being in/at* a place to not being *in/at* it. Likewise, *learning* is a transition into a state of *knowing* something, and *forgetting* is the reverse change, from *knowing* something, to not *knowing* it. Consideration of word meanings without regard to context is part of semantics.

2. Although we cannot be certain, the grade was probably low. By not simply saying "You passed" or "You did very well", and instead bringing in the possibility of failure, the tutor hints that the grade was down near the failing point. Presumably the tutor did not say "You got a low grade" because that could be embarrassing or hurtful. Because we needed to consider alternative utterances that might have been used and because of the uncertain conclusion, this is pragmatic reasoning.

3. *Pick the right lock* can mean 'Choose the correct lock' or 'Without a key open the correct lock'. At least two propositions are involved, one for each possible meaning the sentence can have. We could get additional meanings – and therefore more propositions – by taking *right* in the sense 'right-hand' and *lock* in the 'skein of hair' sense.

4. In 'not trust', 'not regard', 'not like', the verb itself is in the scope of 'not', but for 'prove not' and 'persuade not', something else is in the scope of 'not'.

5. The nonsensical analysis would have the bracketing '(not good) enough'. But *good enough* means 'adequate' and in the given expression it is adequacy that is negated: 'not (good enough)'; negation, expressed by *not*, can alternatively be encoded with the negative prefix *in-*, so the whole expression is synonymous with 'inadequate'.

7. The entailments are as follows: $2 \Rightarrow 1$, $3 \Rightarrow 4$, $4 \Rightarrow 3$.

Chapter 2

1. (a.) They were soundless. (b.) They were silent. (c.) They were noise-less. $(a \Rightarrow b) \ \& \ (a \Rightarrow c) \ \& \ (b \Rightarrow c) \ \& \ (b \Rightarrow a) \ \& \ (c \Rightarrow a) \ \& \ (c \Rightarrow b)$

2. *Awake* and *asleep* are complementaries because *She is awake* entails *She is not asleep*; *She is not awake* entails *She is asleep*; *She is asleep* entails *She is not awake*; *She is not asleep* entails *She is awake*. I take *half-awake, half-asleep* and *dozy* to be different ways of being awake, rather than words denoting an intermediate region between 'awake' and 'asleep'; note that *He's dozy but still awake* is not semantically problematic, in contrast with **He's dozy but still asleep*; and I find the following imaginary conversation fairly plausible: "You're asleep." "No, I'm not, but I admit I'm dozy/half-asleep/only half-awake."

3. The adjectives in the left-hand column are gradable and the "down-toner" sense of *quite* could even be a test for gradability: *How clever is your sister? It is too late now. Families are getting smaller. This is very unusual.* The items in the other column are either members of complementary pairs (*right–wrong, finished–unfinished* and *impossible–possible*) or covert superlatives (*alone*) or both (*impossible*), and complementaries and covert superlatives can be modified by "maximisers".

5. I get biased questions with *young, miserable, pleasant, unpalatable* and *tasty*. With *weak* and *strong* in the 'muscular' sense, only *weak* makes for a biased *how*-question, but in the 'potency of ingestibles' sense, for example with beverages and drugs, both *strong* and *weak* make for biased *how*-questions: "How strong is that tea?" "It's not strong; it's weak." strikes me as a normal interchange; likewise "How weak is that tea?" "It's not weak; it's strong."

6. If, as seems likely, *royal visitor* denotes a royal person who is visiting, then it can be handled intersectively, because such a person is both royal and a visitor. *Royal correspondent* is ambiguous: Queen Christina exchanging letters with Descartes fits the intersective scheme; the case of a journalist, who is not royal but regularly reports on the affairs of royalty, cannot be analysed intersectively; such a person is in the set denoted by *correspondent*, but not in the set denoted by *royal. Heavy eater* is ambiguous: a person who binges on food, but might or might not weigh much, exemplifies non-intersective; if the eater weighs a lot

then an intersective analysis works. *Wise fool,* meaning a professional fool (a clown or jester) who is wise, can be dealt with intersectively; if it means a foolish person who is wise, then it is either a contradiction, with no intersection between the sets denoted by *fool* or *wise,* or it is some clever talk bringing together different aspects of the same person (and probably cannot be analysed intersectively).

Chapter 3

1. For me, a prototype *shoe* has an *upper* and a *sole,* in their turns, the *upper* has a *tongue,* and the *sole* has a *heel.* For some speakers of English, it may be that the *heel* is directly a part of the *shoe,* rather than part of the *sole.* It depends on whether you find it fits your intuitions better to say: "a shoe has an upper, a sole and a heel"; or "a shoe has an upper and a sole; and the sole has a heel". Perhaps *laces, ties, straps* or a *fastener* are parts of your prototype shoe.

2. If the statement is accepted as a reasonable reflection of a competent user of English's knowledge of meaning, then *side* is a superordinate for *top, bottom, front* and *back.* The statement names the latter four as different kinds of *side,* and the relation of incompatibility holds between these four hyponyms of *side.* The "definitions" that follow each colon in the statement consist of the superordinate (side) and a modifier (for example, 'that is down'), which is the pattern for hyponym meanings. The different modifiers of *side* are what make the four hyponyms incompatible.

3. *Mother* and *father* are incompatible. *This is my mother* entails *This is not my father, This is my father* entails *This is not my mother;* however, we do not get entailments from the negative sentences to the affirmative ones, for example someone who is not my mother need not be my father, but could be my aunt or cousin or a passing stranger. The term antonymy is reserved for incompatibility between pairs of adjectives or adverbs; *mother* and *father* are nouns.

4. Some initial ideas: (a) "We don't sell marshmallows here; this is a SHOE shop" would be a memorable objection, but it feels like one that respects the meaning of the word *shoe.* On the other hand, the following objection would strike me as peculiar in meaning: "?We don't sell sandals here; this is a SHOE shop." And it would be just as strange with *slippers* or *boots* substituted for *sandals.*

(b) (c) and, in single quotes, (d). Draw an upside down tree with *shoes*₁ (or *footwear*) 'clothing for the feet, having a sole' as the overall super-ordinate. On three branches below it, put *shoes*₂ 'footwear covering just the feet', *boots* 'footwear covering feet and ankles, at least' and *sandals* 'ventilated footwear'. Hyponyms dangling from branches below *shoes*₂ include *clogs* 'wooden shoes', *trainers* and *sneakers*. (*Sneakers* and *trainers* are a synonym pair. It should not be hard to supply a concise meaning '*shoes*₂ for …'). Hyponyms below *boots* include *football boots* 'boots for football' and *gumboots*. If you know the word, then *jandals* 'waterproof minimal sandals' is a hyponym of *sandals*. (*Jandals* is a New Zealand English word for what many Australians call *thongs*, which are *shower shoes* or *flip flops* to English speakers in some other places.) *Galoshes* and *slippers* are some other words to include.

5. <u>Count</u>

	Count	Mass
(a)	There is a paper lying on my desk.	We use too much paper.
	How many glasses shall I wash?	It can be expensive to re-cycle glass.
	Whole cheeses are on sale at that stall.	Feta cheese is used in spinach pies.
(b)	broadsheet, tabloid	newsprint, typing paper
	goblet, wineglass	window glass, bullet-proof glass
		gouda, gorgonzola

There is another count sense of *paper* with the meaning 'prepared statement'. One of its hyponyms is *conference paper*. *Glasses*, synonymous with *spectacles* and superordinate to hyponyms such as *bifocals* and *sunglasses*, is a count noun, but does not have a singular form, so is not quite right as part of the answer here. I do not know a hyponym for the count noun *cheese*, though I am aware of kinds ranging from fist-sized waxed balls to large round ones with cloth wrappings. Perhaps you know words for some of these.

The mass nouns denote materials or substances. The count nouns denote kinds of thing: newspapers, glass drinking vessels, formats in which cheese is produced.

Chapter 4

1. Talking about the situation after the civil servant's resignation – more than two months later – the sentence ?*The minister resigned the civil servant* might be taken as causative, if a correct understanding of it is: 'an action by the minister directly caused the civil servant to resign'.

This situation could be described by the two-clause formulation *The minister made (the civil servant resign)*, because this covers both direct and indirect causation. However, coming so much later it seems more likely that, if it was the minister's announcement in February that caused the civil servant to resign in May, the causation was indirect. If so, a one-clause sentence ?*The minister resigned the civil servant* would not be an appropriate way to talk about it, because one-clause causatives encode direct causation. Back in February 2002, ?*Who is going to be resigned next?* was probably not a question meaning 'Who will be made to resign next?', but rather a way of catching people's attention with the ill-formedness of the question as a way of getting them to think about the meaning of the word *resign* and, from there, to consider the minister's apparent high-handedness.

2. As an egg, Humpty was "together" (intact) before his 'great fall'. The soldiery failed in the task of getting Humpty back into this previous state of togetherness. *Put* is a causative accomplishment verb in the quoted lines. The restitutive adverb *again* modifies an embedded proposition 'Humpty is together', rather than the main clause action verb *put*.

3. Sentences (a) and (b) are unaccusative, because the referent of the subject does not consciously carry out the action, as confirmed by the peculiarity of these sentences with *carefully*. *The kite carefully flew*, *My heart carefully sank*. Sentence (c) is unergative: reading is something that students do consciously and they can do it carefully.

4. (a) Activity. (b) Accomplishment. (c) Achievement. (d) State. (e) Achievement when talking about a single stop, because the following is not an acceptable way of expressing 'The music waned but continued': *The music stopped stopping*, also because restitutive *again* works straightforwardly. *The music was stopping* is unacceptable unless we interpret this as habitual (meaning 'the music kept stopping'; see Chapter 6) or if it is said with reference to a scheduled stop. On the habitual interpretation, *The music stopped* is an activity. (f) Achievement. (g) Activity. Yes, *the violin* is a definite direct object, but not one that delimits the activity: *Khalid played the violin* does not encode a situation in which he plays until the violin is "finished" (compare *Khalid played the sonata*).

5. In *learn your lines*, the situation is an accomplishment, with 'knowing your lines' as the goal. Only when the goal is reached have you *finished*,

but *stopping* the learning of lines can occur anywhere, before or at the finishing point. *Finish* then means 'stop having reached the goal'. *Playing teenage roles* is an activity. Activities do not have goals; so the difference in meaning between *stop* and *finish* has no significance in (b).

6. In (a) the "material" argument (*this*, referring to the mixed quantity of flour and spices) is the direct object of *sprinkle*. It sets the goal: once all three tablespoonfuls have been sprinkled, the task is accomplished. (The subsequent gentle mixing can spread the flour-and-spice mixture to any peaches missed in the sprinkling.) In (b) the locative argument (*it*, referring to the bottom of the pan) is direct object of *dust*: completion comes when the whole buttered area has been lightly dusted, and there is a good chance that the cook will not, in accomplishing this, use up all the flour in the kitchen.

Chapter 5

1. The person's face "curdled" in embarrassment at what her father, a blood relative, was doing. *Blood is thicker than water* alleges that family links are more significant than others. So it could suggest that Diski's mother's discomfiture was especially acute for being produced by her own father's behaviour, the thickness making the curds more unpalatable. Metaphorical interpretation seems to be open-ended, in something like the way that continued examination of a picture can keep on revealing new features. By contrast, literal interpretation of the word *grimaced* would be rather more a matter of almost instantaneous semantic decoding, with little scope for elaboration. How far you can take a metaphorical interpretation depends on the extent of your encyclopedic knowledge about the metaphorical vehicle; how far you will take it depends on interest and doggedness.

2. Metonymy, using *beaks* as the vehicle and depending on the presupposition 'birds have beaks'.

3. *He's a tube light* was intended to convey that the person in question was slow on the uptake, similar to a fluorescent tube in its delayed response to operation of the switch. The information needed is presuppositional, concerning the salient features of average "tube lights" in Fiji at that time: they were slow to light up and generally rather dim.

4. The two occurrences of *like* suggest the kind of metaphors called simile. However, bees literally do sting, which means that *sting like a*

bee is literal rather than figurative, therefore not a metaphor. But Muhammad Ali was the understood subject – he could have said *I sting like a bee* – and that means that *sting* (*like a bee*) was being metaphorically used, a vehicle to convey the nature of his punches. If the verb *dance* means only 'move in time with music', then butterflies do not do it and nor did Ali when he was boxing, which would make the simile comparison of dancing with the movement of butterflies metaphorical, and so also would be metaphorical his comparison between his movements in the ring and dancing. (That boxing is done in pairs, that boxers circle round each other, "in tune" with each other's movements, of course, bolsters a metaphorical interpretation; and Ali's swift, light, endlessly varied footwork was well expressed through the metaphorical vehicle *butterfly*.) For many users of English, however, *dance* long ago acquired – from repeated metaphorical use – an additional sense of 'make repeated flitting movements', such as those of butterflies. With that in the presuppositions, (*1*) *dance like a butterfly* could simply be taken literally. There is a choice of answers regarding the first half of Muhammad Ali's maxim: it depends on the presuppositions.

Chapter 6

1. *Recently* goes with the past time group that includes *yesterday*. Note the unacceptability of *He is happy recently*, ?*He shops at the corner store recently*, *I will do it recently*. (In connection with Example (6.20) it was noted that *recently* can be used with present perfect forms, for example *I have been over the Forth Rail Bridge recently*, where it indicates that the aftermath – the period between my crossing of the bridge and now, the time of utterance – is relatively short, but note that the period of the aftermath assessed as short is all before now, which is to say it is in past time.) *Soon* is like *then* in Table 6.2, in being acceptable with past and future times, but not present: *I'm eating cake soon* is no good if reference is to the present, but is fine with future reference in *I'm catching a train soon*, even though both of these sentences are present progressive in form. In such cases *soon* is directly anchored on the time of utterance, with the meaning 'a short time after now'. But when *soon* is used with past reference, as in *It began to rain, but stopped soon*, the deixis is indirect, and *soon* means 'a short time after that time'. In the example, 'that time' is the time that the past tense form *began* points to deictically.

2. *Arthur's a tyrant* is a state clause, so it would normally express a relatively long-lasting situation, and probably represents a judgement about Arthur's personality. *Arthur's being a tyrant* is longer than the

other sentence, which encourages a pragmatic line of reasoning: why didn't the speaker use the shorter alternative (perhaps to signal something connected to any difference there may be between the meanings of the two)? The verb BE, which usually contributes to the encoding of states has been marked present progressive in the longer sentence, as if it were an activity verb, inviting the "provisionality" interpretation mentioned in the chapter in connection with Example (6.17b).

3. The verb *told* is past simple; *had saved* is past perfect; *were dying* is past progressive.

before time of report

──────────────────────────── time of report ────────────

The Gov. saves $$$ ↑
The co. told the Gov. ... ↑

People die early.

The report does not allow certainty over how far the grey bar for the duration of early dying should extend to the right: maybe people were, at the time of the report, still dying early from this cause; maybe early smoking deaths had already stopped before the company told the government about it; perhaps the deaths stopped some time between the telling and the reporting. Did the company tell the government "People are dying early" or "People were dying early" or "People have been dying early"? For drawing the diagram it would also help to know whether the company said to the government "You have saved a lot of money" or "You saved a lot of money". These two possibilities, both of which can be reported by means of a past perfect, were mentioned in connection with example (6.21b).

4. *You said you would ...* or *You said you were going to ...* are possible for (c). The request on the previous day might have been any of *Will you ...*, *Would you ...*, *Can you ...*, *Could you ...* or various other request forms. It would be surprising if you had asked by saying *You are going to ...*, because that suggests a high degree of certainty and maybe determination. Your friend can be determined to bring you the book, but if you show that sort of determination in phrasing the request, people might guess that you are a bully or a hypnotist.

Chapter 7

1. The default description without a modal verb is stronger. It is appropriate to use a modal when speakers lack direct information about a state of affairs but are presenting a conclusion based on reasoning from evidence. Therefore, the presence of modal marking invites the conclusion that the speaker does not really know and is relying on inference, with *must* indicating more confidence than *might*.

2. *They must be made from buckwheat* can be either deontic (a demand or strong recommendation that buckwheat be used) or epistemic (speaker infers from evidence – colour or taste, perhaps – that buckwheat is an ingredient).
   We must get up early tomorrow is deontic. What might happen tomorrow is too uncertain to justify epistemic *must*.
   The email needn't have been sent can bear either interpretation: deontically that there was no demand for the sending of the email; epistemically that it is possible that the email has not yet been sent.
   I can hear you now indicates "capability" (mentioned towards the end of Section 7.1.3): sound level, transmission and reception conditions mean that what is coming from you is now being heard. Some semanticists take this sort of modality as similar to deontic: physics and physiology allow something to happen (paralleling the way an authority's permission allows something to happen). Others would classify it as dynamic modality (also mentioned in Section 7.1.3). A pointer to the example being an unusual use is the possibility of removing the modal without affecting the meaning much: *I hear you now* is a paraphrase of *I can hear you now*.
   Although it is possible to use *might* to report permission having been given, Biber et al. (1999: 491) found that almost all instances of *might* in their large samples of conversational and academic English were epistemic. A deontic interpretation of *They might or might not make it* is somewhat implausible because it is hard to imagine permission being given for people to succeed or not succeed.
   You better apologise is deontic. This is a reduced form of *You had better…* or *You'd better…* The idiom *had better* is not used to express epistemic modality; see Huddleston and Pullum (2002: 196). (One of the reasons for calling this an idiom is that, despite containing the form *had*, it is not used to talk about the past.)

3. Lots of different right answers are possible on this. Here are some:
   Guests may check in between 3 pm and midnight is epistemic if someone in the hotel is explaining to a new member of staff on the front desk when

to expect people coming along to check in. But if this is a notice show-ing the permitted checking-in hours, it is deontic.

If a taxi driver says *You must be a musician* while helping a passenger stow a cello case, the interpretation is almost certainly epistemic. The same sentence is probably deontic if spoken by a music teacher to a promising pupil who has said "I wonder if I'll enjoy being a stock-broker?"

If a novice is being given tips on interesting things to notice about antique pieces of silver, then *should* in "Look at it with a magnifying glass; there should be a hallmark" is probably epistemic. But someone who uses *There should be a hallmark* to press the case for quality assur-ance marks on something other than the traditionally hallmarked metals (platinum, gold and silver) is using the sentence deontically.

4. Deontic *may not* is similar to *can't*: negation has wider scope: 'not (possibly (they have an invitation))'. However, epistemic *may not* (see Example (7.28c)) behaves like *mustn't*: modality has wider scope: 'possibly (not (they have an invitation))'. For the comparison of rela-tive scope, it does not matter that *may* is represented as 'possibly', using the same word as was used for *can* in Example (7.28b). The meanings of *may* and *can* share the notion of possibility, the 'negative ruled out' part of their core meanings in Table 7.1.

5. In the situation described *The witness may | not be named* is deontic, with relative scope 'possibly (not (the witness be named))'. This is different from the general pattern for *may* (see Exercise 4 in this chapter), where there is wider scope for negation when the interpretation is deontic, and wider scope for modality with epistemic interpretations.

6. | B ∩ H | is a small number. (*B* represents the set of boats and *H* the set of things that are in the harbour in question). See the examples in (7.29), in this chapter. Taking *few* as a cardinal quantifier, the speaker is just saying that there was a small number of boats in the harbour; the harbour seemed uncrowded by boats. Only the intersection is taken into consideration. Boats that are not in the harbour are left out of the calculation. What number is a small number? That is pragmatically decided by the speaker and relates to the size of the harbour, the density of boats that the speaker is used to, to the fact that they are boats rather than cars or ants or castles, and to the speaker's ideas on what the addressee would regard as a small number in such a case.

7. This is comparable to Example (7.34b) in this chapter. The quantifier

one might have wider scope because it is in the subject noun phrase. On this reading, the sentence describes a single versatile machine that no product escapes being tested by: 'there is one machine (as for every product (the machine tests it))'. But there is an opposing tendency for *each* to have wider scope 'as for every product (there is one machine (the machine tests that product))'. On this reading we are assured that every product is tested by a machine, but it could be a different machine for each different type of product, or a limited number of dual-purpose testing machines; or a couple of multipurpose testers; or ...

Chapter 8

1. Implicature: 'I am someone you know well and from hearing my voice you will recognise me.' It would be a peculiar answer to give if you were knocking on the door of a stranger or someone you knew only slightly. It looks as if the maxim of quantity is being disobeyed, because no new information is supplied. But this can be seen as reasonable if it is taken as a signal that no information is needed because the voice should be immediately recognisable. Reasons for doing it this way: to save time; to deny the information to bystanders; to avoid embarrassing A over not having remembered that B was going to call.

2. Quantity and manner, respectively.

3. B's "I don't know" is an admission of not being fully able to meet the quality maxim, which is the basis for 'perhaps' in the implicature. The excuse also alerts A not to infer anything from B's not simply giving clear directions to the desired section, which is to say that B seems to offer too small a quantity of information. Relevance is also in play: B talking about psycholinguistics books when A has asked about sociolinguistics books can be taken as co-operative by reasoning that B must think that it could be relevant that books in another long-named branch of linguistics are there; specialist branches of the same subject could have similar names.

4. Manner. It is hard to be sure what he wanted to say, but perhaps it could have been expressed by *I fully agree with you*, which has fewer words and does not require the processing of all those negations (*not*, *dis-*, and the hidden ones in *fail* and *less*). An emphatic *Yes!* might have sufficed by itself. But neither of these ways of expressing agreement

carries the implicature: 'I am so clever with language that I can baffle ordinary people', which might have been the point.

5. ?"Her name isn't Moira and his Jon – it's the other way round: his name is Jon and hers is Moira". This seems nonsensical; so Example (8.12e) does not convey an implicature of order. If you are able to sketch a weird scenario in which this denial could plausibly occur, then Example (8.12e) would implicate order in that context.

6. *It seeped into the basement* and its negation *It didn't seep into the basement* both yield the inference that 'It was a fluid'. This inference is cancellable, for example *It didn't ˅seep into the basement; wet rot is a fungus; it GREW there*. Furthermore, reporting the inference in a sentence using the verb *tell* is inappropriate: If X says *It seeped into the basement*, it would be misleading to report this to others as *X told me that the stuff in the basement was a fluid*. It would better to say something like *X spoke about the stuff in the basement as if it was a fluid*. For these three reasons, this inference is a presupposition. The inference that 'It entered the basement slowly' is an entailment because it cannot be cancelled without contradiction (**It seeped into the basement in a sudden rush*) and because it is not inferable from the negative counterpart of the sentence *It didn't seep into the basement*. Note that it is fine to use *tell* in reporting an entailment: if X says to me *It seeped into the basement*, it is entirely alright to report this using the sentence: *X told me that it went into the basement slowly*.

7. The speech act of warning bus riders not to smoke is mitigated by presenting part of it as a speech act of thanking. Thanking presupposes that the addressee has done something appreciated by the bus company. Without the mitigation, some habitually non-smoking passengers might have been affronted by an apparent presumption that they needed to be warned not to smoke.

8. (a) Question, order. (b) Order, offer. (c) Question, statement. (d) Statement, expression of sympathy or condolence. (e) order, statement. (f) Order, expression of condolence. (g) Question, statement (equivalent to 'I have never let you down', this is what is called a rhetorical question). (h) Statement, recommendation.

9. Proper names usually presuppose awareness of the existence of the bearer of the name. It became clear as the conversation continued that B had never before heard of Brooke Shields, so the attempted refer-

ence failed, its presupposition not being met. (There are sentences in which a name would not trigger an existence presupposition, for example *I wonder if anyone would call their child Able Baker Charlie?*)

Chapter 9

1. At least one of the world's Hamish Hendersons was distinguished enough for most of those who might conceivably meet him to have heard about him beforehand. He was a potential topic from the outset of a discourse. People's names count as definite without the definite article *the*. Saying *the Hamish Henderson*, I was indicating I already knew of a noteworthy person with that name. His response played it down by suggesting that there were lots of them.

2. It is a reasonable assumption about prototypical interlocutors that each has a head, which justifies first-off definite reference. And the warning about the step would typically be given in a situation where it is possible for the addressee to experience it directly, for example by looking, or tapping with a stick, again making it part of the background without further ado. The answer is not simply that warnings of this kind may have to be issued in a hurry. Where the danger is not so accessible an indefinite is perfectly feasible: *Careful, there's a snake in there.*

3. The presuppositions (of the kind discussed in this chapter) are the same for a pseudo-cleft and for an inverted pseudo-cleft. The given example presupposes 'Something hit the sofa'.

4. "No, you're wrong: Lucy borrowed the DICtionary." or "No, you're wrong: it was the DICtionary that Lucy borrowed." are both reasonable ways of correcting Tom. Both of them relate to scenario (b), in which Lucy borrowed something, though it was not the atlas. Tom's *it*-cleft presupposes 'Lucy borrowed something' and that is closer to scenario (b) than to (a).

5. The point of the examples in (9.11) was that the active and the passive sentences entail each other. The entailment from the passive sentence that is indicated in (9.11c) itself entails the less informative one presented in (9.12a), that is: *The conspirators liked the scheme* entails 'Someone liked the scheme'. The less informative one had to be presented in (9.12a, a') because the issue there was what is presupposed by – rather than merely entailed by – *The scheme was liked*

by the conSPIrators, and a presupposition is inferable from the negation of a sentence as well as the sentence itself. The negative sentence *The scheme wasn't liked by the conSPIrators* actually contradicts 'The conspirators liked the scheme', but the negative sentence does allow the inference (as an implicature; see Chapter 8) that 'Someone liked the scheme', which is the same as the cited less informative entailment from the affirmative. (The inference from the negative sentence in (9.12a') is an implicature, rather than an entailment, because it can be cancelled: *The scheme wasn't liked by the conSPIrators; and, to be honest, nobody liked it.*)

6. If the *it*-cleft question is addressed to just one person, then it presupposes 'only one came by coach'. If it is addressed to a group, then it presupposes 'only one group came by coach'. This is "exhaustiveness", said to be a feature of meaning that distinguishes *it*-clefts from other structures discussed in the chapter.

Bibliography

Austin, J. L. (1962), *How to Do Things with Words*, Oxford: Oxford University Press.

Biber, Douglas, Stig Johansson, Geoffrey Leech, Susan Conrad and Edward Finegan (1999), *Longman Grammar of Spoken and Written English*, Harlow: Pearson.

Blakemore, Diane (1992), *Understanding Utterances: an Introduction to Pragmatics*, Oxford: Blackwell.

Cann, Ronnie (1993), *Formal Semantics*, Cambridge: Cambridge University Press.

Croft, William and Alan Cruse (2004), *Cognitive Linguistics*, Cambridge: Cambridge University Press.

Cruse, Alan (2000), *Meaning in Language*, Oxford: Oxford University Press.

Dowty, David (2000), '"The garden swarms with bees" and the fallacy of "argument alternation"', in Y. Ravin and C. Leacock (eds), *Polysemy: Theoretical and Computational Approaches*, Oxford: Oxford University Press, pp. 111–28.

Fellbaum, Christiane (2000), 'Autotroponymy', in Y. Ravin and C. Leacock (eds), *Polysemy: Theoretical and Computational Approaches*, Oxford: Oxford University Press, pp. 52–67.

Giegerich, Heinz J. (1992), *English Phonology: an Introduction*, Cambridge: Cambridge University Press.

Grandy, Richard, E. (1987), 'In defense of semantic fields', in E. LePore (ed.), *New Directions in Semantics*, London: Academic Press, pp. 259–80.

Grant, Lynn and Laurie Bauer (2004), 'Criteria for re-defining idioms; are we barking up the wrong tree?' *Applied Linguistics*, 25: 38–61.

Grice, H. Paul (1975), 'Logic and conversation', in P. Cole and J. L. Morgan (eds), *Syntax and Semantics*, vol. 3, New York: Academic Press, pp. 41–58.

Grice, H. Paul (1989), *Studies in the Way of Words*, Cambridge, MA: Harvard University Press.

Griffiths, Patrick (1986), 'Early vocabulary', in P. Fletcher and M. Garman (eds), *Language Acquisition*, 2nd edn, Cambridge: Cambridge University Press, pp. 279–306.

Groefsema, Marjolein (1995), '*Can, may, must* and *should*: a Relevance theoretic account', *Journal of Linguistics*, 31: 53–79.

Grundy, Peter (2000), *Doing Pragmatics*, 2nd edn, London: Edward Arnold.

Horn, Laurence R. (1984), 'Toward a new taxonomy for pragmatic inference: Q-based and R-based implicature', in D. Schiffrin (ed.) *Meaning, Form and Use in Context* (*Georgetown University Round Table on Languages and Linguistics*), Washington: Georgetown University Press, pp. 11–42.

Huddleston, Rodney and Geoffrey K. Pullum (2002), *The Cambridge Grammar of the English Language*, Cambridge: Cambridge University Press.

Imai, Mutsumi (2000), 'Universal ontological knowledge and a bias toward language-specific categories in the construal of individuation', in S. Niemeyer and R. Dirven (eds) *Evidence for Linguistic Relativity*, Amsterdam: Benjamins, pp. 139–60.

Kearns, Kate (2000), *Semantics*, Basingstoke: Macmillan.

Keenan, Edward L. (1996), 'The semantics of determiners', in S. Lappin (ed.), *The Handbook of Semantic Theory*, Oxford: Blackwell, pp. 41–63.

Klein, Wolfgang (1992), 'The present perfect puzzle', *Language*, 68: 525–52.

Lappin, Shalom (2001), 'An introduction to formal semantics', in M. Aronoff and J. Rees-Miller (eds) *The Handbook of Linguistics*, Oxford: Blackwell, pp. 369–93.

Leech, Geoffrey, Paul Rayson and Andrew Wilson (2001), *Word Frequencies in Spoken and Written English*, Harlow: Pearson Education.

Levin, Beth and Malka Rappaport Hovav (1998), 'Morphology and lexical semantics', in A. Spencer and A. M. Zwicky (eds), *The Handbook of Morphology*, Oxford: Blackwell, pp. 248–71.

Levinson, Stephen C. (2000), *Presumptive Meanings: the Theory of Generalized Conversational Implicature*, Cambridge, MA: MIT Press.

Lycan, William G. (2000), *Philosophy of Language*, London: Routledge.

Lyons, John (1977), *Semantics*, 2 vols, Cambridge: Cambridge University Press.

McArthur, Tom (1992), *The Oxford Companion to the English Language*, Oxford: Oxford University Press.

McMahon, April (2002), *An Introduction to English Phonology*, Edinburgh: Edinburgh University Press.

Miller, George A. and Christiane Fellbaum (1991), 'Semantic networks of English', *Cognition*, 41: 197–229.

Miller, Jim (2002), *An Introduction to English Syntax*, Edinburgh: Edinburgh University Press.

Palmer, Frank (1990), *Modality and the English Modals*, 2nd edn, London: Longman.

Papafragou, Anna (2000), *Modality: Issues in the Semantics–Pragmatics Interface*, Amsterdam: Elsevier.

Quirk, Randolph, Sidney Greenbaum, Jan Svartvik and Geoffrey Leech (1985), *A Comprehensive Grammar of the English Language*, London: Longman.

Roach, Peter (2000), *English Phonetics and Phonology*, 3rd edn, Cambridge: Cambridge University Press.

Rooth, Mats (1996), 'Focus', in Shalom Lappin (ed.) *The Handbook of Contemporary Semantic Theory*, Oxford: Blackwell, pp. 271–97.

Saeed, John I. (2003), *Semantics*, 2nd edn, Oxford: Blackwell.

Searle, John R. (1975), 'Indirect speech acts', in P. Cole and J. L. Morgan (eds), *Syntax and Semantics*, vol. 3, New York: Academic Press, pp. 59–82.

Searle, John R. (1979), *Expression and Meaning: Studies in the Theory of Speech Acts*, Cambridge: Cambridge University Press.

Sperber, Dan and Deirdre Wilson (1995), *Relevance: Communication and Cognition*, 2nd edn, Oxford: Blackwell.

Stalnaker, Robert C. (1999), *Context and Content*, Oxford: Oxford University Press.

Stern, Josef (2000), *Metaphor in Context*, Cambridge, MA: MIT Press.

Swart, Henriëtte de (1998), *Introduction to Natural Language Semantics*, Stanford: CSLI.

Swart, Henriëtte de and Helen de Hoop (2000), 'Topic and focus', in Lisa Cheng and Rint Sybesma (eds), *The First Glot International State-of-the-Article Book*, Berlin: Mouton de Gruyter, pp. 105–30.

Tenny, Carol (2000), 'Core events and adverbial modification', in C. Tenny and J. Pustejovsky (eds), *Events as Grammatical Objects: the Converging Perspectives of Lexical Semantics and Syntax*, Stanford, CA: CSLI, pp. 285–334.

Tenny, Carol and Pustejovsky James (2000), 'A history of events in linguistic theory', in C. Tenny and J. Pustejovksy (eds), *Events as Grammatical Objects: the Converging Perspectives of Lexical Semantics and Syntax*, Stanford, CA: CSLI, pp. 3–37.

Trask, R. L. (1993), *A Dictionary of Grammatical Terms in Linguistics*, London: Routledge.

Traugott, Elizabeth Closs (2000), 'Semantic change: an overview', in L. Cheng and R. Sybesma (eds), *The First Glot International State-of-the-Article Book*, Berlin: Mouton de Gruyter, pp. 385–406.

van der Auwera, Johan and Vladimir A. Plungian (1998), 'Modality's semantic map', *Linguistic Typology*, 2: 79–124.

Vendler, Zeno (1967), 'Verbs and times', *Linguistics in Philosophy*, Ithaca, NY: Cornell University Press, pp. 97–121.

Verschueren, Jef (1999), *Understanding Pragmatics*, London: Arnold.

Wales, Roger (1986), 'Deixis', in P. Fletcher and M. Garman (eds), *Language Acquisition*, 2nd edn, Cambridge: Cambridge University Press, pp. 401–28.

Wilson, Deirdre and Dan Sperber (2004), 'Relevance theory', in L. R. Horn and G. Ward (eds), *The Handbook of Pragmatics*, Oxford: Blackwell, pp. 607–32.

Index

Note: Bold print page numbers indicate where some aspect of a technical term is explained. Closely related forms are not separately listed. For example, *ambiguous* and *disambiguation*, are subsumed under the index item *ambiguity*. The exercises and suggested answers have not been indexed, except in a few cases where they add significantly to what is in the main text. The chapter endnotes have been treated very selectively too.